nai010 publishers intend the Refl[...] series to [...] attention socially relevant themes for architecture, urban planning, fine art and design.

Reflect
#10

Previously published in
the Reflect series:

The City as Interface

How Digital Media are Changing the City

Martijn de Waal

nai010 publishers

The City as Interface

Contents

The Future of the City: a Smart City or a Social City?

Several years ago I stumbled upon a column by Microsoft founder Bill Gates in the American magazine *Information Week*. To celebrate its twenty-fifth anniversary, the magazine had invited a number of leading pioneers from the world of computing to look back and to look ahead: what had been the most important breakthroughs in the last quarter of a century and, above all, what did the future have in store?

Gates' column was an eye-opener for me, not so much because of the scenario he outlined but because of the *way* he did it. Somewhat predictably, he began by summarizing the huge progress the computer had made during the last twenty-five yearsa: from expensive mainframes as large as an entire room operable only by specialists, to the affordable personal computers found nowadays in virtually every household, and their ever more awe-inspiring performance, measured in units that are difficult to grasp for ordinary mortals: from kilohertz and bit to gigahertz and terabyte. Impressive, concludes Gates. But, he goes on to say, this is 'only the beginning . . .'

I believe that we're entering an era when software will fundamentally transform almost everything we do. The continued growth of processing power, storage, networking, and graphics is making it possible to create almost any device imaginable. But it's the *magic of software* that will connect these devices into a seamless whole, making them an indispensable part of our everyday lives.[1]

> In a couple of sentences, Gates sketches a vitally important technological development that forms the basis of this book: following the era of the mainframe and the beige PC box placed on or under our desks, we have now entered a new phase. This time around, the computer is becoming invisible and slowly but surely will permeate every aspect of everyday life.

It is a scenario that many people will recognize. The calculating power of the mobile phone we carry around in our trouser pockets is many times greater than that of the first mainframes. This has enormous consequences for our everyday routines: a text message enables us to reschedule a meeting at the last minute or send a quick personal message to a loved one in between all our activities; our smartphones enable us to conveniently look up information about our surroundings ('where is the nearest café, restaurant, ATM?'); thanks to navigation systems, we reach our destinations more quickly, especially if the software is geared to receive live traffic updates and it can redirect us so we avoid traffic jams; mobile social networks such as Twitter and Facebook enable people to keep their 'friends' constantly informed about where they are, what they are doing and what they think of it all.

These are all examples of *urban media*: a collective term that I use in this book for media technologies that in one way or another can influence the experience of a physical location. If it is left to Gates and his colleagues, digital technology will become even more closely interwoven with everyday life. Leading computer multinationals such as IBM and Cisco are currently developing the infrastructure for the city of the future: they envisage a city crammed with sensors and rapid communication networks; all sorts of 'intelligent' technologies will monitor various processes in the city – from traffic circulation to air pollution – and use the collected data to make improvements without human intervention. In his column Gates predicts that 'software can go places it has never gone before.' The factory-floor inventory, the amount of cash in the till, potential burglars around your house, the amount of milk in your fridge – in his column, Gates promises that Microsoft will soon be able to monitor it all for us.

The scenario sketched by Gates is interesting but what mainly set me off thinking was the choice of words in his final sentence: thanks to the *magic* of his software, our lives will soon be even more convenient, more pleasant, more efficient and more agreeable. In that one sentence I suddenly recognized a larger theme I had often encountered in the past. When we talk about new technologies, it is often about their practical application: technology is presented as a convenient solution to real or supposed problems, it promises to make our lives more pleasant and convenient; at the same time, our cities will also become safer, more sustainable and more efficient. In short, technology is an almost inescapable magical power that will improve urban society. But for those who do not believe in magic, this picture mainly raises a number of questions. Sure enough, the new infrastructure of mobile and digital media provides convenient applications for busy city dwellers to organize the practicalities of their lives more efficiently. But what we tend to forget is that this also changes the city as a *society*. Research has shown that the places we visit, the meanings we attach to them and our contacts with others are all changing because of the rise of mobile media.

This is not necessarily a magical process that simply happens to us. As a community – regardless of our role as designers, citizens, policymakers, or consumers – we can make choices about the way we want to deploy technologies. These choices are, in turn, related to the way we think a city should function as a community: ideology rather than magic is one of the central forces behind the way in which technology changes our lives. However, we rarely encounter this philosophical approach outside the specialized worlds of art and science, and it is precisely this which is the theme of this book. 'Technology at present is covert philosophy', argues American communications studies researcher Phil Agre, 'the point is to make it more openly philosophical.'[2] On the one hand technology contains an idea about what the ideal world should look like; on the other hand, the very same technology can also intervene in our everyday world and radically change our experience of and ideas about it. With urban media playing an increasingly prominent role in everyday urban life, it is of great importance to consider this. What are the underlying urban ideals concealed in technologies? And what is the significance of all these new means of communication for urban societies?

In general terms, this debate is currently dominated by two scenarios: the 'smart city' and the 'social city' scenarios, both of which have their supporters and opponents. The smart city embodies Bill Gates' scenario: the city is crammed with sensors, software and networks that enable optimal traffic circulation and energy use. The smartphone becomes an intelligent compass, guiding the city dweller through the bustle and chaos of everyday life. The mobile phone is deployed to personalize the urban experience, for example through software that recommends restaurants or shops that fit the user's profile. It sounds like a splendid vision of the future. Yet this scenario has its critics. American architecture critic Paul Goldberger says that the very media and communication technologies that make life for individual consumers so much easier are a threat to the continued existence of urban society as a whole. Will city dwellers still enter into relationships with their physical surroundings? Will they still participate in community life or will they withdraw completely into the 'cocoons' they create with their mobile phones, thereby transforming the city into an extension of their private domains? Goldberger claims that people who walk down the street using their mobile phones are no longer participating in street life: they are there in body but not in spirit. And it is this very attitude that poses a threat to poses a threat to how the city functions as a democratic community:

> (. . .) the street is the ultimate public space and walking along it is the defining urban experience. It is all of us – different people who lead different lives – coming together in the urban mixing chamber. But what if half of them are elsewhere, there in body but not in any other way?[3]

Not everyone is so pessimistic. Others see the rise of digital and mobile media as a series of aids giving city dwellers more control over urban life, not only as consumers but also as citizens, thus reinforcing the bonds within local communities. They are supporters of the social city scenario. American essayist Andrew Blum for one hopes that bloggers who write about their neighbourhoods can increase a sense of community there. While on the one hand media technologies can link us to global networks, on the other hand local blogs can play a role in developing bonds with our neighbourhood. According to Blum, 'in a community where common ties are electronically buttressed we may be able to reap the global environmental benefit of high-density living without sacrificing the local ties of a medium-density neighborhood'.[4]

It is important not to become fixated on these two scenarios. What matters are the underlying urban ideals they embody. What sorts of philosophical ideals do these scenarios conceal about the way the city as a community should function? I distinguish three: the libertarian city, the republican city and the communitarian city. The libertarian city is based on the ideal of the city as a market. The city is a place where people lead their individual lives in freedom; it is a place where city dwellers have virtually no reciprocal duties or responsibilities. City dwellers are first and foremost consumers of various services, and the city is thus primarily a platform where supply and demand in a variety of fields can meet. In this vision, political and cultural aspects of city life fade into the background or are considered private matters. Many – but not all – smart city scenarios dovetail with this ideal.

Then there is the ideal of the republican city (from the Latin *res publica*, the public interest, rather than a reference to the United States political party). Here, the city also provides the freedom to choose between divergent ways of life, but at the same time city dwellers share responsibility for the city as a whole. Whereas the libertarian thinks it is perfectly acceptable for city dwellers to completely isolate themselves in their private worlds or behind the fences of a gated community, the republican disapproves of such behaviour. The city dweller is first and foremost a citizen and may not completely withdraw from urban society. The philosophical legitimacy of many social city approaches is founded on these concepts.

Finally, there is the ideal of the communitarian city, which is based on the ideal of a harmonious local community in which all city dwellers share more or less the same way of life. In this vision the emphasis is on the common identity of the collective and not on the individual. Nowadays, the idea of the communitarian city is mainly found in nostalgic retrospectives filled with a village-like sense of community. This category includes a small number of social city approaches that mainly deploy digital media to reinforce or invent unambiguous local communities.

But – and this might be counterintuitive - a number of smart city scenarios also dovetail with this ideal. On some issues, libertarian and communitarian principles are surprisingly related. After all, those who use the libertarian freedom to isolate themselves may end up in an unambiguous communitarian world. Remarkably, there is also a certain kinship between the village-like communitarian ideal and modernist ideas that have long played a dominant role in urban planning and that will also occasionally hover in the background in this book. While it is true that at their most extreme the modernists wanted to destroy the old, traditional order, they also proposed a new (modern) collective experience to replace it. The architect was to use scientific methods to determine ideal social relationships and convert them into a physical form that would provide city dwellers with a new collective world of experience: an experiential world that did not arouse nostalgic feelings of togetherness but, instead, a feeling of solidarity that fitted in with the mobility, speed and new technologies of modern life.

The three ideals referred to above are not clear-cut categories. They may overlap and all sorts of intermediate forms are also possible. Here, they are used to make the debate about the role of technology in the city again a philosophical one. I use the three ideals as a gauge to link practical applications of digital media to urban ideals.

The central proposition in this book is that many urban media mainly support the libertarian urban ideal. With their emphasis on efficiency and personalization, they approach city dwellers as individual consumers and increase their freedom to organize life according to their own insights; at the same time, these media also reduce city dwellers' mutual involvement. This is not a foregone conclusion, however: other examples of urban media are based on the republican ideal. They succeed in combining the smart city ideals of personalization and efficiency with the social city ideals of citizenship and connection.

This book can also be read as a defence of the republican city. I defend the proposition that a modern democratic urban society benefits from taking an intermediate position between the communitarian and the libertarian. The city as a communitarian society, where the emphasis is on an unambiguous shared culture, is too coercive and offers little individual freedom; the city that primarily functions as a market offers a great deal of freedom, but that freedom is also so free of commitment that it can ultimately lead to far-reaching fragmentation and segregation, both culturally and economically. The difficult task of finding a balance between freedom and mutual involvement is central to the republican city. My main aim in this book is to study how urban media can or cannot contribute to that task. In order to do this, I will consider not only the future but also the past. To what extent can the three urban ideals be traced in our cities today? Which broader social developments play a role here? And how do urban media fit in with these developments?

A good way to keep this complex question manageable is to

look at the phenomenon of the urban public sphere – the collection of places in a city that serve as meeting places for city dwellers from various backgrounds. The organization of these public spaces plays an important, albeit differently appreciated, role in all three urban ideals. In the communitarian ideal, urban public spaces embody the collective identity: their architecture and design are an expression of this identity and are mainly used for rituals (parades, festivals, commemorative events), allowing city dwellers to participate in a shared culture.

In the libertarian ideal, urban public spaces are markets. By definition, the city consists of city dwellers with varying needs, backgrounds, preferences, aims and convictions. In urban public spaces, they meet in a mechanism of supply and demand, regardless of whether this concerns sellers trying to find customers, believers looking for religious leaders, artists in search of inspiration or members of a specific subculture looking for kindred spirits. The republican ideal is situated somewhere between the two: as in the libertarian ideal, urban public spaces are places where city dwellers from varying backgrounds meet, but these spaces are not commitment-free markets; instead, they are places where all those individual city dwellers can be absorbed into a larger whole, despite their differences. They are places where city dwellers meet, where mutual trust develops, where conflicts are settled, and where city dwellers must ultimately try to relate to each other in one way or another.

The organization, use and experience of the urban public sphere can thus be seen as an indication of how a city functions as a community. Consequently, the way urban media intervene in this process also determines the direction in which urban communities develop. In order to properly research this, we must first look more closely at the phenomenon of the urban public sphere.

The Urban Public Sphere and Urban Publics

The urban public sphere is a complex concept. It usually means a meeting place - 'the urban mixing chamber', as Paul Goldberg put it. But opinion is divided on exactly what sorts of meetings or urban mix should take place in these spaces. Sometimes it is a political debate in which different views clash. A perfect example was the seventeenth-century English coffee house as described by the German philosopher Jürgen Habermas and the American sociologist Richard Sennett. City dwellers met at the coffee houses as citizens to discuss matters of general interest.

But certainly not all examples of urban public spaces are based on the concept of a place for holding rational debates. In their descriptions of the public spaces that developed on the boulevards of Paris at the end of the nineteenth century, Charles

Baudelaire and Walter Benjamin were chiefly concerned with the physical confrontation between different worlds that took place there. The emerging bourgeoisie who sauntered on the boulevards stumbled on paupers from the slums that had survived behind the façades of Haussmann's shiny new buildings. For American urban researcher and neighbourhood activist Jane Jacobs, public spaces were about even more banal everyday interactions: in her famous book *The Death and Life of Great American Cities* she described how trust can develop over time as neighbourhood residents regularly meet on the street, briefly exchange greetings and occasionally have a superficial chat.

What the above examples have in common is that at the places referred to, the interaction between city dwellers always leads to the development of a *modern urban public*: a group of people who are (temporarily) united around a common goal or practice. The way the term 'public' is used is closely related to its two meanings in everyday language: on the one hand, a public is a collection of people who (coincidentally) share a common experience or a common interest. This might be a spatial experience, for example, quite literally the public that is present in a theatre (or on a boulevard) or a mediated experience - the public of a television programme. In addition, 'public' has a second meaning, that of 'making public': something that is 'public' is disclosed to others.[5]

Both aspects come together when we look at how publics in urban public spaces come into existence. Together, city dwellers can form a public (a group of people) by making an aspect of their lives public (accessible to others). Consider again the seventeenth-century coffee houses: citizens went there to drink coffee and read the newspapers but above all to discuss the topics dealt with in the newspapers. In other words, by making their own ideas public (accessible), they created a public (group) with and for each other.

A public is therefore not a passive collective in the sense of an 'audience'. Members of a public are alternately listener and performer.[6] In a similar sense, Marshall Berman used Baudelaire's and Benjamin's contemporary accounts to describe the nineteenth-century boulevards as 'the common meeting ground and the communications line' of the nineteenth century: because the bourgeoisie and paupers came together on the boulevard, it developed into a place where different groups of city dwellers became aware of each other.[7] Through their clothing, habits and manners, city dwellers showed each other who they were and to which group they belonged. At the same time, they formed a public together. The boulevard was the stage on which the inhabitants of Paris and St Petersburg were both performers and spectators.

And not only did they become aware of each other; crucially for Berman, a new public could emerge as a result of this interaction on the boulevard. In a somewhat romanticized account he sketches how the boulevards of St Petersburg contributed to a growing class-consciousness because, while out strolling, workers and proletarians recognized others like themselves. This mutual recognition could give rise to a sense of solidarity and perhaps even political action.

The publics of the English coffee houses and Nevski Prospekt, St Petersburg's main boulevard, were typical *urban* publics. Both publics emerged out of practices that over time had become associated with specific urban locations. Both the seventeenth-century English coffee house and the nineteenth-century boulevard had a set of cultural repertoires: a collection of roles and acts that were connected with and considered appropriate for a particular location. These protocols and repertoires were in turn partly related to the specific urban condition whose essence was the need for citizens to continuously relate to strangers. As Jane Jacobs wrote:

> Great cities are not like towns, only larger; they are not like suburbs, only denser. They differ from towns and suburbs in basic ways, and one of these is that cities are, by definition, full of strangers. To any one person, strangers are far more common in big cities than acquaintances.[8]

In short, the very nature of the city means that we are always sur-rounded by people who are different from ourselves and that most of our fellow city dwellers will also remain strangers to us. Yet in one way or another we must find a way to live with each other.

This idea of the city as a collection of strangers developed in the large cities in the late nineteenth and early twentieth centuries. Chicago School sociologists described how large groups of city dwellers migrated from the country to the city at that time. For many, this literally and figuratively meant arriving in a new world. They left behind their close-knit and orderly traditional communities in the country and arrived in the big city, where anonymity was the norm. There, they were surrounded by innumerable other city dwellers, often from very diverse backgrounds. According to Louis Wirth, the density and heterogeneity of the modern metropolis led to the birth of new urban publics. City dwellers started to specialize, and they also started to become part of various communities and publics for different aspects of their lives.[9]

The urban public sphere playes an essential role in this process. It's the stage or platform where city dwellers show who they are (make their way of life public) and, as a result, become acquainted with other people's ways of life and compare themselves with them. The public sphere is like a cultural or political marketplace: city dwellers can recognize like-minded people and, together with others, be absorbed into new collectives (new publics) or actually distinguish themselves from other city dwellers. In order to research the urban public sphere in today's society, we must therefore look at the way city dwellers make their lives public on our contemporary 'stages' – from the boulevard to Facebook – and how this process then leads or does not lead to the development of new publics.

Parochial and Public Domains

This also leads us to the most important subject in the ideological debate about urban public spaces. In modern cities, residents are continuously surrounded by other city dwellers whom they not only do not know but who are also different from themselves. And yet in one way or another, they must find a way to relate to those other city dwellers. But what is the correct way to relate? The libertarian thinks it is perfectly acceptable if city dwellers isolate themselves and mainly form publics that consist of kindred spirits. The republican wants city dwellers to relate to each other in one way or another despite their differences and in fact actively form publics in which city dwellers from diverse backgrounds come together. The communitarian demands that everyone unequivocally consider themselves members of an overarching cultural community.

In fact, careful consideration shows that the issue revolves around the harmonization of two different domains: the private domain, in which people can do whatever they want, and the urban public sphere as the place where city dwellers from different backgrounds come together and have to relate to each other. Yet this unequivocal distinction between private and public is too clear-cut to get to grips with the social processes that take place in the city: the distinction between the world behind the front door (the private domain) and that of the street (the public domain) is too crude. There are all sorts of gradations in the way we experience the public domain. In some places in the city we feel at home, and sense that we are part of an urban public in which we recognize ourselves or whose members we even know personally. At other places, we do not meet anyone we know and are part of a public of city dwellers with different lifestyles.

In order to do justice to this reality, American sociologist Lyn Lofland introduced a third, intermediate sphere between the public and private: the 'parochial sphere', by which she meant those places in a city where we mainly meet like-minded people. It can be recognized by 'a sense of commonality among acquaintances and neighbors who are involved in interpersonal networks that are located within "communities".'[10] Examples of parochial domains are a Turkish coffee house in a Dutch city neighbourhood, the canteen of a sports club, a gay bar, a local pub in Amsterdam's Jordaan neighbourhood, a bench on some square that has become a hangout for a group of adolescents, and so on. Parochial domains are generally accessible to outsiders but these will probably be received with some suspicion. Lofland contrasts the public domain with the parochial domain. The public domain consists of those places in the city where we mainly come across strangers whom we either do not know at all or whom we only know as members of a category: 'those areas of urban settlements in which individuals in copresence tend to be personally unknown or only categorically known to one another'.[11]

Both the parochial and the public domains are part of the urban public sphere, which consists entirely of places where city dwellers meet and come across each other and together form publics. However, they clearly have a different character: the parochial sphere consists of places that have been appropriated by a particular group; in the public sphere city dwellers mainly come across people whom they do not know. As such, both domains also have an important function: in parochial domains city dwellers can be absorbed into all sorts of collectives, in the public domain they have to relate to each other.

In recent decades, a significant shift has occurred in the relationship between the parochial and public domains, one that plays an important role in this book. Traditional expositions of urban public spaces often idealize nineteenth-century cities such as Vienna or Paris: the centre of the city with its squares and boulevards constituted the public domain, surrounded by all sorts of neatly arranged neighbourhoods that functioned as the parochial domains of local communities. I shall draw on various studies to show that this picture is no longer valid, if it ever existed at all. As a result of increased mobility and the individualization of lifestyles, parochial and public domains have started to overlap more and more. The common Amsterdammer of the past no longer lives in the Jordaan neighbourhood; he has moved to Purmerend or Almere, works in Hoofddorp, shops at an outlet centre in the Flevopolder at the weekends and visits mega-cinemas at the ArenA in the Bijlmer; on Saturday evenings, he likes to briefly return to his old neighbourhood because that is where the most convivial cafés are. His city consists of an extensive network of parochial domains – and this is also true for other segments of the population. Indeed, it is debatable whether there is still a clear-cut public domain, a place where all city dwellers meet. In this, I concur with Maarten Hajer and Arnold Reijndorp, who argue in their book *In Search of New Public Domain* that we must not rigidly cling to the ideal of the nineteenth-century city. They argue that the public domain can also be the product of a temporary overlap of parochial domains belonging to various city dwellers.

This raises the following questions: how do urban media enable us to shape these different domains in new ways? How does the emergence of a new technology shift the balance between parochial and public domains? Does the emergence of new technologies reinforce the parochial domain, and do new technologies make it easier for city dwellers to withdraw to their own 'turf'? Or can they actually reinforce the public domain, which is dominated by mutual interchange?

Digital Media and Urban Public Spaces: 'Experience Markers' and 'Territory Devices'

This leads us to the following curious fact: discussions about the role of urban media in the urban public sphere (the collective term for parochial and public domains) constantly hark back to a number of historical archetypes. The seventeenth-century coffee houses in London, the boulevards in Paris, street life in Jane Jacobs's West Village have also been referred to here. Defenders of the republican urban ideal in particular tend to view digital media in one of two ways: they are our deliverance, restoring an urban public sphere that has apparently been under pressure for decades, or they are the death knell for the republican ideal of an 'open society', a democratic society in which citizens are open to each other and, despite all their differences, attempt to reach an accommodation with each other.

However, if we use yesterday's terminology to describe the future, we risk being wide of the mark, especially as the very emergence of digital media undermines an essential aspect of the historical examples. The urban public sphere in the above examples was always based on the simultaneous use of space. Publics developed out of physical encounters or confrontations with others, however trivial such interaction sometimes was. Thus, in Jürgen Habermas's Lloyd's Coffee House in London, on Walter Benjamin's Boulevard Saint-Germain in Paris or in Jane Jacobs's Hudson Street in Lower Manhattan, an urban public emerged consisting of city dwellers who took notice of each other, entered into debates with each other, simply had a chat or only observed each other. In essence, this is the function of the urban public sphere: it brings city dwellers together spatially who then collectively form a (temporary) public. This might be a public of strangers, in which case we are dealing with a public domain, or it might be a public of kindred spirits, in which case we are dealing with a parochial domain.

However, it is characteristic of the rise of digital and mobile media that the way urban publics do or do not form is no longer limited to a *spatial* process that takes place in the physical urban public space. Fifty years ago, Jane Jacobs argued that 'Word does not move around where public characters and sidewalk life are lacking'.[12] In her view, a modern urban public of 'familiar strangers' could not develop without street life and its associated brief encounters. But what happens if the word does manage to break free of the street? Because that is precisely what is happening with the emergence of urban media: when we blog, tweet or ping what we experience; when we look up information about our surroundings on the smartphone; when we just ring, poke, send text messages and whatsapp someone who is not physically present. We are then part of publics that are partly mediated and partly physical.

It is impossible to give a complete overview of all types of urban media here - the developments are so rapid that such a list would quickly be out of date. Moreover, there is a maze of technological standards, as well as developers and parties with diverging interests who are involved in the development of urban media, each with their own ideals, goals and approaches to urban life.[13] Governments hope to make cities safer with closed circuit television cameras; politicians expect the new digital services to bridge the gap between citizen and government; telephone providers expect to make bigger profits through personalized location services; social workers hope that digital interventions in the public space can reinforce mutual understanding and trust between different segments of the population; artists use the technologies to criticize the 'big brother society' that results from these very technologies; and citizens, companies and consumers in turn use the technologies in their own, often completely unforeseen ways.

The aim here is not to meticulously map out the whole field but to consider the way urban media are qualitatively changing the experience of the urban public sphere. In this book my main interest is in their latent possibilities: media technologies have certain qualities and affordances, but whether they are ultimately used depends on a variety of circumstances. To give just one example: when the radio came onto the market in the United States in the 1920s, this new appliance (often a kitset that the owner had to put together himself) was seen as a means of communication: users could communicate with each other over long distances via radio waves. As a result of legislation, the radio eventually developed into a mass communication medium with only a few parties preparing the broadcasts and the rest of us, as the public, being permitted to listen. Communication was a latent possibility of radio technology but eventually the law – and here the broadcasters' lobby played an important role - determined how the new technology would be used, rather than the affordances of the technology itself. I am inclined to consider urban media in a similar way: what possibilities and promises do they contain? As the development of urban media is now in full swing, it is interesting to look at their possible effects on urban society. Moreover, the very fact that these media are still developing means we can influence their development through policy, regulation, design or use.

Bearing all this in mind, if we consider the latent possibilities of urban media, we can discern two possible applications, which can both take on a variety of shapes. First, we can use urban media as 'experience markers': they can be used to record urban experiences and share them with others. Social media or weblogs enable city dwellers to share their experiences at specific locations with friends, acquaintances and even strangers who are not present at that location. They can take photographs that can then be uploaded using GPS tags so they become visible on maps. All sorts of media files can be equipped with geographic coordinates so they can be linked to specific locations. The public for a particular experience or act is thus no longer limited to the physically present public. Other technologies can automatically record what is taking place in a space. Sensors and cameras can record who or what is present at a particular location, for example, with the aid of face-recognition software or RFID chips. Urban experiences, memories, stories and events can thus be intentionally or unintentionally recorded, stored on databases and made public in all sorts of ways, either immediately or later.[14]

A second series of latent possibilities enables the deployment of digital and mobile media as 'territory devices': an appliance or system that can influence the experience of an urban area. For starters, at a specific location the data files that are linked to that location can be opened again; then it is possible to see who was there yesterday, what sorts of stories or memories absent others have of that place, and so on. The experience of a place can thus extend beyond the here and now. And with aids such as the mobile phone it becomes possible to seek contact with absent friends or acquaintances. Japanese-American anthropologists Mizuko Ito and Daisuke Okabe refer to the mobile phone as a 'membrane': in their study *Personal, Portable, Pedestrian: Mobile Phones in Japanese Life* they argue that the mobile phone is not a 'portal' that teleports us from a physical situation to a virtual world but rather a 'membrane' that enables us to admit mediated contacts to our surroundings and to regulate in the here and now the presence of absent others or media files.[15] Japanese anthropologist Fujimoto argues that this also means we can alter the nature of an urban situation: ringing a friend in a public space means temporarily withdrawing into a private space: 'The *keitai* [Japanese for mobile phone, MdW] is a jamming machine that instantly creates a territory – a personal *keitai* space – around oneself with an invisible minimal barricade.'[16] City dwellers can thus allow virtually absent others access to a physical location, thereby changing the experience of that location.

The reverse is also true: some digital media systems can regulate physical access to a location - smart cards that can be used to open the door of an office building or the communal inner space of a building, or cameras in trams equipped with face-recognition software that emit a signal when someone with a public transport ban boards the tram. Technological systems can also change the experience of a location in more subtle ways – think of billboards in the shape of interactive urban screens whose advertisements are targeted at individual passers-by: this is possible because a camera with face-recognition software 'analyzes' the target group (man or woman, age and so on) to which the passer-by belongs; different passers-by then see a content that is continuously adjusted to specifically appeal to them.

This leads us to conclude that the urban public sphere can no longer be considered as a purely physical construct. If we continue to view public spaces like this, we will miss important new ways in which city dwellers are brought together, take notice of each other and form urban publics. Therefore, instead of looking at physical locations, it is worth focusing on aspects of the process itself: how and under what circumstances do city dwellers take notice of each other and thus form urban publics?

The City as Interface

If we use yesterday's terminology to look at the future, we risk missing a number of important developments in the study of urban public spaces. But what if we look at things from the other end, considering whether concepts used to describe the future can be used to explain past processes; to investigate whether, and to what extent, new technologies indeed cause important social changes.

When we consider urban public spaces from the point of view of digital media, we quickly come across the term 'interface', a rather technical term that according to Webster's dictionary means 'the place at which independent and often unrelated systems meet and act on or communicate with each other'. In the world of computing, 'interface' is either used to describe an environment in which different computer systems can be attuned to each other, or for an environment that converts the computer's bits into humanly comprehensible applications. Bill Gates' Windows is an interface: it translates the logic of the computer into icons that people can understand, enabling users to operate their computers. The TomTom screen is another interface: geographical data and information about traffic flows are converted into a dynamic map that enables us to navigate through traffic. Social networks such as Facebook and Twitter are interfaces too: they provide an environment with specific possibilities and limitations that enables us to communicate with each other.

Can we also use this term to study urban public spaces? Then we would no longer be concerned with the extent to which the interfaces and algorithms of urban media threaten the physical urban public space. Instead, we would look at how urban public spaces have always functioned as interfaces and the extent to which the new interfaces of digital media interfere with this.

The short answer to this question is: yes, we can. First, the dynamic of urban life always consists of an accumulation of all sorts of exchange processes. To a large degree, everyday life revolves around attuning individual and collective identities, attuning the present to the past, and harmonizing the concerns and interests of different urban publics. Seen from this perspective, the urban public sphere has always functioned as an 'interface'. This approach to the city as an interface can be found in the work of Manuel Castells: a city is the material reflection of social relationships and thus creates places where individuals can relate to these social representations:

> Cities have always been communication systems, based on the interface between individual and communal identities and shared social representations. It is their ability to organize this interface materially in forms, in rhythms, in collective experience and communicable perception that makes cities producers of sociability, and integrators of otherwise destructive creativity.[17]

More concretely, specific social, cultural and economic practices, traditions and power relations are given a material form in the city: the market, a church, the town hall, a square where a variety of events are held. By using these urban spaces, city dwellers learn 'hands on' how to master the logic of these different social systems. They can gear their individual lifestyles to collective habits and practices, or try to gear collective rhythms to their individual wishes. They can identify themselves with the rhythms of urban society or resist them. The physical city is an 'interface' where collective practices take shape, and when these collective practices change, the shape and meaning of the physical environment change with them. Thus, the coffee house, the boulevard and the city street in West Village should also be seen as 'interfaces': places where different city dwellers came together and attuned their lives within the framework of social conventions that have developed over time.

Moreover, interface is a particularly apt term because it shifts attention from the spatial aspect (the coffee house, boulevard, street) to the question of the relationships themselves. Who is relating to whom? How are these groups brought together? Who is excluded? Which protocols apply to communications between those present, and who determines this? What sorts of new publics or communities might emerge as a result of this process? And on what sort of common elements are those publics or communities based?

The advantage of looking at urban life using the interface 'frame' is that an analysis can include all sorts of non-physical structures and practices. Moreover, this term also forces us to look at the role of the interface itself: interfaces are not neutral environments; they partly determine how a possible interchange or harmonization comes about. The term enables us to look not only at the 'outcomes' of these processes – how are mobile media used and how does that change urban society – but also at the interface subject itself: what sort of urban ideal does it actually embody?

Platform, Programme, Protocols

When looking at the city as an interface, we are not so much concerned with the question whether certain locations can be regarded as parochial or public domains; instead, we look at how city dwellers organize themselves as publics and at the nature of these publics: are they mainly like-minded people who become linked to each other? Or is there in fact an overlap between city dwellers whose ways of life differ?

If we wish to analyze this process more thoroughly, we can consider five related aspects: platform, programme, protocol, filter and agency. By platform I mean the environment in which city dwellers are brought together, make their lives public and harmonize with each other. This might be a physical environment - a street or square can function as a platform - but it might also be a software environment such as a smartphone's 'operating system'.

In general, a platform only becomes useful thanks to a programme: a specific use of the platform. This might be an archi-tectural programme (a street can be designed with shops 'in the plinth' or designated as an exclusive residential area), a social programme (a neighbourhood centre where activities are organized) or a software programme (a Facebook app for the iPhone). Such a programme always imposes a certain order on the publics it creates. For example, through the Facebook app, communication is shaped by the possibilities and limitations inherent in the programme. For instance, Facebook allows a person to reveal something about his identity by filling in catchwords in a number of categories invented by Facebook. But urban designs and social policies also categorize city dwellers according to a particular logic. Designs always contain specific notions about urban publics and this labelling process (and the associated issue of power) plays a role in the way interaction takes place.

Connected to this is an interface's function as a filter. An interface makes it possible to harmonize specific elements from different worlds and exclude other elements. Finally, interfaces function according to a 'protocol'. A protocol is a specific behaviour that is experienced as generally applicable in a specific social context. If we look at Facebook again, we see that the status updates and the use of the 'like' button have developed into important protocols. In urban life, protocol is more concerned with all sorts of everyday behaviours that have become customary over time. Sometimes this concerns tacit agreements about which neighbour parks his car in a particular parking spot or who sits on a particular bench in the park and when, at other times it concerns practices that have been laid down in regulations or even laws.

Taken together, platform, programme, filter and protocol play a role in the way urban publics can be shaped. An underlying issue that will arise in this context over and over again is that of agency. Who has the opportunity to influence the way in which the city as an interface is shaped? Is it the architects and policymakers, who determine the urban programme? Is it the technology companies, which shape the protocols through which city dwellers can communicate with each other? Is it perhaps city dwellers themselves, who individually or collectively are given more possibilities to 'reprogramme' the urban space using their mobile phones? This is an important question: all sorts of protocols can be established in computer algorithms but who determines precisely which legal and cultural codes are laid down in the software computer codes? As Eric Kluitenberg writes:

> If the initiative lies exclusively with the constructors, the producers of these enriched spaces, and their clients, then the space we are living in is liable to total authoritarian control, even if there is no immediately observable way in which that space displays the historic characteristics of authoritarianism. The more widely the initiative is distributed between producers and consumers and the more decisions are made at the 'nodes' (the extremities of the network, occupied by the users) instead of at the 'hubs' (junctions in the network), the more chance there is of a space in which the sovereign subject is able to shape his or her own autonomy.[18]

In other words, who shapes the urban interfaces of the twenty-first century? Who determines the manner in which the city as interface functions? Are our future urban interfaces closed systems? Or do they in fact consist of open platforms? To put it in black-and-white terms, are citizens at the mercy of protocols that are laid down by the state and commercial parties or do they have the opportunity to exercise influence directly?

Test Cases: Scenarios for Tomorrow's Urban Society

It is still unclear how the city, as a result of the emergence of urban media, functions as an interface. We are in the middle of an era in which urban media are being shaped: smartphones, navigation systems, location services, sensors, RFID chips, 'smart city' protocols are all products and services that are currently being developed, implemented and slowly becoming part of everyday life. And this is why it is so important to explore possible future scenarios now, without losing sight of historical continuity.

At the same time this is also difficult, because the rise and use of digital media have not yet crystallized. Different scenarios are possible and these partly depend on the approach underlying the use of digital media in urban planning as well as on policy measures and the extent to which users will embrace these media. In order to avoid this difficulty, I study the role of urban media in urban public spaces using a number of 'test cases'. These test cases are diverse and include a work of art that conveys a specific view of interactive design, an iPhone app that directs city dwellers to view the city in a particular way and the emergence of commercial practices that address specific publics. These test cases allow us glimpses of a possible future; they show us the different directions in which the 'city as interface' might continue to develop.

This approach is based on the idea of the 'cultural probe', a methodology borrowed from the world of design. As part of the design process, designers sometimes use cultural probes - objects presented to a test panel as part of a research project. Sometimes the object is a prototype whose functionality is tested, at other times it is an object that is not intended to be produced but rather to elicit reactions from the test panel that the designer can then use as inspiration.

Cultural probes are used by designers to stimulate imagination; the designer takes the role of 'provocateur' and the information collected is 'inspirational data (. . .) used to acquire] a more impressionistic account of [people's] beliefs and desires, their aesthetic preferences and cultural concerns.[19]

The test cases are similarly intended as a 'philosophical gauge' that I can use to measure feelings in the debate about digital media and the city, or even as a 'philosophical provocation', intended to provoke a debate. The test cases are always the occasion or springboard for a number of discussions that make clear what might be at stake: how does the rise of urban media change the way in which urban publics can emerge? And what are the consequences for the way in which a city functions as a society? I follow two lines of investigation: in the first three chapters I will consider how the parochial domain is created and in the last three chapters I will consider the public domain.

In both cases it is important to explore the future scenarios without losing sight of historical continuity. By looking at the historical examples of the way the city as interface has functioned, we can demonstrate important qualitative and normative shifts in the way urban media interfaces interfere in urban public spaces. After all, the urban media software is not a magical force that will, abracadabra à la Bill Gates, improve life for everyone in the city. According to computer scientist and anthropologist Paul Dourish, software is an attempt to lay down a particular model of reality or vision of society in computer codes:

It creates and manipulates models of reality of people and of action. Every piece of software reflects an uncountable number of philosophical commitments and perspectives without which it could never be created.[20]

A two-fold development is taking place: on the one hand, digital media influence the way the city is experienced and the way urban publics might be shaped; on the other hand, the design of these digital technologies is based on specific historical concepts of what a city is and of ideals of urban life.[21]

This study of the role of urban media in urban society therefore begins with a return to the past: in order to explore the future, we travel to the Pendrecht district, which was built on the south bank of the Maas river in Rotterdam in 1954. Pendrecht developed into an icon of Dutch architectural history, not least because of Lotte Stam-Beese's urban development plan: in line with the neighbourhood planning concept popular at the time, her plan was intended to result in the emergence of a completely new type of urban community. Although urban media are the great absent factor in this scenario, it provides a first clue to how an urban designer working on the basis of a republican city ideal approached her work as an 'interface designer'.

Pendrecht: a Brief History of the Paro- chial Domain

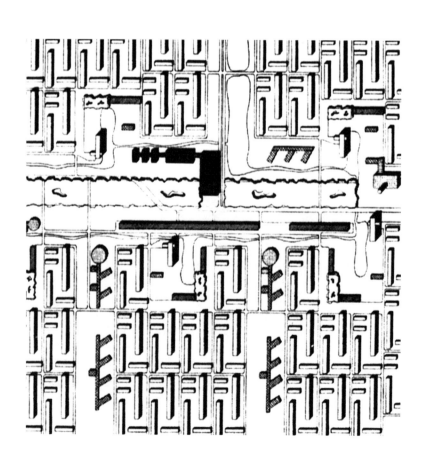

Mario Bosch has lived in Rotterdam's Pendrecht district nearly all his life. In 1964, at the age of five, he moved from Almelo in the east of the Netherlands to the then new district on the south bank of the Maas river in Rotterdam. On the weblog about the district that he has kept since the beginning of this century he takes an unsentimental look at the past. He remembers the creaking and groaning of the heavy diesel locomotives that rumbled over the port railway line right next to Pendrecht, the water fleas he caught with his father in the ditch at the district's boundary and the little doorbell at the tobacconist's where he frequently bought hand-rolling tobacco for his father when he was a young boy.

What is immediately striking about his memories is the small scale of life in the neighbourhood at the beginning of the 1960s. The baker and the milkman still called at the house and other shopping could be done nearby. The tobacconist's, greengrocer's, barber's and grocer's were just around the corner at one of the many local shops. Pendrecht was a respectable district in those days - not a posh residential area, but a decent neighborhood for workers who at that time often worked in the port of Rotterdam and at the shipyards. Although there was no central heating and the windows were often covered in frost in winter, Pendrecht was considered a desirable, modern neighbourhood with what was considered luxury housing at the time. It was not possible to simply move to Pendrecht: there was a great housing shortage and before houses were allocated an inspector would visit potential new residents to see whether they were 'domestically civilized' enough.[1] Clubs and societies flourished - Bosch still recalls Pendrecht's aquarium club. And when the rubbish was collected once a week, the residents put out their zinc rubbish bins in a tidy line at the edge of the street.

Bosch stayed in the neighbourhood all his life and now frequently gives guided tours to people whose interest has been roused after coming across his blog. And many people are interested: Pendrecht is internationally renowned for its monumental urban planning pattern, which was designed by Lotte Stam-Beese in the 1950s. After a turbulent life, this architect ended up in the Netherlands in the middle of the 1930s. Before that, she had studied at the Bauhaus, where she had an affair with its director, Hannes Meyer. When he was dismissed because of his communist sympathies, Stam-Beese followed him to Russia. Through her lover she became involved in various urban planning projects, and was impressed by the systematic and scientific approach to urban planning that was popular in Russia at the time.[2]

This experience can be traced in the plan that Stam-Beese developed for Pendrecht. As with many Russian housing projects that she worked on, her plan for Pendrecht consists of a repetitive pattern of housing blocks grouped around a common garden, creating a 'stamp': a unit that is repeated over and over again in the district. This stamp is one of the first aspects that Mario Bosch shows during his guided tours of Pendrecht. From a field about the size of a football pitch, he points out the unit's separate elements: to the left, a long four-floor block of flats, to the right a three-floor block. Located perpendicular to these are three blocks of terraced housing at the front and back of the stamp, one of which was specifically designed for the elderly. The whole district consists of an uninterrupted repetition of this basic pattern.

The garden between the housing blocks was intended as a meeting place for residents: it was meant to develop into a parochial domain where residents could meet regularly. This idea fitted in with the instructions that Stam-Beese received from the Rotterdam city council: the new districts that were built in Rotterdam-Zuid were to be designed in the spirit of the 'neighbourhood concept', a vision of urban planning that was formulated by the Bos committee during the Second World War. In its report, *De stad der toekomst, de toekomst der stad: Een stedebouwkundige en sociaal-culturele studie over de groeiende stadsgemeenschap* (literally: 'The city of the future, the future of the city: an urban planning and socio-cultural study of the growing city community'), the committee concluded that the rapid modernization and industrialization of Rotterdam before the war had led to alienation and social isolation. The city had become a 'brick desert' where it was no longer possible to really meet up with other people. The modern city dweller had become a 'nomad' - someone lacking an identity and points of contact with a local community, someone who 'thinks of his house as a camping spot, with which he is satisfied today but which he can just as easily swap for a different one tomorrow'.[3]

The neighbourhood concept that the Bos committee introduced in its report promised to reverse this development by creating new neighbourhoods in such a way that a local community could flourish again. This was not only an architectural exercise but above all a philosophical one: the post-war reconstruction of Rotterdam entailed not only physically rebuilding the city itself but first and foremost reinstating the lost urban community. Would a renewed focus on community life succeed in eliminating the unease about modern life? And what sort of community should be created at the neighbourhood level? And how could designers achieve this? In other words, how could the neighbourhood function as an interface, as a platform where residents harmonized their lives with each other in such a way that they would automatically blend into a local community? What sort of programme was needed to achieve this and which protocols were considered desirable?

The Bos committee had a communitarian ideal in mind: the district had to become the parochial domain again of the community that lived there. We shall see that Stam-Beese had different ideas about this: her starting point was closer to a republican ideal in which Pendrecht was to develop into an urban environment - a place where there was room for different communities to live next to and among each other. The Bos committee and Lotte Stam-Beese did have one thing in common: both cherished the hope that architects would be able to create a new type of society through their designs at the neighbourhood level.

This ideal was not fully realized, as becomes clear during the rest of Mario Bosch's guided tour. In the next two streets the gallery flats are enclosed by fences, behind which the bulldozers and cranes with demolition balls are at work. The obsolete flats are being demolished to make way for modern dwellings. In order to retain the design's monumental pattern, they will be neatly built within the contours of the existing stamp, although for some blocks the public gardens will now be closed off: what was once intended as a publicly accessible parochial domain will now be privatized.

This restructuring is the result of a period of decline that began in the early 1990s. The long-time residents of Pendrecht - many of whom were now elderly - started to leave the district in large numbers. Hardly any of the neighbours with whom Mario Bosch grew up in the 1960s still live in the district, and their children would rather live in the new suburban housing developments in Barendrecht, a few kilometres away. An additional factor has been the economic malaise resulting from declining employment opportunities in the port of Rotterdam since the 1980s.

As a consequence of all these developments, the dwellings that became vacant from the beginning of the 1990s onwards mainly attracted underprivileged residents, including many migrants who had only just arrived in the Netherlands. The old Pendrecht residents who have remained behind feel less and less at home in the district: they consider the satellite dishes that appear on the façades as proof that the new residents are not oriented towards the neighbourhood. Moreover, from the end of the 1960s many of the old residents themselves became less oriented towards their immediate surroundings. Their initial enthusiasm about this development, made possible by the advent of modern life with its cars, television and the telephone that release us from the duty to be part of a local community ,had by the 1990s given way to increasing concern about the consequences of this development. With residents being connected with like-minded people in other places through the media, Stam-Beese's common gardens lost their function as local parochial domains and, in the end, many residents lost the sense of belonging to a local community.

At the turn of the century these issues returned to the political agenda: a variety of programmes were aimed at restoring the sense of community in the neighbourhood. The pendulum that had swung towards republican and even libertarian concepts in the 1970s now swung back towards the communitarian ideals of the 1950s: the neighbourhood must become a community again, although this time it was not architects and urban planners who hoped to achieve this through their physical interfaces but policymakers with their social programmes.

In the developments that have affected Pendrecht since the 1950s, a number of interesting themes are visible that today are at the heart of the debate about the neighbourhood or, more precisely, about the interplay between the use of space and urban publics. Can the shared use of space (as in an urban neighbourhood) lead to the development of a community or an urban public? And if it can, what sort of public should it be and how should its members relate to each other? Or does the dynamic of the modern city actually work the other way around: do publics appropriate certain areas in the city, creating their own 'neighbourhoods'? This is, in a nutshell, the issue of the parochial domain, whose origins in Pendrecht can be traced to the introduction of the neighbourhood concept at the end of the 1940s.

Time for a New Programme: the 'Neighbourhood Concept'

It is not hard to link the emergence of the neighbourhood concept to a general sense of unease about the modernization of society. In a colourful 1948 folder intended to popularize the neighbourhood concept W.F. Geyl wrote that 'In the past, life was more harmonious; there was a connection between work and lifestyle, celebrations, religion and knowledge; the results and significance of one's work were clear, social problems were not so overwhelming, cities were more manageable and one's ideas about life were not called into question.' [4] Developments during the last century had disturbed this ideal: the rise of science and the Industrial Revolution had led to a 'spiritual poverty, the loss of a simpler and more balanced way of life'. Increases of scale in the economy and governmental centralization resulted in alienation, the erosion of community feeling and a growing gap between citizens and the state. This called for a new programme: 'Something must be done to promote a sense of community and contact between government and citizens (. . .) We must not allow any further descent into chaos!' [5] Geyl argued that the solution to the problems of the modern city must be sought in the 'neighbourhood concept', a planning vision for the city that propagates the design of small, conveniently arranged districts.[6]

The basis for the neighbourhood concept was laid in the Second World War by a committee led by A. Bos, the director of public housing in Rotterdam. According to his optimistic account, urban planning could provide the solution to the problems that had been pointed out. His committee commissioned urban planners to create an environment 'that can be a framework for people and communities, providing opportunities for personal development and inviting people, as it were, to enter into many different forms of cooperation and community.'[7]

In his manifesto Bos emphatically rejected the modernist Le Corbusier-inspired urban planning programmes that were influential at the time, with their attempt to get a grip on the chaos of the city through zoning. In Bos's view, the development of separate residential areas, commercial districts and shopping centres, made possible by the increase of motorized traffic, actually created the very problem they were supposed to solve: the deterioration of urban life. The large scale of such designs led to a loss of cohesion and order, resulting in residential districts that merely provided an 'amputated life'.[8] Bos argued that instead, local communities could be created through the facilitation of all sorts of everyday acts; for example, casual contacts would grow naturally through the presence of neighbourhood shops. In the following passage, which is strongly reminiscent of the insights that would make Jane Jacobs famous fifteen years later, he wrote:

> Women can just go shopping in their housework clothes (though perhaps without wearing their aprons) (. . .) Human contact in this context is of the greatest importance to them, they are interested in what happens in the circle of people they meet daily and they search for the links and controversies between the shops and neighbourhood residents.[9]

The neighbourhood is not the setting for great and weighty matters, says Bos, but rather a platform for small-scale, human and perhaps trivial meetings, a place where neighbourhood residents can make their everyday lives public. All these local interactions added up would lead the city dweller – and this was essential for Bos – to consider the neighbourhood his or her *own*. For these reasons, Bos also argued for the construction of other meeting places such as community 'auditoriums and handicraft centres' that could be used by both schools and youth organizations.

But a spatial programme that created an overlap between the worlds of local residents was not sufficient to achieve this. The neighbourhood concept could only be implemented successfully if a social programme was also in place. Clubs and associations, which should be stimulated by the government, were given an important role. Bos regularly emphasized the importance of social control:

'A great deal depends on those who provide leadership in the buildings: they will have to be able to win over local residents to participate in community life in a variety of shapes and forms.'[10]

Bos's ideas were not unique: similar ideas developed in the United States, as can be seen in the work of planner Clarence Perry and sociologist Horton Cooley.[11] In the years before the Second World War, Cooley had developed a sociological theory in which face-to-face contacts played an important role in group-formation processes. Perry translated this idea into a planning principle, the 'Neighborhood Unit Concept', one of its central tenets being the construction of communal spaces that would allow communities to emerge.[12] He defended the importance of a central square where ceremonies could be held: 'Here [on the square] on Independence Day the Flag will be raised, the Declaration of Independence will be recited and the citizenry urged to patriotic deeds by eloquent orators.'[13]

The emphasis on the creation of a local community that encompassed the whole of life did not mean that Bos unreservedly yearned for a bygone traditional form of community life - he was well aware of the modern city's positive aspects. The basic principle of the neighbourhood concept is that society must be stratified: the city must not become a collection of 'urban villages' (unrelated parochial domains); instead, communities at the district level must be part of the larger whole of the city. The neighbourhood is part of a district, which in turn is part of one of the urban quarters that together form the city as a whole. Most everyday facilities should be organized at the district level but specific functions of urban life should be organized at the city level. Bos and his committee were certainly conscious of the advantages provided by the anonymous urban public spaces that have developed at the central-city level. One could lose oneself in the anonymous mass there:

> Here, one [experiences] a unique freedom that is not experienced anywhere else (. . .) It satisfies people's frivolous tendencies, creates a relative independence towards other people and frees the individual from the critical and suspicious eye that often makes life in the small community so troublesome, and some- times even unbearable.[14]

The charms of public life, however, could only be enjoyed as a supple- ment to a locally rooted existence: 'The complexity, the strangeness, the unfamiliarity that characterize the modern metropolis can only captivate and enrapture if the city also provides its residents with an orderly and familiar environment.'[15] The public domain could only charm if city dwellers could also return to the parochial domain of the local community.

In the Bos committee's book the issue of urban society is

dominated by a communitarian vision. Above all, the ideal city had to be a place where individuals could develop as part of an all-encompassing community that distinguished itself from the 'mass culture' of footloose, instinctive individuals. Such an urban public could be created by an emphasis on small-scale developments, combined with a mixing of functions and a targeted social programme. But shortly after the Second World War, when Lotte Stam-Beese was commissioned to implement these ideas in a plan for the neighbourhood that would later be called Pendrecht, she shifted the emphasis in her own design philosophy to a republican programme.

The City as the 'Homestead of Democracy'

Pendrecht was intended to be the second Rotterdam district, after Zuidwijk, that was based on the principles of the neighbourhood concept. In Zuidwijk, the neighbourhood concept had led to an important social breakthrough. With his communitarian ideal, Bos aimed not only to reverse the alienation of the modern city but also to break down the compartmentalized social structure known as *zuilen* (literally, 'pillars':the segregation of society along socio-political lines), which had had the Netherlands in its grip since the nineteenth century. Different groups, from socialists and liberals to Catholics and Protestants, had segregated themselves from each other, and social life - from sports clubs to housing corporations - mostly took place via organizations that were connected to one of these 'pillars'. It was therefore revolutionary that shortly after the Second World War the city council decided that a single housing corporation without ties to an existing 'pillar' should be allowed to develop the Zuidwijk district: the specially founded Stichting voor Volkshuisvesting Tuinstad Zuidwijk (literally, the Garden City Zuidwijk Public Housing Foundation).[16] In Zuidwijk every tenant automatically and compulsorily became a member of the Zuidwijkse Gemeenschap ('Zuidwijk association'): this was how the association was to form the collective within which the residents must develop themselves.[17]

This ideal was under pressure at the time Pendrecht was being developed. For starters, Lotte Stam-Beese, the architect, favoured a generous interpretation of the neighbourhood concept in her design: she exchanged the communitarian way of thinking that regularly appeared in Bos's *De stad der toekomst* manifesto for a republican vision for the local community. While Bos had emphasized the importance of the sense of community among district residents, Stam-Beese emphasized the freedom of the individual. According to Stam-Beese, Pendrecht must not become a village but a city. And the most important quality of a city, in her view, was that it provides its residents with the possibility to choose from different ways of life: 'The choice that the city offers regarding housing, work, relaxation, mutual communication, is the essential element of an urban society and *au fond* the difference between a city and a village.'[18] For her, city dwellers were modern individuals who must be allowed to shape their own lives, and this meant that freedom of choice was important. Consequently, the problem of the modern industrial metropolis was not so much its modern character but rather its monotony and associated lack of choice and variety:

> The modern city (. . .) should be spatially organized in such a way that there is space for the one and for the other; in this regard it is irrelevant how open a city is, how much wider the streets have become (. . .) What does matter is whether, in relation to spatial variety, this diversity and alternation is present to give the human being who is moving and present in it the feeling that he has the freedom to choose from many options.[19]

However, this freedom of choice did not mean the city dweller was permitted to ignore the alternatives that he did not choose. Stam-Beese argued that the city dweller was also automatically part of the democratic urban community: 'Our democratic system preferably excludes the exception, the "not being part of". We stand in a space and are part of it.' And this also meant that city dwellers would have to relate to all those other city dwellers:

> The city dweller shares with many others the ground on which his house is built, on which he walks and rests; he uses things and institutions that are used by innumerable others besides himself. He is not one, but one within the framework of many others. His wellbeing will therefore greatly depend on his relationship with his surroundings, his fellow human beings. After all, the nature of this relationship can either mean the development and enrichment of his own self as an individual or the destruction of his own self.[20]

To Stam-Beese, the city was thus the 'homestead of democracy', [21] and the architect must therefore first and foremost design a spatial environment that expressed this precarious republican balance between the freedom to choose on the one hand, and an involvement in a greater whole on the other.

This was also the approach she took to her Pendrecht commission. She did not consider it her task to design a beautiful residential district with elegant avenues and monumental buildings. Stam-Beese argued that the identity of Pendrecht should not be sought in the architecture of the buildings themselves; instead, the district's unique character would lie in the way she tried to shape it socially:

'The primary aim was not to strive for an incidental aesthetic solution; the structure of a social constellation itself was used as a design element. A "grid" was sought within which these conclusions could develop in their own way.'[22] According to the terminology used in this book, Stam-Beese saw herself primarily as an interface designer.

In Pendrecht her ideas were given shape in the design for the repetitive residential unit: the 'stamp' of buildings around a communal garden that could easily be repeated. The final plan for Pendrecht consists of a pattern of dozens of adjacent 'copies' of this stamp. Adjacent residential units were mirrored in order to avoid monotony - something she also tried to avoid within the residential units: the different types of buildings within the residential units were intended for residents with different lifestyles.

Mixing different ways of life served two purposes for Stam-Beese: on the one hand, the mix of different types of city dwellers would provide the opportunity to avoid a suffocating social control. Stam-Beese argued that mixing lifestyles in a differentiated environment would 'better meet his [the city dweller's] need for freely chosen, mostly erratic contacts.'[23] On the other hand, Stam-Beese hoped that a form of social solidarity would develop within the residential unit, partly because all the residents shared the communal garden. Ultimately, it was the social relations developing in the residential units that should give Pendrecht its character. The social connections that would grow between the seventy to eighty families who were to live in each residential unit would form the actual bricks and mortar of the new neighbourhood, as far as Lotte Stam-Beese was concerned. In her explanation of the plans for Pendrecht, she wrote:

> A deliberate choice has therefore been made to reject the creation of a senseless variety based on outer form, trusting instead that an inner social variety of residential groups will come to the fore and manifest itself in the use of the dwellings and the communal garden, in the activities of the residents and their mutual relations, thus counteracting the apparent uniformity and monotony.[24]

The architect's task is therefore to spatially connect different lifestyles in such a way that social relationships can develop. But which lifestyles are and are not allocated a place in that design? How are the different lifestyles labelled and codified in the design? And to what extent does this labelling in itself play a role in the way social relationships are shaped? This discussion was relevant at two levels in Pendrecht: at the level of the individual residential units and at the level of the district as a whole. It is worth considering this in detail because a similar discussion is currently ongoing regarding the emergence of digital media: who labels the lifestyles that are allocated a place in the interface design (regardless of whether it is for a neighbourhood or a mobile phone screen) and how are these different lifestyles ranked?

For the implementation of her residential units in Pendrecht, Stam-Beese made meticulous use of data from the Rotterdam city council's statistics department. She divided the population into groups of people who were in one of five different phases of life: singles, the elderly, families with no children or only one child, small families, and large families. She considered one or two types of dwelling appropriate for each group, varying from the single-family dwelling and flat to high-rise blocks. She calculated exactly what proportion of Rotterdam's population was formed by each group, and those details in turn informed the design of her residential unit: at the time the elderly made up 6 per cent of Rotterdam's population and exactly 6 per cent of the dwellings in the residential units were therefore made suitable for the elderly. She made similar calculations for the other groups. The city's articulation, with all its different lifestyles, was thus concentrated in the smallest possible unit, the residential unit. And the residential unit, with its seventy to eighty families, must therefore be a representative reflection of the whole city - a sort of 'micro version' of Rotterdam grouped around a communal garden.[25]

At the district level, lifestyles were arranged completely differently: in Zuidwijk a single housing corporation, uniting all Zuidwijkers, had successfully developed the district but this was politically no longer feasible when it came to the development of Pendrecht. The district was parcelled out in nine neighbourhoods that were marked out using Roman numerals. These neighbourhoods (Pendrecht I to Pendrecht IX) were then assigned to each 'pillar's' housing corporation. In addition, part of the district was also developed by private developers. Pendrecht was divided into a number of neighbourhoods that all acquired their own character: Pendrecht I and Pendrecht VII were allocated to the socialist *Onze Woning* housing corporation, the Catholic *Voor het Huisgezin* housing corporation developed Pendrecht V and the Protestant *Patrimonium* housing corporation developed Pendrecht IV, while Pendrecht VIII was developed by the *Rotterdamse Droogdok-maatschappij*, which eventually mainly provided housing for the employees of this dry docks company. As a result, the different neighbourhoods in Pendrecht developed into somewhat segregated parochial domains for the different 'pillars' of the population. The distinctions became particularly clear on specific holidays, for instance when part of Pendrecht suddenly turned into a sea of red for the socialist flag parade as part of May Day celebrations - a survey of residents in the 1950s showed that this was how at least some residents experienced it: 'There is a division into the reds and the blacks here, and we belong to the latter. On 1 May we got the shock of our lives because this looked like a communist village.'[26]

To provide a counterweight to this geographic compartmentalization, Stam-Beese paid considerable attention to the public spaces between the different parts of the district in the overall design. Facilities such as churches and schools were built on a number of green strips that radiate from the heart of Pendrecht in four different directions. These green strips create the edges between the different neighbourhoods, merging in the fields and the Zuiderpark that borders the district on the other side. By locating them next to each other, Stam-Beese hoped that the different groups would meet each other there. In addition, a large square was constructed in the middle of the district at the intersection of the green strips and the main roads. This square accommodated large-scale facilities at district level and was intended to develop into a central area to be used by all the district's residents. 'It was meant to be an urban square filled with different activities in the same way that Pendrecht as a residential area was intended to be an urban district and not a dormitory city.'[27] The aim was for all Pendrecht residents to meet regularly at this central square and thus be absorbed into the local community.

The hope for the neighbourhood concept was that carefully thought-out interventions in the programming for districts such as Pendrecht would create a platform from which a local community would develop. Local shops within walking distance and public spaces to be used by different groups would ensure that residents met frequently. Communal facilities such as the shared gardens in Pendrecht were meant to create a sense of 'ownership', and, hopefully, a sense of solidarity. However, reality was not so easily managed: not all residents in the district wanted to become part of a local community; moreover, when the district was finally finished, television and cars were on the rise, which meant that many residents' parochial domains began to reach far beyond the district they lived in.

'The Death of Distance' and the Neighbourhood as 'Ethereal Zone'

Perhaps one of the most striking aspects of the neighbourhood concept was the principle that community and neighbourhood coincide: everyone who lived in a particular neighbourhood was expected to be part of the local community. It was this very link between parochial domain and urban neighbourhood that quickly made the concept controversial. At the end of the 1950s a new generation of academics publicly rejected this geographic principle of the neighbourhood concept. They argued that modern media and means of transport, which hardly featured in the neighbourhood concept, actually heralded a new era. They frankly declared that the neighbourhood was out of date as a meaningful social entity: from now on publics would form around the television screen and, thanks to the car, they would no longer be tied to a fixed geographical location. This went hand in hand with increased attention to the wishes of the individual in the philosophical debate about the urban community. The communitarian and republican ideas of the 1950s now had to compete with a libertarian perspective.

This development first became apparent in various surveys of residents in Pendrecht and adjacent Zuidwijk in the 1950s, which made it clear that many of the new residents were quite happy in these districts. This was hardly surprising: due to the housing shortage they had lived with their parents or parents-in-law until recently, sometimes for a long time after marrying.[28] Nevertheless, most residents did not experience the district as a clear-cut community, pointing to the considerable contrasts between population groups. In both Pendrecht and Zuidwijk residents reported the regional contrasts that could be found in the district: 'My greatest objection to this district is that all sorts of people live together here. You live here with 8 families using one flight of stairs, and they're people from Indonesia, Groningen, Friesland and Rotterdam. They don't get on - it simply doesn't work.'[29] Barends and De Pree, who conducted surveys in adjacent Zuidwijk, concluded that there were few contacts in the neighbourhood due to this diversity. Physical proximity alone was not enough: brief encounters mainly developed when neighbourhood residents also shared a number of cultural points of contact. However, it is worth noting that cultural differences between people from other Dutch provinces such as Brabant and Friesland apparently faded over time.

The most important question in the surveys was whether residents were keen on the design's collective nature. In adjacent Zuidwijk it quickly became apparent that many residents were not the least interested in contacts or communal ownership. They would rather choose their own social contacts than be forced to participate in them. Barends and De Pree wrote in a report at the end of the 1950s:

> The residents of this type of housing are part of a commune against their will (. . .) A number of residents object to this: they prefer the anonymity of families in types of mass housing where there is less social control. These residents are not looking for contacts within their housing environments but rather through clubs, societies, and the like - that is, selected contact.[30]

In Pendrecht, too, many residents were not interested in intensive involvement in the neighbourhood. Some people even thought it was the residential units and gallery flats that made it possible to live alongside others pleasantly without having any contact:[31] As they put it in one survey of residents, 'All sorts of people live here but thanks to the gallery flat you hardly notice this', and 'I think the gallery flat is pleasant because you don't have anything to do with each other. You don't even know who your upstairs and downstairs neighbours are.'[32] Many neighbourhood residents indicated that they preferred superficial relations with neighbours to close bonds with neighbourhood residents because they feared the social control that is an inevitable component of a close-knit local community.[33]

The results are diametrically opposed to the Bos committee's communitarian vision for the role of the neighbourhood as a community, and not everyone wanted to hear this at the time. In the middle of the 1950s researcher Van Doorn-Janssen concluded that residents in Zuidwijk were not necessarily interested in the imposed sense of community either; her report was withheld and was only made public in 1965.[34] Yet her findings were not completely unexpected.[35]

The young sociologist J.A.A. van Doorn caused uproar at a conference when he challenged the theorists behind the neighbour-hood concept by arguing that urban neighbourhoods are by their very nature composed of people with completely different back-grounds. The idea that a new, all-encompassing community could be built from those different ways of life was merely wishful thinking: 'The very social heterogeneity of the new districts (. . .) means that the possibility of a more or less total organization of district life is a lost battle, nothing more than an illusion. The social fields within which the various component groups move have no point of contact.'[36]

Internationally, a similar shift could be observed in different academic disciplines. In the United States and England 'community studies' were still an important strand of thought within sociology during the 1950s and 1960s. Its academics were interested in the extent to which urban society still accommodated clearly recogniz-able communities; for example, did the traditional workers' districts still form a local community?[37] However, this focus on local community life gradually lost ground. In Germany, for example, Hans Paul Bahrdt argued in *Die moderne Grossstadt* that modern city dwellers actually found local communities suffocating. He contrasted the idea of the neighbourhood as a community with the idea of the city as a market. The city exists as a focal point for interactions: it is the sum of all those transactions between individuals, who all act from self-interest and their own ideas. By 'transactions' Bahrdt not only means economic examples but also processes of cultural exchange.[38] Rather than the neighbourhood, the city as a whole functions as an interface where city dwellers harmonize their lives with each other. There is no clear-cut, over-arching community, but that is not necessarily a loss.

This libertarian approach, which is based on the individual

rather than on the local community, also gained ground in the Netherlands during the 1950s and 1960s. Here, too, modern means of transport and the rise of communication technologies such as the telephone allowed individuals to organize their lives independently of geography. The media (the rise of television) could make the sense of involvement palpable on an even larger (national) scale. Young up-and-coming academics concluded that the neighbourhood was nothing more than an 'ethereal zone', the place where people happened to live but that was of little further interest to them. This 'death of distance' thinking at the time can be found in the work of urban researcher Groenman. In a 1971 article for *Intermediair*, aimed at a larger public, he wrote:

> Man's orientation towards his environment has a rhythm that can be geographically fixed and sociologically interpreted. He has a strong domestic focus, that is, he is focused on his family, his house and its immediate vicinity. The surrounding area is an 'ethereal zone' to him. He uses it only instrumentally, passing through it in his car without knowing it. Only a much greater whole takes shape for him, but only in outline. In his case this might be a big city and its surroundings, or perhaps even the whole country about which he has been fed so much information by the mass media that he can now join in conversations about (. . .) the renewal of a political party, the unrest in the east of Groningen, the mine closures, the Delta plan, [Minister of Foreign Affairs] Luns' pinstriped suits, and so on.[39]

It is interesting that Groenman's discussions of the city include the role of the media, which until then had been largely absent in debates about the neighbourhood. The emergence of mass media had enlarged the city dweller's world, so that he was now involved in a larger social unit. The city dweller was only involved in his immediate environment because he happened to live there. But the neighbourhood, the district and perhaps even the city were no longer territorial units that he felt connected with or that gave him the sense of belonging to a community. The rise of mass media had widened his horizon to include the nation. For the city dweller, it is as part of the media public that the 'larger whole' is shaped. Involvement in this case is non-committal, it is the rough outlines (the unrest in the east of Groningen) that the individualized city dweller is given and that are occasionally filled in with a bit of detail (Luns's pinstriped suits).

This way, the feeling of being part of a collective was detached from a physical location (the neighbourhood) and linked with the circulation of symbols in a media landscape. And the city dweller became so footloose that he turned into a 'nomad': there was not one particular location where he felt at home. While the Bos committee had considered 'nomad' a negative term denoting someone who could not put down roots, the term now had a positive connotation. Modern man was a nomad who could choose which communities and publics to join. This did not mean he was completely rootless - it simply meant he no longer put roots down into the ground but up into the air in the form of the television antennae that began to proliferate on roofs at the time.[40] With the mass media starting to function as a landscape for cultural exchange, distance and location hardly seemed to matter any more. According to this theory, the television screen had become the most important interface and the city street was nothing but a place we occasionally drive through.

The rise of the media and increasing mobility contributed to the development of a new type of public in the decades after the Second World War. Although people had fewer contacts in the neighbourhood, this did not mean that they were lonely but that the context in which they organized themselves changed socially. The collectives that city dwellers joined were increasingly based on shared interests and professional relationships and less related to the neighbourhood they lived in. This is not entirely at odds with the neighbourhood concept. Lotte Stam-Beese also emphasized the importance of freedom of choice: city dwellers should be granted this choice but at the same time a minimal mutual involvement at the neighbourhood level was also necessary for the continued existence of the city as a community. In her view, the neighbourhood played an important role as a meeting place for city dwellers with different networks. This function gradually faded in both the broader debate and urban policy.[41]

This did not mean that the neighbourhood entirely lost its function: while it was no longer the exclusive location where city dwellers must try to live together, after the 1960s the neighbourhood continued to be the place where a considerable part of everyday life took place for many city dwellers.[42] The lifestyles of city dwellers differed but they also occasionally overlapped. In that sense, the neighbourhood was not an all-powerful collective. Instead, American academic Suttles observed the development of 'communities of limited liability' at the neighbourhood level in the United States. In his book *The Social Construction of Communities* he described how neighbourhood residents from different backgrounds lived among each other. They did not form close-knit communities but some residents were still involved in local affairs, often organized around a local institution (a school or café). However, they often did this on a voluntary basis and were frequently involved in many other communities at different levels as well. Involvement in the local community tended to be somewhat noncommittal - people could also withdraw. And such publics often became concrete only when there were external threats or problems in the neighbourhood.[43]

This development, in which the neighbourhood is no longer seen as an a priori community but rather as a latent public, was initially considered a blessing by many. From the mid-1990s onward, however, it gradually became a worrying issue. The role of the neighbourhood as an 'interface' returned to the agenda when it clearly started to falter as a result of various developments. By the end of the twentieth century, the role of the neighbourhood in urban society gradually came into focus again. Whereas freedom of choice and the city dweller's nomadic life had been the main focus of attention until then, the emphasis now shifted to the mutual involvement that modern urban society also requires. But what exactly should this consist of and is the neighbourhood the best place to shape this mutual involvement?

The Neighbourhood: from Parochial to Public Domain

On 16 January 2007 a number of residents from Sint-Annaland street in Pendrecht met to formulate a number of 'street rules'. The meeting was part of Rotterdam city council's 'Mensen maken de stad' (literally, 'People make the city') programme that was introduced in 2002 to improve the quality of life in a number of neighbourhoods in the city through interventions at street level. The evening involved a gimmick: a barrel of water that appeared to be on fire - reaching agreements between the street's residents was apparently difficult, but the idea was that now they had seen water burn they should surely be able to get over that hurdle. At the end of the evening a number of rules were indeed drawn up: residents promised to greet each other, to keep the street clean, to park their cars properly in the parking spaces and to ensure that their children did not cause trouble; they also agreed to regularly organize activities together.[44] These sorts of street rules have been agreed upon in several streets in Rotterdam since 2002 and they form one of the spearheads of the policy that the new municipal executive implemented following the election victory of the newly formed Leefbaar Rotterdam ('Liveable Rotterdam') party. According to the executive's programme, 'Rotterdam has developed into a world city' but the result of all these changes is that some people no longer feel at home in the city:

> One result of the changes that has received little attention is the lack of connectedness between Rotterdammers and their city: newcomers do not feel at home yet, and the original inhabitants feel less and less at home. Many Rotterdammers see the city as a place to live rather than a place where they live together.[45]

The concern expressed here by the Rotterdam city council is not isolated: it is part of a broader shift in the debate about the city.

The modern exposition that sang the praises of individual freedom of choice is increasingly resisted as a result of renewed attention to community connections. Globalization, migration and the neoliberal politics of flexibility have led to a growing sense of economic and cultural insecurity among different groups in society. In 2005 the Scientific Council for Government Policy observed that these developments had led to a decline in 'social cohesion':[46]

> Recently, general satisfaction has given way to increasing concern about civil society and democracy in the Netherlands. There has been a noticeable decline in people's involvement with each other (social trust) and with their democratic institutions (political trust). This declining social cohesion has negative social consequences such as anonymity, alienation, a lack of security, criminality, and a dwindling sense of well-being (and perhaps also of prosperity).[47]

These changes became visible in Pendrecht in the 1980s. Until then, Pendrecht had been a district for the lower middle class where residents were generally satisfied. But this gradually changed: employment opportunities at the port of Rotterdam declined, partly as a result of the bankruptcy of the RDM shipyard, which had once been one of the main employers in the district, and the relocation of shipbuilding jobs to countries such as Korea; in addition, many of the original residents started to age and moved from their flats to more comfortable dwellings elsewhere. Their children now preferred to live in the new suburban housing developments such as Carnisselande in Barendrecht - the once modern houses in Pendrecht were now considered small and noisy and mainly attracted migrants and tenants from the lowest rungs of society. Furthermore, the neighbourhood was rapidly becoming more multicultural and many of the Dutch residents felt less and less at home. A growing number of residents are now considering moving out of the neighbourhood.[48]

The underlying mechanism in such developments has been described well by Arnold Reijndorp in his book *Stadswijk* (literally: City District): newcomers, often migrants and in some cases also 'new city dwellers' (well-educated young people from the 'creative class'), have left their mark on the neighbourhoods of a number of Dutch urban districts over the last two to three decades.[49] This has left many long-time residents feeling that the neighbourhood is no longer theirs. In the past, many original residents considered their old city neighbourhood their parochial domain and now feel that they are slowly losing control of it. According to Reindorp, 'Strong social changes lead to a lack of clarity about the rules. New groups are apparently not prepared to unquestioningly comply with existing norms, instead following their own rules.'[50]

This is a potential source of mutual incomprehension and

conflict. Dieteke van der Ree elucidates this process using surveys of residents in Zuidwijk, the Rotterdam district adjacent to Pendrecht. She observes that residents became less satisfied from the 1990s onwards, partly as a result of the arrival of new residents who were unfamiliar with the unspoken rules that had developed over the years, or who sometimes did not even speak the language. 'Changes in familiar surroundings often mean that the experienced social space becomes smaller,' says Van der Ree, 'a growing number of strangers are part of it and the sense of familiarity slowly crumbles.'[51] The arrival of foreigners in particular leads to a feeling of 'expropriation', for example 'because other groups take over familiar places.'[52] As one resident put it:

> If you go to the park when the weather is nice, all you see are Turks or Moroccans or whatever. They all sit around barbecuing in the park. The park doesn't really belong to the Zuidwijkers any more, in terms of what you [with a nod to her husband] used to do, going to the canoeing pond or whatever. That's something you needn't even try to do anymore, it's all been taken over by the foreigners. You don't feel at home there anyway. Because you're alone against a bigger group - the balance is gone.[53]

In 2007, the then Minister of Integration and Housing Ella Vogelaar summarized this development, which did not apply only to districts such as Pendrecht or Zuidwijk, as follows: 'Many of the residents who have remained in the district have seen their district change, and they experience the new situation as threatening. Encounters with other residents are becoming fewer and fewer.'[54]

The alleged lack of social cohesion resulting from such situations could be mended at the neighbourhood level. This time it is not the architects and urban planners but the policymakers and politicians who see the neighbourhood as a 'pretext'[55], as the appropriate location for their interventions. For example, in 2002 a national programme tackling forty problematic *krachtwijken* (literally, 'power districts') was one of the spearheads of a new policy on large cities. A special programme for 'social recovery' was also to be introduced. The central issue in these programmes, which always include Pendrecht, is what could be called the 'tuning' of the neighbourhood as an interface. How can social trust and social cohesion be restored? The apparent lack of 'connection' with society is thus reduced to a lack of connection with the neighbourhood. We see in this respect different strategies to intervene in the 'programming' for the neighbourhood. Activation is used in attempts to involve neighbourhood residents in community activities and make them conform to a collective protocol. Restructuring using interventions in a neighbourhood's physical programme is an attempt to attract new groups of residents to the neighbourhood who are expected to enhance its 'social cohesion'. A third group of researchers and policymakers argues that all these attempts to create a new sense of community at the neighbourhood level should be abandoned in favour of smaller-scale interventions that might stimulate brief encounters between neighbourhood residents, in the hope that these will result in the development of mutual trust.

The 'Mensen maken de stad' programme as it was implemented in places such as Pendrecht is an example of 'activation'. This programme includes the activation of and appeals to Rotterdam's residents to reach agreements with each other at the street level. The city council also refers to an 'urban etiquette': a number of basic rules drawn up by residents that are intended to make coexistence on the street possible. This urban etiquette is meant to function as a code of behaviour or protocol; without this basis, coexistence of city dwellers with diverse backgrounds is not possible. It is remarkable that the programme presupposes that a matter-of-fact protocol on its own is not enough. Neighbours are also encouraged to collectively organize and participate in activities. It is hoped that they will then feel they are 'joint owners' of their physical and social surroundings and want to become committed to them. Commitment is what the city council calls 'social and normative cohesion'. Social cohesion means that residents know each other and participate in social activities; normative cohesion means that residents share a set of norms, values and patterns of behaviour. If the street does not automatically function as an 'interface', where social and normative cohesion result from everyday meetings, then the state must intervene and provide a framework within which this can still take place. Reactions to this active form of 'programming' vary: in an evaluation of the 'Mensen maken de stad' programme, the sociologists Duyvendak and Uitermark observe that 'impressive results' have been achieved in a number of places; they emphasize that it is naïve to think that, certainly in *krachtwijken* ('power districts' – the central government euphemism for depressed neighbourhoods contained in its policy on large cities), residents will start initiating all sorts of things of their own accord, and an activating programme can therefore be important. At the same time, they emphasize that not everyone wants to participate:

> 'Social cohesion does not mean that everyone in the street knows each other and maintains friendly relations with other residents. In the 'Mensen maken de stad' reality, it appears that the street is *the* framework for social relations for only a limited number of residents.' But those few residents can in fact play an important role in managing the neighbourhood.[56]

Another way to improve social cohesion in a neighbourhood is 'restructuring': getting new population groups to commit themselves to a district. Restructuring consists of partly demolishing and rebuilding a district. Using the metaphor of the neighbourhood as an interface, we can see restructuring as a refinement of the filtering mechanism that determines which groups of city dwellers are brought together at the neighbourhood and district levels. The new houses are intended to attract new, often better-educated and better-off target groups to the district. Just as Stam-Beese spatially organized different lifestyles in the residential unit, the aim is now to mix social groups at the district level. Active intervention in the spatial organization of different lifestyles will give the less well educated new 'chances to meet', providing them with the chance to extend the social networks that they can call upon. At the same time, the advent of new population groups can boost spending power in a district, thus ensuring the continued existence of meeting places such as shops, cafés and restaurants. This restructuring policy is partly based on neighbourhoods, at least those in problem districts, not being too one-sided in their composition: if they become the exclusive domain of one (disadvantaged) group, the fear is that this can lead to exclusion.

Reference is often made in this regard to American research showing that a 'culture of poverty' has developed in some neighbourhoods: because hardly anyone has paid employment, the norm within the neighbourhood changes, and unemployment is seen as normal. Moreover, a lack of casual contacts with other networks excludes the possibility of finding work through those channels. The neighbourhood then becomes conceptualized as a parochial domain within which norms and values are interchangeable. As a result of a lack of contact with wider society, deviant values and norms develop and thrive.[57]

A number of policymakers and critics have serious reservations about activation and restructuring. Geographers Musterd and Van Kempen, for example, argue that the physical 'mixing' of lifestyles does not automatically lead to more contact between different groups and a broadening of social networks. It is more likely that different social groups develop at the neighbourhood level that indeed live among but not necessarily with each other.[58] There is also criticism of activation at the neighbourhood level: many social problems do occur in the neighbourhood but they are not necessarily problems arising in the neighbourhood but rather structural socioeconomic problems that would be better approached in a different way, for example, through training programmes.

Moreover, a number of critics consider the emphasis on activation and participation contrary to the ideal of freedom of choice for city dwellers. Why should neighbours in a particular street be compelled to organize social activities together? Arnold Reijndorp considers that far too much emphasis is placed on 'cohesion' and 'harmony' in urban policy. He argues that the real task is not the creation of a new togetherness but rather creating a framework for heterogeneity.[59] The neighbourhood does not have to become a local community, as long as it is a place where different residents can trust each other. A republican rather than a communitarian ideal should be the aim: the neighbourhood is a public domain in which different worlds overlap rather than a local community's parochial domain.

We have thus gained a picture of the different ways in which urban planners, working from their underlying urban ideals, have tried to create specific publics at the neighbourhood level through interventions in 'programming'. However, the city dwellers themselves have faded from this picture. So, how do parochial domains actually develop in city dwellers' everyday use of space? This question requires a different, more 'bottom-up' approach, which we find in the work of people such as Jane Jacobs.

The Neighbour-hood as an 'Interface' in Everyday Life

When a decisive council meeting was held in the mid-1950s to discuss Robert Moses's plan to construct a big motorway straight through the southern part of Manhattan, New York's 'master builder' lost his self-possession. His proposal to extend 5th Avenue and largely demolish Washington Square Park in the process had hit upon opposition from the residents of nearby Greenwich Village: they did not want a modern ten-lane motorway on concrete posts right next door; they would rather keep the neighbourhood park, where they could walk their dogs and the children could play in peace and quiet. Moses, the powerful urban planner, found it hard to swallow all this small-town quaintness putting paid to his visions for Progress. He tried to persuade the council that no one was actually opposed to his plan: 'there is nobody against this – nobody, nobody, nobody, but a bunch of . . . mothers!'[1]

The leader of this bunch of mothers was Jane Jacobs, journalist, writer and, according to *The New York Review of Books*, neighbour-hood activist with a Napoleonic gift for mobilizing a civilian army of alarmed residents. From the beginning of the 1950s she success-fully defended the 'everydayness' of neighbourhood life in fiery polemics against the large-scale master plans of powerful architects and modernist urban planners. Jacobs argued that although they promised progress, they actually threatened to wipe out the traditional city street and its associated urban dynamics. Of course their wide boulevards look splendid, with their elegant trees, symmetrical lay-out and monumental buildings, she said in one of her articles, but none of that has anything to do with life in the city, as she made clear in the punchline that followed these laudatory words: 'They will have all the attributes of a well-kept, dignified cemetery.'[2]

It was quotes such as this that made Jacobs famous and that have made her book *The Death and Life of Great American Cities* a classic that is still read fifty years after it was first published. But the book is more than simply a polemic against the established order: what makes it interesting is Jacobs's attempt to explain why the city street plays such an important role as an 'interface' in urban life. She argued that a neighbourhood feel can develop out of the apparently chaotic accumulation of everyday interactions. This is not a communitarian, village-like sense of neighbourhood solidarity. Rather, it leads to a republican or even libertarian urban public of familiar strangers.

Jacobs was not alone in paying attention to everyday life. From the 1950s onwards a wider interest developed in the way city dwellers give meaning to their lives through a series of more or less trivial everyday acts. Sociologist Erving Goffman described in *The Presentation of Self in Everyday Life* (1959) how people behave differently in different situations, linking specific protocols and behavioural repertoires to specific locations. Not much later Kevin Lynch described in his classic *The Image of the City* (1960) how city dwellers, from their everyday lives, also attribute symbolic meanings to places. A decade later saw the appearance of Lyn Lofland's study of how a number of these aspects coincide: *A World of Strangers: Order and Action in Urban Public Space* explores how groups of city dwellers appropriate particular urban locations.

What all these studies have in common is that they explicitly or implicitly describe the city as the 'theatre of everyday life'.[3] The city is the stage where we perform the various roles we take on at various times, being actor and public simultaneously. The very fact that we show who we are allows us to compare ourselves with others and identify with or distinguish ourselves from them. The places *where* we do that can then acquire an emotional or symbolic meaning on top of that. Everyday routines can create a feeling of involvement – the square I walk across every day becomes *my* square. In the long run, such everyday practices can also lead to a process of collective symbolic appropriation: this is the bench where the elderly people always sit and have a chat at morning teatime; that is the square where juveniles show off their souped-up scooters; this is the street where chic ladies do their shopping, here is the nightlife street that is well known in the gay scene. The bench, the square, the street then become their bench, their square or their street: parochial domains are the sum total of everyday acts.

Half a century after they first appeared in print, the observations made by Jacobs, Lynch, Goffman and Lofland are still useful for understanding the process that leads to the development of parochial domains. But of course a great deal has changed since Robert Moses's bulldozers threatened to flatten Jane Jacobs's urban neighbourhood. The most significant sociological development since then has been the emergence of what American-Canadian sociologist Barry Wellman has labelled 'networked individualism': individualization does not mean that we are increasingly left to our own devices and that we have broken our ties with others; rather, it means that we have more say about the various groups we are part of. This in turn means that many city dwellers are part of a large number of networks that only partly overlap.

Spatially this has led to a two-fold development. On the one hand, parochial domains have gained in importance on all points: specific groups of city dwellers choose to settle in parts of the city where they mainly live among other people like themselves – think, for example, of neighbourhoods where a single ethnic group or lifestyle is overrepresented. On the other hand, many parochial domains can no longer be described as clearly defined areas. Rather, they consist of a network of places spread over a city or even region. The authentic working-class Amsterdammer from Amsterdam's Jordaan or Pijp neighbourhoods now lives in the suburbs of Purmerend or Almere. But on Saturday evenings he still returns to his local pub in his old neighbourhood. In the meantime, a Turkish teahouse has opened next door, and next to that there might be a coffee bar where trendy young people have a cappuccino. Different parochial domains can thus overlap spatially. Geographically, the distance between these different worlds – the local pub, teahouse and designer coffee bar – is small; symbolically, it is huge. To put these recent developments into perspective, we shall first return to the 1950s, to Lower Hudson Street, Greenwich Village, where Jane Jacobs, armed with her Remmington typewriter, did battle against the army of professional planners.

Jane Jacobs's 'Web of Public Respect and Trust'

One of the most influential theories about everyday urban life is still Jane Jacobs's, which is surprising because her book *The Death and Life of Great American Cities* dates back to 1961. Can her observations about street life in 1950s New York still teach us something about how the twenty-first century city functions as an interface? On the one hand, this is hard to imagine: the deli that belonged to Joe Cornacchia, with whom Jacobs sometimes left her house-key, is now probably owned by a new generation of migrants whose origins do not lie in the old world but in Asia or Latin America. Nowadays Lower Manhattan has few job opportunities for the dock workers who lived in the neighbourhood, and in recent decades many middle-class families have moved to the suburbs of New Jersey or Long Island. Of the innumerable butchers in the nearby Meat Packing District only a few remain. Some of them have retained their original function as workplaces, albeit of a different kind, having been transformed into loft-type cafés where the creative work on their laptops developing websites, advertising campaigns or policy memoranda.[4]

On the other hand, Jacobs's book is still relevant not only because she shared her observations about street life as it was half a century ago but mainly because she introduced a method of observing and analyzing that still provides interesting leads. Her central thesis is that the city street plays an important role in the process through which urban communities develop at the neighbourhood level. Jacobs did not favour a village-type sense of community, and the street is thus crucial in building up trust between all those different city dwellers who have to live together. The book is a study of *catalysts* that can start that process.

This trust, says Jacobs in *The Death and Life of Great American Cities*, develops as follows – and it is worthwhile considering the following long quotation in some detail:

> The trust of a city street is formed over time from many, many little public sidewalk contacts. It grows out of people stopping by at the bar for a beer, getting advice from the grocer and giving advice to the newsstand man, comparing opinions with other customers at the bakery and nodding hello to the two boys drinking pop on the stoop, eyeing the girls while waiting to be called for dinner, admonishing the children, hearing about a job from the hardware man and borrowing a dollar from the druggist, admiring the new babies and sympathizing over the way a coat faded. (. . .) Most of it is ostensibly utterly trivial but the sum is not trivial at all. The sum of such casual, public contact at a local level – most of it fortuitous, most of it associated with errands, all of it metered by the person concerned and not thrust upon him by anyone – is a feeling for the public identity of people, a web of public respect and trust and a resource in time of personal or neighborhood need.[5]

Jacobs claimed that mutual trust can develop over time from the repeated everyday and even trivial interaction between neighbourhood residents. As a result, a neighbourhood can grow into a local public of people who recognize each other but also maintain a certain distance from each other. The main question is then: under exactly what circumstances can this 'web of public respect and trust' develop? Which catalysts play a role in whether such an urban public actually develops? Jacobs names several, four of which are particularly relevant: the first two correspond with the insights of planners and policymakers referred to in the previous chapter. A local public can only develop if there is a platform where different residents regularly meet. For the design of urban neighbourhoods like Greenwich Village, where residents performed many everyday activities on foot, Jacobs therefore argued for the development of a grid street plan with small blocks: if streets regularly intersect and users can take different routes, the chance that people will casually meet is increased.[6]

But only creating such a platform is not enough; the second point is that residents must have a reason to actually use the potential meeting places. Jacobs's advice was to mix different functions: the combination of housing, shopping and work ensures that there is always someone on the street in her neighbourhood. A certain 'programming' is therefore required that elicits simultaneous spatial use. This leads us to the third point: exactly which people must be brought together through such a programme? What sort of 'filter mechanism' is required so that mutual trust can flourish? Jacobs argues for a good balance between regular users and strangers. In her view it is important that enough people are present who have a certain sense of 'ownership' and involvement regarding a neighbourhood's meeting places. An urban neighbourhood is not the residents' segregated parochial domain; it also functions as a public domain where strangers constantly come and go. This creates a certain tension: the presence of too many strangers in a neighbourhood can erode the residents' sense of trust: they no longer recognize the other users and this undermines the sense of 'being at home' in the neighbourhood.

It is therefore important that a number of key figures such as shop owners are active in the neighbourhood: recognizable 'public figures' in Jacobs's terms, who are always recognizably present; at the same time, they have an interest as shop owners in being vigilant and maintaining 'street order'.[7] If such public figures are absent, a negative spiral can develop as a counter-reaction: the residents still living in the neighbourhood will move out because they no longer feel they are with familiars; this further reduces the number of people who feel involved, and the feeling of insecurity continues to grow. This means that either a certain filter mechanism is needed to ensure there is a balance between regular users and strangers or a form of supervision or control to ensure that those present comply with the protocol.

Fourthly, Jacobs considered it important to achieve a certain harmonization between a neighbourhood's private, parochial and public domains. If neighbourhood residents interfere too much in each other's lives this can lead to a suffocating social control that Jacobs considers undesirable. The neighbourhood must not be a place where a single group determines which codes are dominant – there must be room for diversity. The goal is for neighbourhood residents to deal with each other on the basis of 'familiar public terms'. Jacobs did not like communality: 'Togetherness is a fittingly nauseating name for an old ideal in planning theory. This ideal is that if anything is shared among people, much should be shared.'[8]

Jacobs's vision of the city is thus based on a more libertarian ideal of urban society: all individuals have their private lives; an overly emphatic parochial atmosphere at the neighbourhood level is undesirable. Society consists of the sum total of all these private lives, and individuals are free to join or not join the communities they choose. Society as a whole exists thanks to a minimal degree of solidarity, where people leave each other's private spheres as intact as possible. As Jacobs put it:

> For all our conformity we are too adventurous, inquisitive, egoistic and competitive to be a harmonious society of artists by consensus, and what is more we place a high value upon the very traits that prevent us from being so. (. . .) Under this system it is possible in

a city-street neighborhood to know all kinds of people without unwelcome entanglements, without boredom, necessity for excuses, explanations fears of giving offence, embarrassments respecting imposition or commitments, and all such paraphernalia of obligation which can accompany less limited relationships. (. . .) It is possible to be on excellent sidewalk terms with people who are very different from oneself, and even, as time passes, on familiar public terms with them.[9]

The most interesting question when reading *Death and Life* half a century after its publication is not whether the specific way in which these catalysts functioned in 1950s Greenwich Village can still work in our times. The more interesting question is whether the abstracter categorization of these catalysts can still be made applicable: can platform, programme, filter, control and harmonization between the public, the parochial and the private be attuned in such a way that they also lead to social trust in restructuring districts such as Pendrecht?

Consulting Jacobs's work for answers and comparing her insights with the discussions about Pendrecht, one is struck by one thing: on the one hand, her ideal urban neighbourhood consists of the private domain of city dwellers, which is of no concern to anyone but themselves, and on the other hand it consists of the parochial domain, which might belong to everyone but on which no one in particular can leave their mark. One could say that the city street creates a minimal neighbourhood feel. While Lotte Stam-Beese linked mutual encounters to a democratic ideal of mutual involvement, this republican objective disappears in Jacobs's approach.

This minimal involvement is made possible by a shared protocol which everyone seems to comply with: the protocol of small talk, the distant chat for politeness' sake in which the speakers reveal as little as possible of their individual identities. This protocol ensures that despite all the differences between residents, a certain mutual trust and recognition can develop through which residents start to experience the neighbourhood as *their* neighbourhood. It is remarkable that Jacobs does not describe these protocols in more detail. The etiquette in her 1950s neighbourhood was apparently so self-evident that it formed an invisible layer in social interaction; like the private identities of the residents of Hudson Street, it was a fixed given for Jacobs.

However, in discussions about today's urban districts it is precisely this 'self-evidence' of protocol that is disputed. Discussions are often about how city dwellers' diverse protocols relate to each other. Understanding this issue requires more than a purely functional approach to the neighbourhood as a platform. The street is not only a stage where we showcase existing identities according to fixed protocols; the content of these identities and protocols can also change in the everyday interactions between neighbourhood residents. The work of sociologist Talja Blokland provides a number of interesting leads: she shows the role played by the neighbourhood as the theatre of everyday life in the process of identity formation and the construction of protocols.[10]

Talja Blokland's 'Public Familiarity'

In Rotterdam's Hillesluis district the older residents still recall how the inhabitants kept a close eye on each other on Sunday mornings. From behind their windows they watched in which direction everyone walked; that way the stay-at-homes could see which church the passers-by were going to and thus also determine which local parish they belonged to. This morning ritual has now lost its meaning: Sunday church attendance has declined sharply over the past decades, and besides, a large number of Hillesluis's current residents are actually more likely to attend the mosque. Still, this example from sociologist Blokland's *Urban Bonds* study is characteristic of her thinking: people constantly categorize the world and those around them; they constantly compare their own lives with those of others. And the categorizations they make in this process form the basis for social identifications: to which groups do we or do we not belong?

This process of identification, of the appropriation of group characteristics and collective symbols, is largely a spatial process. Blokland agrees with the insights of British sociologist Richard Jenkins, who argues that people express their solidarity or identification with specific collectives or communities in both everyday and special acts. Community is expressed in:

> (. . .) saying this or that, participating in rituals, mounting political protests, fishing together, or whatever. It is in and out of what people do that a shared sense of things and a shared symbolic universe emerges. It is in talking together about 'community' – which is after all a public doing – that its symbolic value is produced and reproduced.[11]

It is in performing all sorts of everyday acts, routines and rituals that we express who we are.[12] Weekly church attendance was a way for Hillesluis's residents to express which group in the district they belonged to: they made an aspect of their lives public. Both their fellow worshippers and those who watched from behind their windows could deduce from the ritual Sunday morning procession which group everyone belonged to. Every community has a cultural repertoire of acts and symbolic expressions, from Sunday morning church attendance to specific ways of greeting, from local accents to clothing preferences. This repertoire is not static: it can be expanded with new elements, and customs can become obsolete or change in their everyday use. The importance of church attendance has declined over the years and has been replaced by other customs and rituals.

The neighbourhood can play an important role in this process. In *Goeie buren houden zich op d'r eigen* (literally, 'Good neighbours keep to themselves') Blokland describes how Hillesluis, a district near Pendrecht whose social composition is somewhat comparable, was for a long time an important platform for many residents where their everyday lives were played out. For some residents, says Blokland, the neighbourhood is indeed the most important stage 'for expressing their membership of groups and perpetuating the group and its norms and values.' Residents could compare their own lives to those of others and distinguish between 'us' and 'them'. As a consequence, the neighbourhood did not automatically develop into a community. Not all neighbourhood residents were part of the same communities and, vice versa, communities present in the neighbourhood did not limit their expressions to its geographical territory. It is simply a given that different ways of life come together in the neighbourhood.[13]

However, repeated interactions with neighbourhood residents can lead to a different type of public that is based on what Blokland calls 'public familiarity'. This public familiarity develops when neighbourhood residents regularly meet in the neighbourhood - while out shopping, at the school gate or because their paths cross when they are going somewhere. Over time, a picture of the other develops from these encounters and, according to Blokland, this does not even require interaction: what matters is that residents can also observe each other from a distance and take notice of each other. In the course of time, other residents' customs and habits can become more familiar, and similarities with and differences from one's own lifestyle gradually become clear. The public familiarity thus established then plays a role in processes of identification:

> The very visibility of behaviour leads to social distinctions and thus to social identifications: they are less neat and tidy, less organized or less civilized than we because they go to the bath-house, do not clean properly, live on the benefit, gossip or hang out the window.(. . .) Public familiarity was a precondition for these distinctions.[14]

Through these encounters people know where they stand with each other and what to expect from each other – precisely through this superficial knowledge based on personal experiences. This way, the neighbourhood functions as an interface again: it is a place for the harmonization of different ways of life. Residents display their own ways of life there and these are also given shape through this process:

neighbourhood residents can or cannot identify with the 'performances' of other residents and harmonize their own ways of life with the collective practices and habits of others, with whom they do or do not identify. The neighbourhood thus functions both as a public domain – a place where different groups of residents have found a way to live together – and a parochial domain - because public trust can develop, everyone feels at home despite the differences.

This form of public familiarity resembles Jacobs's 'familiar public terms' but there are a number of significant differences. Firstly, Jacobs emphasized familiarity with specific individuals; Blokland's concern is rather with a 'categorical knowledge': what matters is not so much familiarity with particular neighbourhood residents but familiarity with members of more generic groups that all have their own habits and customs. We identify with one group and not with another, and – crucially – this very identification is what allows us to feel at home in a neighbourhood: we recognize ourselves in the presence of others and in the prevailing protocols. This does not mean that we must be able to identify with all neighbourhood residents, but we must be able to place other neighbourhood residents and we need enough categorical knowledge about them to be able to make distinctions. This again requires the right balance between 'familiar' and 'strange': these are not, as with Jacobs, the *geographical* categories 'neighbourhood residents' and 'visitors from outside'. Rather, the terms are related to the different lifestyles displayed in the neighbourhood in which residents do or do not recognize themselves. If a neighbourhood develops into the exclusive parochial domain of a specific group, the balance will be disturbed: the other neighbourhood residents might no longer recognize themselves in the neighbourhood and the prevailing everyday protocols that govern behaviour. In this respect, the neighbourhood functions not only as a neutral platform where different lifestyles can be distinguished and given shape; gradually, the places where different groups manifest themselves also acquire a symbolic value. Recognition then means not only the recognition of people with comparable ways of life but also a sense – or lack of sense - of involvement with the locations that have become intertwined with those ways of life. Studies of the symbolic value of urban locations provide more insight into that process.

Eric Gordon's 'Placeworlds' and Lyn Lofland's 'Home Territories'

A year before Jane Jacobs published her *Death and Life of Great American Cities*, another book had already made a deep impression: *The Image of the City* by American urban planner Kevin Lynch. In this book Lynch argued that the value that particular locations have for city dwellers cannot be imposed from above by planners.

A symbolic value can only develop when aspects of an urban 'land-scape' resonate with city dwellers' needs. Although this is primarily an individual process, collective meanings also develop because groups of people usually attribute similar meanings to a city's spatial elements.[15] Sociologists became interested in this process as well: urban sociologist Herbert Gans used the twin terms 'effective' and 'potential' surroundings to shatter the concept of 'physical determinism', that is, that a particular environment can exact a particular type of behaviour. For example, a planner can design a beautiful park but it is only in its use, in the process of appropriation in which individuals and groups use the space for their own goals, that this space acquires a meaning.

An important concept for understanding this process is Eric Gordon's 'placeworld': a group's collection of knowledge and cultural repertoires (the characteristic acts, practices and meanings as a whole) that is related to one or more specific places. As specific elements from a group's cultural repertoire are linked to specific places, they also acquire a symbolic significance: they are not merely places - for members of a group they grow into 'our' places. Gordon harks back to the anthropologist Geertz's term 'local knowledge', a group's shared frame of reference that is linked to specific locations. This might be a concealed passage between two blocks of flats in a district; the consensus about which café serves the best coffee; an unspoken agreement about who has the right to sit on a particular bench in the park; or shared memories of bygone times. The crucial aspect of 'local knowledge' is that it develops from processes of social interaction. Gordon argues that in social situations in a neighbourhood this sort of knowledge is or is not exchanged tacitly.

At the same time, the 'local knowledge' that is built up this way is not only a source of practical information: it is also a shared world of experience that plays a role in binding a public together. A 'we' evolves to whom the shared location-tied knowledge and rituals belong.[16] The collection of a group's location-bound meanings and practices are what Gordon calls a 'placeworld':

> A placeworld, therefore, is a group-defined horizon that is specifically oriented around geographical location. Sharing information about the secret cemetery entrance, for example, is communicative action that results in a placeworld. It is the product of local knowledge.[17]

A 'placeworld' can thus be understood as the collection of places that have a symbolic meaning for the members of a group. This does not mean that a 'placeworld' has a one-to-one correspondence to a geographical location: different groups that live in the same neighbourhood often use different 'placeworlds'; and the reverse is also true: a group that is spread all over the world can also derive a shared identity from, for example, their country of origin. Groups can use a 'placeworld' to distinguish or even segregate themselves from others. As a result, locations or areas can develop into the more or less exclusive domain of a specific group.[18] How this process takes place had already been shown in two studies by American sociologist Lyn Lofland. She referred to the development of 'home territories' and 'urban villages'. A 'home territory' is an urban location that is dominated by one group or another; it results from a gradual process during which a location is appropriated by a certain group that uses it more and more frequently, starts to feel at home there and slowly but surely leaves its mark on the location, so that 'this bar is taken over by homosexuals, that cafeteria by elderly ladies, this hot dog stand by motorcycle buffs, etc.'.[19] The location itself then slowly but surely becomes part of the symbolic repertoire of the group, and the combination of location and its associated activities form a placeworld.

Similarly, on a larger scale, cities can see the development of 'urban villages', neighbourhoods that are dominated by a certain group of city dwellers. Neutral public spaces can be (temporarily) appropriated by groups that leave their mark on that space. This process, during which part of an urban public space is claimed as a parochial domain, does not go smoothly: often a 'symbolic battle' takes place between different groups of users. All sorts of external factors can also play a role in this process – think of policy measures to stimulate or actually prevent a specific group claiming a location as a parochial domain. The 'mosquito' is a good example: this device emits irritating tones that are audible only to the young and is aimed at preventing them from claiming a space as a hangout. Policy measures can also be used to either prevent or stimulate the symbolic representation of specific groups in a neighbourhood – a mosque, for example, or a commercial party that sees a chance to make a profit by developing a location whose design, marketing and price will appeal to a target group with a specific lifestyle.

Together, all these factors produce a certain spatial 'filtering' at the city level: groups of people who recognize each other's lifestyles seek each other out both in terms of where they live and in their leisure pursuits. Lofland had already shown that this is not only true for adjacent areas: in 1973, she wrote that 'Technology is the key to successfully creating and maintaining a village in the midst of the city'.[20] The technology Lofland referred to was the car, which enables city dwellers to easily link together the different parochial areas of the collectives they are part of.

Lofland saw a significant shift in the 1970s, partly caused by the emergence of this technology (the car). In the past - Lofland returns to the Middle Ages here - the symbolic order was linked to a person's appearance. Nearly all city dwellers made very intensive use of a city's public domains, and all sorts of functions that now often have their own, specialized locations overlapped. A city dweller's outward appearance made it possible to recognize which group he or she belonged to - indeed there were laws regulating the clothes people were allowed to wear: Elizabethan England, for example, avoided confusion by making it illegal for the 'ordinary man' to wear clothing made from luxurious fabrics such as velvet.

But in the modern industrial city of the 1970s, Lofland observed the development of a codification that was based on spatial order: an increasing number of urban functions were acquiring their own specialized locations in the urban landscape - the shopping centre here, the university campus there, here a middle-class residential district, further up the road Chinatown. She concluded that 'The ideal of the modern city is like the ideal of a well-ordered home: a place for everything and everything in its place.'[21] In a mood resonant with the optimism of progress, she presented cities such as Los Angeles and Detroit as the epitome of urban civilization and planning: their public domains had dissolved into a mosaic of parochial domains, each with its own specific function. Lofland saw this as a logical process: 'to segregate is human', she wrote, 'to integrate divine.'[22]

This process of parochialization is reminiscent of the principle underlying the neighbourhood concept, but now shaped by bottom-up processes rather than by means of a top-down plan. After all, certain neighbourhoods can, through these processes, develop into the parochial domains of residents who share a particular lifestyle. Yet this is not one-to-one correspondence: while such neighbourhoods do accommodate groups of residents who share specific cultural codes, this does not mean that they form a community. The role of the neighbourhood is a different one: it is not a functional frame-work for integration or the defined territory of an all-encompassing community. The neighbourhood now acquires the function of a symbolic core around which a community is 'imagined': one lives in a particular neighbourhood and derives part of one's identity from this fact; one identifies with others who also live in the neighbour-hood, one recognizes and appreciates the symbolic meanings of specific locations and expressions of groups that live in the neigh-bourhood. Bourdieu, for one, argues that the neighbourhood is an expression of the social status that certain residents arrogate to themselves.[23] The use of specific places then becomes a way to express which collectives people consider themselves part of. This does not mean, however, that people actually have much contact with others who use the same place or that life mainly takes place in the neighbourhood.[24] These housing domains thus lead to a particular mix of different spheres. Considered symbolically, they are parochial domains: to a large degree, residents derive their identity from the neighbourhood and recognize themselves in its symbolic aspects. Considered culturally and socially, it is much less a parochial domain: residents generally do not form a close-knit community but rather an instrumental control relationship with each other.[25]

In some cases, these symbolic neighbourhood ties go a step further: even people who do not live in a neighbourhood can still feel a symbolic connection with it, either because they have lived there in the past or because they work there, go out there, or identify with the symbolic meaning of the neighbourhood in some other way.[26] The neighbourhood thus becomes the central element around which an 'imagined community' forms: people recognize themselves in the symbolic meaning of a place and feel connected to others who also feel connected with it, without necessarily knowing all those others personally. Through mutual interaction, the members of a community or public thus create a framework of stories, memories and qualities they identify with and from which they derive part of their identity. These stories then create the element that binds the public together. This is why Talja Blokland refers to 'imagined communities': they 'exist as mental images of the "we belong together" way of thinking and feeling, and as the everyday practices through which we express which group we belong to and through which we either include others with "us" or exclude them from "us".'[27] Symbolic locations can play a significant role in such 'imagined communities'.

We also see a shift in the function and meaning of the neigh-bourhood: the question is not so much how a local public can develop from a neighbourhood (a shared territory), but how different publics appropriate spaces symbolically. The parochial domain that develops from this does not necessarily limit itself to a neighbourhood – it can consist of a network of different places. Moreover, the mutual ties between the members of its public can vary greatly: a type of urban public can develop around a neighbourhood that is based on a combination of symbolic proximity and personal distance.

Regarding these conclusions, however, it must be noted that the development of theories about parochialization is largely based on research carried out in the United States and it is often several decades old. To what extent are the analyses outlined here also applicable to Dutch cities at the beginning of the twenty-first century? For the answer, we turn to the interesting insights contained in the work of Arnold Reijndorp and others.

Arnold Reijndorp's 'Network City'

At first glance, developments in the Netherlands have run fairly parallel with the picture of parochialization outlined in Lofland's studies. This trend had been observed as early as 1970 by urban researcher Frans Grünfeld. In his doctoral thesis *Habitat and Habitation* he showed that there was a relationship between lifestyle and preferred place of abode: to an increasing extent people appeared to live in a neighbourhood where they could recognize themselves, that is, where people lived who shared their lifestyles to some extent.[28] Increasing prosperity played an important role in this: partly thanks to the advent of the car, the middle class was able to start living further away from their place of work and this made it easier for them to find a house at the location of their choice. Since then, similar conclusions have frequently been reached: in the last decade, for example, De Wijs-Mulkens and Buys and Van der Schaar have shown that the place of abode is increasingly becoming a social expression, the selection of a neighbourhood being connected to preferences associated with specific lifestyles.[29] Yet Lofland's picture of Detroit and Los Angeles as ideal 'cities of the future' is not applicable: the formation of domains in the Netherlands does not go nearly as far as in the United States where, for example, part of the middle class with-draws into 'gated communities'.[30] In the Netherlands this formation of domains is much more limited: in certain districts people with certain lifestyles are slightly more emphatically present than others.

Remarkably, in the Netherlands this limited formation of domains went hand in hand with a development that has seen a large number of neighbourhoods actually become more mixed. Arnold Reijndorp calls this development 'urbanization'. In his book *Stadswijk* he observes this process in a number of older urban districts in the big cities. The increasing variety of lifestyles is caused on the one hand by the influx of migrants and on the other by highly educated young people who also settle in the traditional workers' districts of some of these cities. Reijndorp calls this group the 'new city dwellers'.

At the same time, the world of these new (and in many cases also of the old) residents extends beyond the neighbourhood itself. They use a network of places that is spread over the whole city and sometimes even further afield. Reijndorp therefore refers to the rise of a 'network urbanism'. Cities such as Rotterdam and Amster-dam are part of a larger urban field, which no longer consists of a single city centre surrounded by a periphery containing residential districts; rather, it consists of a network of places with different functions and symbolic meanings that vary for different city dwellers. From this palette, the city dweller puts together his own city: he lives in one place, shops at the shopping centre next to the motorway but also sometimes in the city centre, and in his spare time he visits places that meet his requirements:

> This [network city] is much less the result of urban planning than of government and market strategies for social control and economic development, and of the individual urban planning of

the inhabitants of that city. (. . .) The network city provides a differentiated supply of housing environments, places of employment, education and training, and of cultural, recreational, service and care institutions. The inhabitant of the network city compiles his or her own 'package' from this supply.[31]

At the city level this leads to a mixed picture. On the one hand, geographical networks of parochial domains belonging to different groups develop in the network city. At the same time, they also overlap at a number of places. In some old urban districts we see different groups. Some of the original residents of these urban districts, for example, have moved to the suburbs of large cities, but still regularly return to a few isolated locations in their old neighbourhood: the local pub in Amsterdam's Jordaan neighbourhood – now jammed between a Turkish coffee house and a lounge café for trendy young city dwellers – the sports club or the market. Their parochial domain is thus no longer the neighbourhood where they live; instead, it consists of a collection of different places in the urban region.[32] The reverse is also true: the neighbourhood in the old urban district now consists of a number of different parochial domains; geographically they are next to each other but there is little overlap between these parochial domains: it is now 'living together apart' – different lifestyles all live among but more or less uninvolved with each other.[33]

These developments are connected with an important, broader sociological development that American-Canadian sociologist Barry Wellman calls 'networked individualism'. Individualization means that the modern individual has freed himself from the traditional community and starts living his life according to his own views. But, says Wellman, this does not mean that we are increasingly thrown back on our own resources as individuals: it mainly means that we have more choice regarding the collectives of which we consider ourselves part. We are no longer part of a single overarching collective, but of all sorts of diverse publics, each with its own functions, roles, associated repertoires and parochial domains. According to Wellman:

Rather than relating to one group, they [people] cycle through interactions with a variety of others, at work or in the community. Their work and community networks are diffuse, sparsely knit, with vague, overlapping, social and spatial boundaries. Each person is a switchboard, between ties and networks. People remain connected, but as individuals, rather than being rooted in the home bases of work unit and household. Each person operates a separate personal community network, and switches rapidly among multiple sub-networks.[34]

In their book *Kiezen voor de kudde* ('Following the herd') sociologists Jan Willem Duyvendak and Menno Hurenkamp refer in similar terms to 'light communities': the increasing freedom of choice does not mean that people are no longer part of collectives that they consider meaningful; it's just that the bonds within such collectives are less coercive and membership is no longer automatically for life:

> Groups still determine the (choice) behaviour of people and people still want to belong to groups. They are just not the groups of the past. To an increasing extent, the constriction of close social ties seems to be avoided and temporary and exchangeable ties are becoming more popular. (. . .) Weak or loose bonds, memberships that can be cancelled instead of lifelong associations are frequently preferred to strong ties. And this less collective nature of the new networks also makes it possible to be simultaneously connected to more than one network. It leads to more transient ties but also to more connections. We see the development of light communities.[35]

Together, all these developments mean the parochial domains of the twenty-first-century city can be given shape in at least three ways. First, there are places – think of the nightlife street for some subculture – that clearly belong to a particular public. They have a clearly recognizable character and a symbolic value that are inextricably linked with that public. Different publics or communities have networks of such locations in the city at their disposal that together can always form an 'urban village'. At these places, their users feel 'at home'.

Besides this, parochial domains also develop where it is the symbolic aspects that are decisive. Residents of certain districts can feel connected with a neighbourhood without there being an actual public or community. They feel at home in a neighbourhood or at a location because they recognize themselves in its symbolic meaning but do not necessarily have many contacts or friends there. The neighbourhood is then a 'parish without parishioners'.

A final way in which a parochial domain is given shape was one we found in Jacobs's and Blokland's work. This parochial domain is very close to the public domain: it is given shape by people with different ways of life who regularly go there and relate to each other, as in Jane Jacobs's Hudson Street. The relationship between 'familiar' and 'unknown' there is such that people can identify sufficiently with the location and with others present there to be able to feel at home. In the course of time, neighbourhood residents begin to recognize each other and because all those present comply with a number of shared protocols, this repeated interaction can lead to a sense of trust between the neighbourhood's residents.

This last form of the parochial domain is under a certain amount of pressure. According to Talja Blokland, this is partly because processes of identity formation and public familiarity linked to the neighbourhood are past their peak. Everyday life is concentrated less on the neighbourhood, and collective and individual rhythms have become increasingly divergent. In the past, says Blokland, different aspects of everyday life at the neighbourhood level were much more closely intertwined. Shop owners, for example, often lived in the neighbourhood and therefore had both social and economic ties with the neighbourhood. Networks of solidarity were often also organized at the neighbourhood level, for example through the local church, and the same was true for political networks. Because many of the various social roles for city dwellers were tied to the neighbourhood, residents also regularly met each other in different roles. These encounters did not lead to the formation of a close community but could certainly contribute to a sense of recognizing each other and, thus, to public familiarity.[36]

In general, the rhythms of life of today's neighbourhood residents are less parallel than in Jane Jacobs's day. City dwellers use a more extensive network of places that are spread over the entire city. The first two manifestations of the parochial domain (as the defined 'home territory' or 'urban village' of a specific group or as a symbolic 'parish without parishioners') have become more meaningful as a result.

This development is not entirely unambiguous. There is a process of domain formation in which city dwellers with similar ways of life seek each other out spatially but, at the same time, these spatial networks partly overlap, even if the symbolic distance is sometimes great.

This is the background against which we must see the emergence of digital technologies and new media. Digital media play an important role in the way individual city dwellers coordinate and combine their involvement as 'networked individuals' in various networks. In addition, they also form a new platform on which city dwellers can make their way of life public. What is the significance of these possibilities of digital media for the way in which parochial domains develop and are maintained? Do they reinforce the process of domain formation and thus contribute to an increasingly libertarian urban ideal in which city dwellers can do whatever they like? Or do they, conversely, give rise to new possibilities for creating a local public from the shared use of an urban neighbourhood, thus contributing to a more republican urban ideal? In the next chapter we shall explore these scenarios for the future using three test cases.

Digital Media and the Parochial Domain

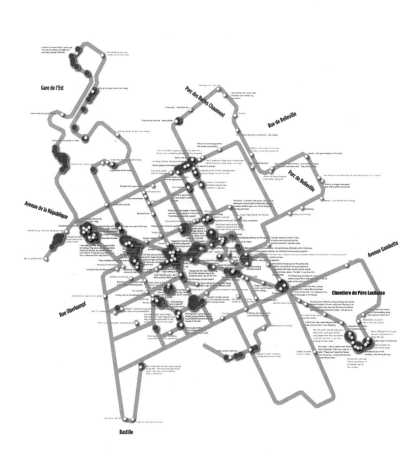

In his book *Me++*, the late American urban researcher and new-media guru William Mitchell describes the rise of digital media using the same literary technique applied by James Joyce in *Ulysses*: Joyce repeatedly refers to the Irish capital Dublin as 'Doublin' to make clear that the city by definition is a place where thousands of life stories criss-cross. As a result, every square, every street corner and every local pub leads a double life. The experience of all these places consists not only of their physical design but also of the dozens, perhaps even hundreds, of stories circulating about each place. Nostalgic memories, recent news items and projected desires, at times articulated in the conflicting claims of various population groups: they all play a role in the way we absorb the world around us.

Due to the rise of digital media and especially the way in which they function as 'experience markers', Doublin is no longer just a metaphor, says William Mitchell. Stories, experiences, memories – many people share these with each other through social networks. Even if we do not actively participate in social networks, we passively leave our trails behind in innumerable digital data-bases. The electronic eyes of security cameras record our presence, the supermarket maintains a database of our purchases thanks to customer loyalty programmes, and transport companies keep a record of our transport patterns with the aid of smart cards that are replacing the old paper tickets. This all means that everyday experiences have a double life in the digital world:

> Multiplying thousands of electronic eyes and ears continuously capture the city's unfolding interwoven narrative threads and spin them out into cyberspace. Some of these threads are ephemeral and disappear instantly. Others sit on voicemail, email and other servers for a while, then are deleted or automatically fade away. Yet others accumulate permanently to form an expanding, long-term electronic memory trace.[1]

Remarkably, the Joycean 'doubling' of urban life that digital media make possible leads to the simultaneous 'de-spacing' of urban experience and the *intensification* of one and the same spatial experience. This in turn has consequences for the way in which parochial domains develop.

This 'de-spacing' is fairly self-explanatory: digital media allow us to share experiences with others who are not present. Urban publics are no longer formed only through simultaneous spatial use but to an increasing extent through all sorts of online platforms, for example, when we use social media to share with our 'friends' where we are and what we are doing. We shall see that in the case of Japanese teenagers, this leads to a changed perception of 'presence': it is no longer necessary for friends to be physically present in order to feel they 'joined in'.

But the doubling of urban experiences can simultaneously lead to an intensification of spatial experiences. Digital media are perfectly suited to symbolic spatial use – how we use the places where we are to show who we are. Thanks to Joycean doubling, we can use digital media platforms to make this symbolic spatial use known to those who are not physically present as well. Specific places in a city can then take on a symbolic meaning in a new way: with digital media we can see that members of a specific subculture have started using a specific hangout, café or restaurant more often and now consider that place *their* place; people can also identify with such places online without actually visiting them. Specific places can thus develop into the centre around which an 'imagined community' of people develops who feel connected with each other and with that place.

Together, digital media can thus reinforce the parochialization of urban society: wherever we are, we mainly remain in contact with people from our own networks, and it is also easier than ever to find the parochial domains of the groups we consider ourselves part of. But this is precisely why all these parochial domains can spatially criss-cross: thanks to the use of mobile media as 'territory devices' we can feel at home anywhere in a city or pick out exactly those places in the vicinity that are relevant to us. This can stimulate the development of what I referred to in the previous chapter as 'living together apart', when different ways of life at the neighbourhood level overlap. Although this appears to threaten the republican urban ideal – while different groups share the same space, they do not care about each other – this same spatial overlap may also provide a new chance for this republican ideal. Might these very urban media cause these different worlds to again take notice of each other? Might the neighbourhood still grow into a parochial domain? In order to see how all this works in practice, we shall return to Pendrecht. This time we shall zoom in on Mario Bosch's neighbourhood blog, one of the many examples of digital *doublins* in everyday life.

Test case 1: Mario Bosch's Neighbourhood Blog and Other Social Networks in Pendrecht

For several years now, Mario Bosch has been writing a brief daily update on his Pendrecht weblog: we read that on Tuesday 24 May 2011 the Bavo church clocks are working again; on Monday 23 May he noted that while he was out cycling, he saw Frans and Maja den Hollander watering the plants at Vlissingenplein; the day before, Bosch informed guests at the Zuiderkroon restaurant that Wim van de Pot, a regular guest, was recovering well from a stroke; other bits and pieces of news that came along in the days before: the supermarket is to be renamed, the computer lessons in the kiosk at De Zijpe shopping centre have been cancelled, and the music festival at Plein 1953 – held under the motto 'Pendrecht is just like a village' – was a success: church elder Tjark Jansen sold refreshments and Elly Kamperman ran the information stall. Billiards was very popular at the Zuiderkroon that day but Cees Dorsman said there would be a summer break in July and August. And so it goes on: virtually nothing in the district escapes Mario Bosch's attention and he faithfully describes both the events and all sorts of everyday rituals and minor changes in the neighbour-hood. The people concerned are usually mentioned by name and they are often also photographed.

Mario Bosch is perhaps the most fanatic but certainly not the only online chronicler of everyday life in Pendrecht. A number of pages on Hyves, a social network popular in the Netherlands at the time of research, are also dedicated to the district, so residents and former residents can exchange messages and memories. Residents also use other social networks to share what they are doing or going to do in Pendrecht. Everyday routines and special occasions that take place physically in the district thus acquire a second, digital life.

A number of optimistic media gurus hope that the emergence of such platforms will breathe new life into the neighbourhood. Will these platforms make it possible to reverse the development that has seen neighbourhood residents' rhythms of life run less and less parallel and neighbourhood use decline? Talja Blokland concluded that this development was the reason why the number of chance street encounters declined and the basis for building up mutual trust also disappeared. Can weblogs such as Mario Bosch's encourage neighbourhood residents to start noticing each other again so that the neighbourhood again grows into its residents' parochial domain?

Thanks to his weblog, Mario Bosch has now become what Jane Jacobs called a 'public figure' in Pendrecht. He is emphatically present in the neighbourhood, both online and offline, making him a recognizable point of contact for fellow residents. But is it possible for people such as Wim van de Pot, Tjark Jansen and Elly Kamperman to become familiar strangers by regularly visiting the blog but without meeting them physically every time? Will the city street, now that it has become a 'hybrid city street', recover its function as the theatre of everyday life, as the arena where local publics can be formed? Lily Shirvanee, for one, hopes that location-tied media will lead to what she calls 'social viscosity': through blog messages or other annotations, neighbourhood residents might be able to trace memories or experiences that they cannot perceive in a physical space:

> This viscosity of space is perceived as a bond that may exist not only between people with established relationships who can find each other 'on the street' in a mobile context, but also between strangers, thereby inspiring a new community and, possibly, creating the potential for a more democratized public space.[2]

In recent years, several studies have attempted to establish whether this hope is well founded. One of the best known is sociologists Wellman and Hampton's study of Netville, a new middle-class suburb in Toronto, which was carried out at the beginning of this century. The results provide a number of interesting insights. The houses in Netville were equipped with broadband Internet, something that was very progressive at the time. A mailing list for residents was also set up. The researchers describe how, as a result of this combination, residents' spatial practices quickly became interwoven with the use of new media: residents often sat in front of their houses in the evenings and watched the comings and goings in the neighbourhood; at the same time, some residents also regularly used the mailing list. Both practices reinforced each other:

> The residents of Netville literally had their 'eyes upon the street' [a reference to Jane Jacobs]. The neighborhood email list (NET-L) became an extension of those eyes, allowing residents to share information easily and quickly about what they had observed from their porches.[3]

The study makes clear that residents in the neighbourhood did indeed use the Internet to get to know each other and to initiate contacts with other residents in the district. And those who had a lot of offline contact with neighbourhood residents were also active online, and vice versa.

Yet studies such as the one of Netville show that the 'doubling' of a district with the aid of digital media does not automatically lead to a closer-knit local community.[4] One important conclusion is that people mainly use the technology for personal ends: they use digital media to maintain all the different networks that they are part of as 'networked individuals'. They use the technology to maintain contacts with both neighbours and friends who do not live in the district, and within the neighbourhood, too, they mainly maintain contact with like-minded people. The motivation for using the neighbourhood mailing list is largely a practical one: keeping each other informed about developments, the search for a new babysitter, and so on. In other words, the mailing list is not used because people are so keen on forming a community with each other but mainly because it can be very convenient.

This individual approach can lead to stronger neighbourhood ties in contexts like Netville, a newly-built middle-class suburb with a fairly heterogeneous population composed of highly educated young families. Neighbours become acquainted precisely because they have to organize practical things together, and these sorts of contacts can result in a sense of community. Yet this sense of community is partly based on the fact that the neighbourhood residents already share many aspects of their way of life.

In itself, setting up a blog, mailing list or other platform for a neighbourhood does not automatically lead to exchanges or contacts between residents.[5] Above all, such networks must be personally and practically useful and they are usually most effective if neighbours already have a shared interest in or tie with the neighbourhood that can then be reinforced through digital communication. Digital communication can turn a neighbourhood that functions as a 'parish without parishioners' into a 'parish with parishioners' again. A similar development may also result from external circumstances: if a neighbourhood or way of life is threatened by an external intervention such as the construction of a shopping centre, neighbourhood residents often use digital media to organize themselves as a local public.[6] But the less neighbourhood residents identify with each other, the less should be expected of such new platforms as binding instruments.

Still, blogs like the one about Pendrecht might contribute to public familiarity: if a resident who is a member of the Turkish community visits Bosch's blog to read a report about the Iftar meal, he will also come across a report of the music festival or a performance by the Pendrecht Theater in the Bavo church. In this case, Mario Bosch functions as a 'bridge' who, from his interest in the district, connects the various activities that take place there. It is a precondition that bloggers such as Bosch move between all these different worlds: he must know how to build bridges between all these different publics and also have something to offer to each of them. The programming of a weblog like Bosch's can then create an overlap between different local publics. This overlap can lead to a platform where a new public develops consisting of neighbourhood residents with from various backgrounds who take notice of each other.

This is unlikely to happen spontaneously. Jane Jacobs taught us that in her city street a mixed programme was of the greatest importance: it meant that neighbours would start to use the street intensively and that it would gradually develop into a parochial domain of familiar strangers. A comparable online mechanism might act as a similar stimulus. The more such a platform has to offer to various publics, the greater the likelihood that different residents will actually meet each other there.

The Pendrecht Hyve and Symbolic Neighbourhood Use

Mario Bosch is not the only Pendrecht resident to use digital media as an 'experience marker': a number of Pendrechters are also active on the Hyves social network. However, they do not use this digital platform to build bridges between different local publics but rather to attribute a symbolic meaning to Pendrecht, starting from their own ways of life.

One example is a page about Pendrecht that was set up in 2007 by 'Edwin' as 'a Hyve for all current and former residents of the Rotterdam district of Pendrecht'.[7] In March 2013 there were 744 members and, although the site is no longer used very actively, the discussions that were held there in recent years can still be accessed. The district's identity was discussed in a number of forums, and it is remarkable that a number of the participants no longer lived in the district – their places of abode included suburbs of Rotterdam such as Rhoon, Barendrecht and Ridderkerk. On the one hand, former residents recounted warm memories of specific places in the neighbourhood where they grew up - the primary school they attended and the snack bar that was run by 'Piet Paddestoel' (literally, 'Piet the Toadstool').[8] On the other hand, a number of participants said they were glad they no longer lived in Pendrecht: 'I lived in ellewoutsdijkstraat, had a nice time,' writes 'Ineke', 'but wouldn't want to return. Live in the old part of Barendrecht now, all peace and quiet.'[9] And there were more former residents who thought the district had greatly deteriorated since they left. Current residents also discussed the district's image: some of them thought that Pendrecht was going downhill - 'Ton' wrote, 'No, Pendrecht is doing well (. . .) when it comes to planting flags and sticking its head in the sand when there are problems. Luckily there are still a lot of old residents who wish Pendrecht well.'[10] Others defended the district and wrote that they still enjoyed living there.

What we see here is partly a 'remediation' of the social process that Talja Blokland described in Hillesluis: neighbourhood residents compare their lives with the lives of others and distinguish between an 'us' and a 'them'. 'Ton', for example, considers himself part of a group that wishes the district well while others (who are not directly named but whose identities are taken for granted) are clearly not part of that group. Hyves is thus not only a stage where residents can become acquainted with each other's ideas or a place for reflection; the Pendrecht district is also deployed symbolically to express the individual identities of the Hyves visitors, regardless of whether they live in the district. An 'imagined community' thus develops around the district, consisting of former and current residents who use the district to create a shared framework of memories and stories. A story about Pendrecht is collectively constructed, and it is one that participants can identify with or distance themselves from; above all, their distinction between 'us' and 'them' says something about themselves. This way, a district such as Pendrecht acquires a symbolic function online because residents, by displaying their affinity with or rejection of its depiction in the 'story', actually express their own identities.

The symbolic use of a neighbourhood is not new but the way in which it is given shape has changed, as American scholar Danah Boyd's study of social networks makes clear. An important aspect of social networks is that users describe themselves with words and sometimes also photographs or film clips, often via a number of categories established by the owners of the social network. Boyd shows that the creation of a profile and maintaining status updates on social networks such as Facebook and MySpace are very similar to the behaviour of city dwellers that Erving Goffman described in his book *The Presentation of Self*.[11] On social network sites, users constantly check how others in the network present themselves and they adapt their own profiles and status updates accordingly. They are constantly occupied with what Goffman called 'impression management': what impression does the way I present myself make on my public, and was this intended? How can I adapt my presentation in order to meet the applicable norms and my own intentions? While Goffman was often concerned with unconscious processes, this impression management now often takes on reflexive forms in social media: '[This] is the first generation', writes Boyd, referring to the current generation of American teenagers she studied, 'to have to publicly articulate itself, to have to write itself into being as a precondition of social participation.'[12]

In other words, social networks play an important role in the way users present themselves to the world; they are one of the stages where users make part of their lives public. Physical practices and networked exchanges are closely intertwined here: the American teenagers in Boyd's study meet at the shopping mall and in between encounters they stay in contact through social media. Events at the shopping mall are also recounted through social media. Cultural practices such as comparison, harmonization and the construction of individual and collective identities and norms take place in both worlds simultaneously, with a double use of place apparently being the norm. On the one hand, physical places function as the stage where teenagers make their lives public, and their publics are extended through social networks – absent classmates can simultaneously or at a later date be informed of their activities. On the other hand, different places also start to play a symbolic role in the performance that Boyd's teenagers perform for each other through social media: by emphatically announcing where they are, they indicate which groups they consider themselves part of.

To illustrate this, let us again look at the role that Pendrecht fulfilled for a few users of the Dutch social network Hyves. Hyves asks users to create a profile of themselves using a number of categories devised by Hyves. Two of these are directly related to 'place': 'Hometown' and 'Hangouts'. Users are asked to reflect on places that play an important role in their lives and that are symbolic of their lifestyle. A number of users from Pendrecht chose to fill in 'Hometown' with 'Pendrecht' and not 'Rotterdam'; the district was thus labelled as the place where they 'felt at home'. It is striking that the neighbourhood was claimed as 'Hometown' by various online users with very different identities: the symbolic meaning of 'Hometown Pendrecht' is therefore not clear cut.

At the same time, most users symbolically appropriated not only Pendrecht but other places as well: consider the profile of 'Ghis', one of the Hyvers whose 'Hometown' was given as Pendrecht. The places she described as 'Hangout' are spread over the entire country: Heineken Music Hall (Amsterdam), Hollywood Music Hall (Rotterdam), McDonald's (a so-called 'non-place', where she can feel at home all over the world), Pathé de Munt (a cinema in Amsterdam), Scheveningen beach.[13] The 'Hangout' category can partly be seen as an attempt to name the parochial domains of collectives that users consider themselves part of. Anyone who clicks on 'Show on the map' in the 'Hangout' category is presented with a geographical overview of the different places where Ghis said she likes to go, a network of places spread across the entire Randstad conurbation in the west of the Netherlands. This map is not so much the parochial domain of a single collective that Ghis considers herself part of, but consists of the interface of the different publics that she is occasionally part of.

In his doctoral thesis about 'place blogging', Tim Lindgren links these descriptions of place and the development of network individualism with city dwellers participating in diverse, partly overlapping networks. Individuals fulfil different roles that are less and less cohesive and location-based. A weblog or a profile page on a social network can actually provide the framework for bringing together the various facets of someone's life in order to construct a coherent identity again. In other words, we are part of all sorts of networks and collectives, but it is difficult to bring these under a single, overarching denominator. An identity – or, more practically, a way of life - is therefore best understood as the interface between all these different networks. A weblog or page on a social network literally maps the overlap between all these networks and from this we construct a new whole. This way, weblogs, profile pages and status updates integrate various aspects of a single person into a composite identity. Location can also play a significant role in this process: people use location to indicate the collectives they consider themselves part of. Individuals and collectives can then claim certain places: people like me come here!

Both developments converge in what Eric Gordon and Adriana de Souza e Silva call 'net-locality': the experience and symbolic meaning of a place result partly from exchanges in a physical space and partly from media networks. A 'placeworld' (the sum total of knowledge, meanings and rituals linked to locations that are important for a specific group) is thus increasingly interpreted through digital media platforms. De Souza e Silva and Gordon predict that mobile media will play an increasingly important role in this process. The mobile phone will become an 'experience marker' for 'net-localities':

> Mobile annotation applications have enabled us to locate things and to be located ourselves, and the availability of GPS and the affordability of mobile devices have fueled the popular adoption of these tools. Now that our devices are location aware, we are much better positioned to be location aware ourselves.[14]

They expect that we will increasingly use mobile media to show who we are, partly by showing where we are. At the same time we can use the same mobile phone to access the experiences of others. We can also see who attributes particular symbolic meanings to particular places. This in turn can have consequences for our own use of space and the way parochial domains are created. This process is the subject of the next test case: the living map.

Test case 2: The Living Map

Imagine being able to look at a digital map and see everything that is happening around you: from the exact location where various people are to the movements of all buses and trams; from shop and restaurant reviews – left by visitors – to the inspection reports of the food standards agency; from (former) residents' cherished memories of a place to tourists' photographs or Twitter messages; from all the film images on security cameras located in a city to statistical details about residents or visitors to a location; from historical background information to future building plans.

This is roughly the idea behind the 'Living Map', a concept introduced by the Rathenau Institute as a thought experiment.[15] The idea extrapolates a number of recent technological developments: an increasing number of objects and people leave a digital trail behind them through all sorts of sensor networks, from public transport smart cards to cameras on motorways that photograph the number plates of passing cars. Parts of the living map already exist: spaces can be annotated via Google Earth; Foursquare,

Google Latitude and Apple's Find My Friends app allow users to share their location with friends; Yelp and Google Local make it possible to view reviews of shops and restaurants in the user's vicinity; and 'augmented reality' mobile phone apps such as Layar enable users to see the future construction plans for a location.

But what if all these details combined with innumerable other data sources could be represented on a single map, for example using a platform such as Google Earth or the TomTom navigation screen? The user would then constantly see a digital map with himself always in the centre; around him all sorts of dynamic information about 'useful places'[16] as well as about his 'friends' would appear.

During the meetings that the Rathenau Institute organized about the living map, two themes kept recurring: the first was the need to balance 'empowerment' and 'control'. Many participants in the meetings found the living map very convenient because it can help one use the city effectively. But then there was the issue of privacy: to what extent do users have control over what is recorded and who gets access to these data?[17]

The second theme discussed was the balance between 'predictability' and 'spontaneity'. The Living Map is not only a dynamic representation of all sorts of details; it also filters these details. It is impossible to reproduce all available data on a single map, and the user and/or designer of the map would have to install mechanisms that users can use to view specific details about their location. This raised the hope *and* fear that users' personal preferences would become the dominant filters in living-map types of systems: users would be able to see where their 'friends' are on the map, the location of cafés in the neighbourhood that matched their personal preferences and so on. The system could become a personal filter or 'guide' that makes the city with all its functions manageable for the city dweller. This would be convenient, but could it also mean that spontaneous encounters would disappear as well? What about serendipity – fortuitously stumbling upon something interesting while one is actually looking for something else? Would living maps encourage the parochialization of urban public spaces?

To answer these questions, we must first examine two underlying mechanisms: systems such as the living map might change the way in which we experience nearness and presence. With the living map's filtering mechanisms events, places or people that are only a few metres away might remain more or less invisible, while users of such living maps (or whatever shape such a system may ultimately take) can see what is happening a few kilometres away or even on the other side of the world. That which is 'nearby' is not that which is physically present in our surroundings but whatever or whomever we can easily view using, for example, mobile media; 'social nearness' might thus become more important than 'physical nearness'.[18]

A number of studies show that this development has already taken root. After all, thanks to the mobile phone it is already possible to make contact everywhere and anywhere with others who are not physically present. Japanese-American anthropologist Ito has shown that this might even mean that our concept of 'presence' will start to change. In her book *Personal, Portable, Pedestrian* she describes the mobile phone as a 'territory device', a device that can change the perception of a place because the user can use it to contact absent people and download information or other media contents.[19] Together with her co-authors, Ito describes the implications of this for the way Japanese teenagers experience the city. When a Japanese group of friends meets in the city, there is contact with both those who are physically present and others from the group who are not present. Text messages and photographs are sent backwards and forwards, and when the physical meeting is over, the friends remain in contact with each other using the mobile phone. The Japanese teenagers in the study constantly divided their attention between the physical situation they were in and mediated contacts with others:

> The mobile phone makes these situations contiguous rather than disjunctive, stitching them together into a technosocial gathering that extends beyond the time and space of physical co-presence. (. . .) Keitai [the Japanese term for a mobile phone] e-mail constructs a space of connectivity that relies on a pulsating movement between background and foreground awareness and interaction as people shift from lightweight messaging to chat to 'flesh meets'.[20]

This changes the concept of who is present in a situation. In the same volume Okabe describes, for example, how some groups of friends or loved ones are regularly in contact with each other through-out the day because they send an occasional email, text or chat message. This gives the impression to those involved that these others are always present in the background.[21] In yet another essay in *Personal, Portable, Pedestrian*, Matsuda also refers to a 'full time intimate sphere'. The mobile phone can be used to create an intimate private sphere that is available on demand everywhere.[22]

The mobile phone as a 'territory device' can thus be used to turn every urban situation into a personal or parochial experience: wherever one is in a city, one's own network of friends and family can be activated at the press of a button. Matsuda describes how this also affects the way in which Japanese teenagers and students use the city. Before the advent of the mobile phone, they met at a number of fixed locations that were characteristic of the group they were part of, for example a café at or near the university campus. This usually happened without a pre-arranged plan - the students went to these places and checked whether there were any people there whom they knew. This hardly ever happens now, according to Matsuda. Instead, they ring their friends to meet somewhere in the city. The Japanese students thus experience urban public spaces as locations where they can arrange private meetings using the mobile phone: for them, the whole city is a potential parochial domain.[23]

According to Norwegian anthropologist Rich Ling, this has implications for the way we maintain communities and publics. His research shows that, thanks to the mobile phone, we are paying more and more attention to the people in our network and are making less contact with people we do not know:

> The mobile telephone is the tool of the intimate sphere. (. . .) while generally we must be open to both intimated and strangers when we interact in daily life, the mobile phone tips the balance in the favor of the intimate sphere of friends and family. In a situation where there otherwise might have been the opportunity for talking with a stranger (e.g. waiting for a bus or standing in a checkout line), we can instead gossip, flirt, or joke with friends, intimates or family members. It allows us to pick up the threads of ritual interaction when and wherever the urge moves us.[24]

The 'telecocoon' scenario threatens: while we move around the city, we use the mobile phone and living map to wrap ourselves in a cocoon that hinders all spontaneous interaction with unknown others; we are constantly connected with people we know and guided to places where we are again surrounded by familiars.

Yet the question is whether developments will indeed lead to such far-reaching isolation. The idea of a 'territory device' that city dwellers use to define a personal space and withdraw from public space is not new. Indeed, it is part of the essence of modern urban life – we constantly maintain an appropriate distance towards all those unknown others whom we meet, whether by hiding behind a newspaper or behind the screen of a mobile phone. Urban life demands continuous adjustment: sometimes we opt for social interaction with our direct surroundings, at other times we with-draw into our 'internal world' and use all sorts of signals to indicate that we are not interested in interaction.[25] What is new is that we do not so much withdraw from social interaction as such, but from social interaction in a particular physical location; instead, we take part in social interaction that partly proceeds through digital networks, and this might indeed lead to an intensification of the parochial experience. At the same time, the very use of living maps might lead to the intermingling of all these parochial domains. Wherever we are in a city, the living map would show those elements in our surroundings that are relevant to us. Grindr, a 'living map' that is offered as a 'dating app' for the smartphone, shows how this scenario might take shape.

Grindr: Living Together Apart

Grindr is an app for the mobile phone aimed at a specific subculture: it brings homosexuals looking for a date in contact with like-minded men who happen to be in the user's vicinity - in the makers' words: 'Grindr is 'the largest all-male location-based mobile network tool'. It is the simple implementation of a living map: the screen displays a map of the user's location with a projection of the profiles of other users who are in the mood for an escapade at that moment: an online marketplace where supply and demand are both figuratively and literally brought together.

This is associated with an interesting development: in many subcultures, the opportunity to meet like-minded people is linked to specific, symbolically meaningful locations. The homosexual subculture is one of the most clearly recognizable parochial domains in many cities - certain streets are known as the scene for gay nightlife. In San Francisco, for example, the Castro developed into *the* gay district, with rainbow flags flying from every second or third building. There is a gay scene in both the literal and the figurative sense: a public of like-minded people who can recognize each other at the location where they happen to be.

But thanks to Grindr, every shopping centre, square, park or office complex can become a meeting place. The software works like a filter that is able to recognize appropriate people in an anonymous mass anywhere in a city. Living maps like Grindr disconnect a cultural scene (a group of people with a shared way of life) from its geographical scene (the specific places where this group meets):

> Simply download the Grindr app to view who's around and start chatting with a local guy. Trade your stats, show off a photo, or send an instant message to any guy you like. Share your location on a map and make plans to meet up right away. Or just browse the local scene.[26]

This scene is no longer necessarily linked to a particular geography, but can – at least theoretically – be called into existence anywhere. There is one precondition, however: the likelihood of actually 'scoring' with Grindr is greater in places where there is a high concentration of diverse individuals.

American scholar Anthony Townsend predicts that similar practices might lead to an intensification of urban life; at different places, several cultural protocols and systems of meaning will criss-cross:

> The mobile phone then might lead to a dramatic increase in the size of the city, not necessarily in a physical sense, but in terms of activity and productivity. No massive new physical infrastructure

will emerge; rather, cities might witness the intensification of urban activity – the speeding up of urban metabolism. . . . Urban theorists such as Michael Dear argue that postmodern urbanism is particularly characterized by fragmentation. The mobile phone certainly reinforces these patterns; it substitutes chaotic decentralized networks for centralized ones.[27]

On the one hand, living maps may pave the way for parochialization, because users are mainly updated about events in their own network; on the other hand, the location of these parochial domains may become more flexible and they may start to criss-cross. Wherever individuals are, they carry their own parochial domains with them, and as 'networked individuals', living-map users can also quickly switch between the different maps of their various networks. This might reinforce the development of 'living together apart'.

The users themselves can install the filters they require: do they want to see their colleagues on the living map? Their friends' favourite restaurants? Or would they rather have an overview of potential dates in the vicinity? A new generation of interfaces provides an additional function: the digital traces that city dwellers leave behind can be consolidated and used as a basis for making collective rhythms and meanings clear. Some programmes use these data to create user profiles; this information can then be used by a living map to recommend new places, services and people. A living map can thus partly lead its own life - the underlying algorithms determine what one ultimately sees on a map. But who programmes these algorithms and to what ends? And to what extent do users have 'agency' to appropriate these living maps in ways they find useful? These issues are addressed in the following test case.

Test case 3: Funda's Lifestyles

Potential home-buyers accessing the Dutch real estate site Funda in search of a house in Pendrecht in 2007 were shown not only which houses were for sale there; they were also presented with a picture of the neighbourhood and its residents. A house that was for sale in Tholenstraat was advertised by Funda with the following information: the future neighbours' hobbies included 'puzzles and brainteasers', 'walking' and 'fitness'; the newspaper boy mainly delivered women's magazines like *Libelle* and *Margriet* and *Plus* magazine for 50-plussers; Opels, Fords and Volkswagens were parked in the street; and Tholenstraat's residents mainly got their news from the *Algemeen Dagblad*, *Rotterdams Dagblad* and the *Telegraaf* newspapers; the average household consisted of 1.63 people, and families with young children made up only 5.9 per cent of the total population – as against 42.7 per cent older couples without children. Altogether, according to Funda, the neighbourhood was predominantly populated by three types of city dwellers, who were classified as 'financially limited', 'price-conscious consumers' and 'nightlife youth'.[28]

Potential buyers who wanted a more detailed picture of how the residents in the area comprising 'postcode 3086 AA' arranged their lives could visit another real estate website, Dimo.nl, which informed them that Pendrecht was mainly populated by city dwellers who fell into three categories: 'social seniors', 'active trend followers' and '"out-of-district" neighbours'. All three lifestyles were minutely described: the 'social senior', for example, had the following words put into his mouth by Dimo.nl:

> My neighbourhood is quite sociable, nice people live here with whom I sometimes have a cup of coffee. Most of my neighbours have tightened their belts, we don't need a big house that needs lots of maintenance any more, especially if your partner has already died – half of the people here live on their own. I haven't worked for a while and my partner only works a couple of hours a week. We don't really have a big income but we have a modest house and don't need that much. If you walk through my neighbourhood you notice that people are often at home. People spend their time playing bridge, on handicrafts or crossword puzzles. Health is important and that's also why many of my neighbours do voluntary work to stay active. In the basket under the side tables you see magazines like *Plus*, *Reader's Digest* and other health magazines. Their indoor activities are often accompanied by quiet music on Radio 1, 4 or 747 AM.[29]

Similar lifestyle profiles are compiled by specialized, often international, companies such as Claritas and Experian. These companies collect all sorts of details from innumerable databases, varying from publicly accessible data banks containing information about age composition, income and work to details collected by companies through, for example, customer loyalty programmes such as the 'Bonus card' issued to customers by Albert Heijn, the Netherlands' largest supermarket chain. By aggregating and analyzing data it is possible to discover collective patterns that are often linked to zip code areas, creating a picture of where different lifestyles are located.

These details can also be used to intervene in a neighbourhood. Chain stores that target specific lifestyles can establish themselves near their target groups or skip particular neighbourhoods. Housing corporations also work with such profiles, for example, the Nieuwe Unie housing corporation, which manages a large number of houses in Pendrecht, makes use of specific 'customer groups'. While Lotte Stam-Beese based her master plan on lifestyles such as large and small families, the Nieuwe Unie now distinguishes between 'survivors', 'discoverers', 'the neighbourhood-oriented', 'dynamic individualists', 'well-off families', 'average-income seniors', and 'well-off seniors'. Each of these groups is accompanied by an extensive profile that can be translated into a number of housing requirements. By using these customer groups, the Nieuwe Unie hopes to attract a number of them to Pendrecht when it has been redeveloped.

This creates a double dynamic: our purchases and our use of space and time are recorded in databases. The information collected from these databases then provides the basis for compiling profiles that are used by shops, governments, housing corporations and other parties to programme the city – and thus the stage of our everyday lives.[30] According to geographers Burrows and Gane, the publication of such lifestyle profiles on websites like Funda's can actually reinforce certain patterns. Potential residents use the details to see whether they can identify with the current residents and whether they do or do not want to live among the 'social seniors' and 'financially limited': '[B]y making more and more geodemo-graphic information available on-line', they argue, '(some) people are being given express encouragement to "sort themselves out"'.[31] This might lead to a circular development: once certain lifestyles have 'colonized' an area, it will attract more and more people with similar consumption patterns and lifestyles.

The practice of linking data produced by city dwellers and their lifestyles to neighbourhoods or zip code areas is not new. This practice has existed for nearly a century but there have been a number of significant changes in the way the information is linked. Initially, this practice had a social purpose: at the beginning of the twentieth century, British shipping magnate and social reformer Charles Booth pioneered the literal mapping of different lifestyles; he produced his own map of London's East End and coloured it in according to the nature of the population he found there, ranging from yellow for the better neighbourhoods to black for the 'seats of vice'.[32] This map was intended as a programme of action: a single glance showed which neighbourhoods needed intervention in order to improve living conditions. Even today's computerized lifestyle analyses were originally intended as policy instruments. In the 1960s, demographer Jonathan Robbin was commissioned by the US Department of Housing and Urban Development to analyze different lifestyles in a variety of neighbourhoods in American cities. Follow-ing riots in different parts of the country, the ministry wanted to use the geographical analyses for the distribution of housing subsidies. In England, economist Richard Webber worked on a similar project at the London Centre for Environmental Studies.

However, the computerized databases with zip codes and life-styles that Robbin and Webber developed quickly attracted commercial attention and they both left academia in order to refine their analyses for a variety of commercial parties that could use the details for targeted marketing campaigns and for decisions about whether or not to invest in a particular area. Burrows and Gane consider this an important transition: it symbolizes a shift in who had agency when it came to labelling social groups. The state's primacy gave way to a number of commercial parties. Parallel with this development, consumer behaviour also became an increasingly important basis on which the lifestyle categories were founded.

With the rise of mobile media – and their use as 'experience markers' in particular – we enter a new phase in the way lifestyles are labelled by various parties. First, the amount of data that can be registered and stored on databases is increasing. How people move about the city, the places they visit (both online and in the physical city), the messages they leave via social networks, the searches they do via the (mobile) Internet, all these details can be stored, analyzed and converted into new profiles. Moreover, these details can be accessed again in real time, both by users on their mobile phone screens and by all sorts of parties that use the profiles to offer targeted services to specific groups.

What does this development mean for the way parochial domains develop? Two examples illustrate two different developments: CitySense is an app that collects users' mobility details and uses them as a basis for recommending new places to visit; *i-500* is an artwork that actually collects data from all users of a place to depict a collective rhythm. In the one case, the use of profiles leads to a reinforcement of 'urban villages' - CitySense directs city dwellers to those places in a city where they will feel at home; in the other case, *i-500* shows the overlap between the various users of a place and it can therefore contribute to a parochial domain that is based on 'familiar strangers'.

CitySense is an iPhone app developed by Sense Networks, an American company whose mission it is to predict the use of space by groups of city dwellers. The company describes CitySense as 'an innovative mobile application for real-time nightlife discovery and social navigation, answering the question, "where is everybody going right now?"'[33] It works as follows: the user downloads an app for his smartphone. This app then registers the owner's spatial use; CitySense gathers the details of all the service's users and projects these aggregated data onto a map of the city, on which users can see – live – which part of a city is most crowded, and whether it is actually busier or quieter than normal.

Sense Networks promises that a new edition of the programme will also be able to make recommendations to the user: 'In its next release, CitySense will not only answer "where is everyone right now" but "where is everyone *like me* right now".'[34] In order to do this, the programme will analyze the mobile phone owner's spatial use and compare it with others' spatial use. Based on this information, a number of 'tribes' will be named and the user will then always be able to see the pattern of his own tribe's collective activities: 'Four friends at dinner discussing where to go next will see four different live maps of hotspots and unexpected activity.'

CitySense is thus also an interactive service: users receive recommendations about which places to visit, based on the input of their own spatial movements. A service like this is also referred to as 'discovery', to use a buzzword from the Internet industry: it encourages users to discover places or activities they have not previously visited. However, a number of critics are concerned that such 'discovery' services might actually lead to ghettoization in cities. The French Orange Labs researchers Aguiton and Smoreda argue that:

> Showing a typology of a user in the city is of course useful to a person searching for a place to go, especially if one visits an unknown city. Nevertheless, if the majority of individuals look for the places crowded with people similar in age, education, taste, sexual preferences, etc., providing this information can intensify the segregation tendency and, in the long run, contribute to a kind of 'ghettoization' of the urban space.[35]

This risk of 'ghettoization' is certainly not unfounded. Yet a number of other developments also play a role here that could steer the effect of services such as CitySense in a different direction. At present, CitySense still aggregates a user's patterns in a number of 'tribes' or, to use this book's terminology, different publics, each with their own collective characteristics. Each individual is categorized in one of these 'tribes' and can thus access his own tribe's collective repertoire of places. In his book *The Numerati*, Stephen Baker describes how these lifestyle categories may only be an intermediate step: all sorts of parties are trying to refine the algorithms behind this profiling.[36] This might increasingly lead to individual profiles instead of group profiles:

> The ultimate goal (. . .) is to build versions of humans that are just as complex as we are – each one unique. Add all of these efforts together and we're witnessing (as well as experiencing) the mathematical modeling of humanity.[37]

A similar approach can already be seen in the way Amazon and Google approach their users: these companies' recommendations of books, websites or advertisements are not based on the collective purchasing patterns of one group; instead, both websites have compiled highly individualized profiles of their users, based on earlier searches, purchases and 'click' behaviour. For these services we are, as American writer Dalton Conley argues, a 'group of one'.[38]

Services, products or places that fit in with our earlier consumption pattern are constantly recommended to us but there is no single collective that we are considered part of.

In the Internet industry this principle is also called the 'Long Tail': compiling and comparing customer profiles produces an increasingly detailed picture of the customer, which makes it possible to draw their attention to tiny niches that might be of interest to them. We ourselves are the centre of this universe, and recommendations specifically targeted at our profile orbit around us.

Similar mechanisms can also contribute to the formation of new, hyper-specialized publics. In his 1975 article 'Towards a Subcultural Theory of Urbanism', sociologist Claude Fischer described why it was in cities that new subcultures arose: the density of cities combined with looser social control leads to the development of a critical mass of city dwellers who share specific preferences, interests or concerns out of which new subcultures can develop. The city is also, in a cultural sense, a marketplace: it is where people with related interests meet each other and, if there is sufficient critical mass, a new subculture may develop. Could more refined versions of 'discovery' services such as CitySense, regardless of whether they are combined with the use of social networks, contribute to bringing together critical masses of city dwellers so that new publics develop around small-scale interests? The advent of these and similar digital services could lead to a paradoxical development: the total diversity in the urban landscape might increase, but this might be accompanied by parochialization, with the result that the urban individual's world of experience actually becoming more monotonous; at the same time, all these different domains might also increasingly criss-cross, and this overlap might again lead to the development of a new local public, as the examples of Arch-OS and *i-500* show.

Arch-OS and *i-500*

Arch-OS is an 'operating system' for buildings, by which the developers mean a system that can collect all sorts of data about the use of a building, ranging from temperature and the number of people present (for example through camera detection) to the amount of data that is downloaded via Internet in a building.[39] These data can in turn be linked to different output mechanisms, including practical applications - air-conditioning or a sunscreen that reacts to temperature or air quality, or a mobile wall that moves in accordance with the number of people in a space.

But there are also more poetical applications, for example, making visible many of the invisible processes that Arch-OS measures. Artists Paul Thomas, Chris Malcolm and Mike Phillips developed the data visualization artwork *i-500* for the new

chemistry faculty building at Australia's Curtin University. *i-500*
makes use of the data that Arch-OS collects about the use of the
building: these data are converted into moving coloured patterns
that are projected onto the ceiling of one of the shared spaces in the
faculty building. The visualizations cannot be traced directly to a
particular activity; the idea is that over time the building's
permanent users will be able to recognize patterns in the visualizations and thus become familiar with the building's users and its
rhythms. Paul Thomas, one of the system's designers, compares
this manner of perception with Walter Benjamin's description of
the *flâneur*. According to Thomas, Benjamin's *flâneur* is someone
who becomes part of urban life by being completely absorbed by it;
someone who, as a result of a linked series of experiences, is able to
grasp and reflect on urban life. *i-500* is similarly intended to
provide a stage 'for the chemists flâneurs, enabling them to amble
through the space whilst perceiving subtle rhythms or recognising
complex patterns.'[40] *i-500* is not unique: there are now several
projects that collect data of social processes and visualize these in
different ways. Architect Lars Spuybroek, for example, has also
made a number of real-time installations that are based on such
data. One of the best-known is the D-tower in the Dutch city of
Doetinchem: the idea is for this sculpture to reflect the mood of the
city's residents.[41] A number of residents have been invited to
complete an Internet questionnaire about their states of mind, and
the results are expressed in the tower's lighting programme.

These projects are interesting for a number of reasons. *i-500*
shows that the advent of digital media makes it easier to realize
such projects. This also means that the power concealed in the
labelling of relevant categories and collectives shifts: initially, that
power lay primarily with government institutions and later with
marketing companies, but now it can be shaped more easily from
the bottom up. Systems such as Experian are mainly based on consumption patterns: the aim is to divide consumers into categories
that are relevant for producers. But *i-500* now opens up possibilities
to start from other patterns, for example by using the rhythms of a
specific place as a basis.

The rhythms, moods or events at a location can be collected,
analyzed and visualized using systems such as Arch-OS and *i-500*.
They can also be translated back into the physical design for a
location. Such possibilities might turn architecture into what
architect Kas Oosterhuis calls a 'time-based discipline': a building
is no longer a static fact, a fixed form in the city; its shape or in any
case its atmosphere can change.[42]

Can the collection of facts about urban practices thus contribute to a feeling of being at home somewhere – for example,
through the visualization of the collective rhythms of a city, neighbourhood or location? And if so, does this in turn reinforce the

process of domain formation, with specific groups recognizing themselves in collective rhythms? Or can such a design contribute to a sense of public familiarity because, through the visualizations, they gradually become familiar with the collective rhythms of a particular place?

It is too early to give a clear answer to these questions but projects such as *i-500* do show that city dwellers' digital traces can be used in different ways: on the one hand, they can contribute to the libertarian ideal of a far-reaching personalization of urban experiences, encouraging city dwellers to 'discover' those places where they will find like-minded people; on the other hand, it is certainly possible that new publics will form around collective rhythms or practices, in line with the republican urban ideal.

Digital media thus play an extremely complex role in the way in which parochial domains develop. The doubling of city life made possible by digital media reinforces the city's function as a cultural market where like-minded people can find each other. Mobile media also make it possible to maintain and coordinate contacts with various publics, which can in turn reinforce the development of network individualism and 'light communities': 'living map' types of mobile phone interfaces show the city dweller as a flashing blue light, always at the centre of his own universe, with his relationships and places and people that are relevant to him neatly positioned around him. Nearness and presence are no longer purely physical concepts but rather social categories. As a result, the notion of a parochial domain is less exclusively linked to a specific location: the use of the mobile phone as a 'territory device' means it can be accessed anywhere.

As part of this process, the urban individual is on the one hand 'dismantled' because different technological systems - from the 'Bonus card' issued by the Albert Heijn supermarket to his mobile phone - follow (some of) his activities, store them in databases, aggregate all the details and then use them to offer services that are based on his personal preferences. On the other hand, social media also make it possible to reassemble all these different aspects in a single profile: a renewed image of an urban individual is created when he makes public all his roles and memberships of different publics. Urban places often play a symbolic role in this process: by naming specific places in, for example, status updates, city dwellers can show which groups they consider themselves part of. Agency then seems to shift to the city dweller himself: he has more influence over the publics he wants to be part of and can exercise more control over his role in them. But commercial parties also play a significant role in collecting data, setting up profiles and labelling categories that then play a role in both the physical shape of a city – for example, through all sorts of 'discovery' mechanisms – and in the way it is perceived.

Looking at the city from the perspective of *locations*, a different picture emerges: at first, the emergence of digital media appears to reinforce a process of parochialization – filtering different lifestyles in the city. City dwellers can, after all, seek and find likeminded people and their locations more easily. But all these different parochial domains can again criss-cross so that digital media might reinforce the principle of 'living together apart'. For 'networked individuals' this may even be convenient, because they do not consider themselves part of a single group and can thus quickly switch between the different publics they are part of and their accompanying geographical locations.

At first sight, this seems to lead to a somewhat chaotic urban landscape but a digital media layer might provide each individual with a certain order. However, the two developments - spatial sorting and living together apart – are not mutually exclusive: it is quite possible that certain (parts of) cities will increasingly be characterized by spatial sorting while other (parts of) cities become more heterogeneous.

This discussion about the parochial domain is also inextricably linked to the question of the public domain. Until now we have seen how city dwellers form publics that are based on their mutual similarities and shared protocols. But how do city dwellers with different lifestyles relate to each other in the city? What exactly happens when different parochial domains overlap?

This leads us to the issue of the public domain. We may conclude that the developments outlined here increase the risk that the public domain will be eroded: is there a threat that the city might fall apart into a vast collection of parochial domains? Or are there still places where city dwellers with different backgrounds and interests can meet? Might new forms of overlap develop, with the aid of urban media, as we saw above? These questions will be addressed in the next three chapters, which look at the city from the perspective of the public domain.

The Eternal Crisis of the Public Domain

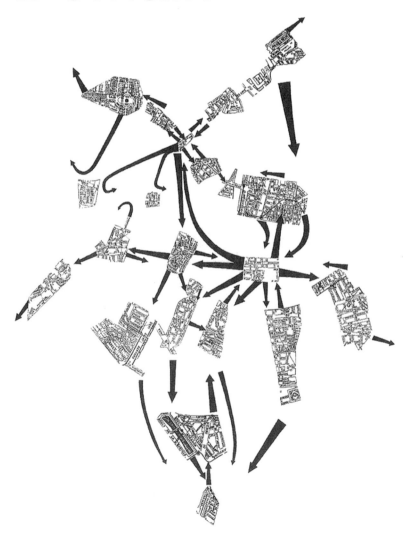

In 2006 the Dutch *Open* magazine devoted a special issue to the emergence of digital and mobile media and its consequences for the urban public sphere. The issue's contents page gave cause for optimism: it included an essay about the way artists made use of urban media to breathe new life into the public spaces of cities; another article described how inhabitants whose neighbourhood had been destroyed by an explosion at a fireworks factory used a website to keep their memories alive; and guest editor Eric Kluitenberg described a series of activist strategies that could be used to stimulate public participation in 'hybrid urban spaces'. It was a rosy picture. Yet in a large number of articles there was an underlying concern that urban media might actually be a threat to the continued existence of the public domain.

This concern was expressed by senior editor Jorinde Seijdel. Her editorial opened with a reference to Hannah Arendt, a philosopher whose most important work was published at a time when radio and newspapers were the dominant media. For Arendt, the public sphere was first and foremost a physical meeting place that she characterized, as quoted by Seijdel, as 'a place where people act, thus creating a common world full of differences'.[1] Will this basic principle survive, now that our cities are pervaded by digital media networks?

At the time, *Open* was not the only publication to hark back to Arendt's work. In their book *Mediapolis*, which also appeared in 2006, Schuilenberg and De Jong referred to this philosopher when discussing the role of the public domain in the city:

> The reality of the public domain is founded on the simultaneous 'being there' of innumerable perspectives and aspects in which the communal world manifests itself and that can never be measured with a common criterion or classified under a common denominator.[2]

Arendt was also quoted in *The Situated Technologies Pamphlet Series* that dealt with the implications of 'ubiquitous computing' for disciplines such as architecture and urban planning.[3] According to Mark Shepard and Adam Greenfield, for example, Arendt described the public space as:

> (...) the place where we encounter the stranger, a space of friction that breeds tolerance through encountering differences in opinion, social standing, ethnicity, economic background, etc.[4]

In all three references, the writers use Arendt's work instrumentally. They are not so much concerned with a critical reflection on Arendt's work as a whole; rather, her vision of the elusive phenomenon of 'public space', 'public sphere' or 'public domain' is always concisely summarized to support their own arguments. What remains of Arendt's ideas usually comes down to this: the public domain plays an essential role in the republican ideal of a democratic urban society. It is the place where city dwellers with different backgrounds meet, are confronted with each other and must come to terms with each other. The spatial aspect that Arendt assigns to her public sphere is of great significance: at those places where citizens with different backgrounds and ideas come together spatially and can look each other in the eye, a common world can develop in which matters concerning the common good can be discussed.

Put the other way around, public spaces that function well in a city lead to the development of a specific type of public: a democratic public that is open to all city dwellers, with all their different backgrounds. As the writers Frei and Böhlen aptly put it in their powerful image, 'The public realm is like parentheses that hold together the differences between people.'[5] The (urban) public domain acts like the parentheses that keep together the differences that are always an essential part of a society's composition.

But what if these parentheses disappear? The point the philosophers, architects and essayists quoted above were making when they referred to Arendt was that the rise of digital media might threaten the continued existence of such public spaces.

In itself, this is not a new note in the debate – the concepts of 'public sphere' or 'public space' are mainly invoked in alleged 'crisis situations', when this highly esteemed element of urban culture is apparently threatened with extinction or dilution. Indeed, Arendt herself argued in the 1950s that processes of individualism, privatization and commercialism were undermining the function of the public domain as a physical exchange landscape. Similar concerns were voiced in the decades that followed: increasing prosperity combined with the advent of the car, the suburb, the shopping mall and the television would all undermine the public domain as a meeting place for city dwellers from different backgrounds, it was feared.

But digital media have added a new perspective to the debate. How do they change the experience of public domains? And what are the implications for the way urban publics can take shape in these domains? Do they really mainly lead to the parochialization of urban society, as we saw in the previous chapter? And does this mean that common meeting places will disappear from urban life?

At the same time, it is worth considering whether the focus on Arendt's work and the importance she attached to physical meeting places is still relevant. Now that digital media are used as 'experience markers' that 'double' the city, physical encounters might be less important. But might there be new ways in which the programmes and protocols of digital technologies can lead to the development of publics that consist of city dwellers from different backgrounds?

The role of digital media as 'territory devices' may completely change the way a public sphere is created. In Arendt's theory, the public sphere is diametrically opposed to the private sphere. But the very use of digital media as 'territory devices' means that private, parochial and public spheres have started to overlap in all sorts of ways. In the previous chapter we saw how parochial domains can be accessed anywhere in a city. But what if the opposite is also true, and it is possible to create the public domain in all sorts of places using digital media? In short, will the 'parentheses' that hold together city dwellers from different backgrounds disappear from the urban landscape forever? Or are there new ways in which can they be placed around yet to be formed urban publics?

To find answers to these questions, it is first necessary to examine the theories about the public domain. How does the public domain function as an interface? That is, precisely which people meet there, under what conditions and with which motives? Which protocols apply and who has the initiative? These questions are particularly relevant to the republican urban ideal. The city can only survive as a community of strangers if city dwellers from different backgrounds actually continue to meet.

Opinions vary on how this process should take place. For Hannah Arendt and Jürgen Habermas, the public domain is primarily a neutral meeting place where city dwellers shed their individual identities and meet as citizens in order to enter into discussions with each other on the basis of rational argument. Richard Sennett takes an interesting position: he also argues for a public domain that is protected against intimacy or personal relationships; it is precisely by maintaining a certain distance from each other that city dwellers can live together. These theories are noteworthy because they have laid the foundation for a public domain where citizens can act collectively without necessarily having to form a clear-cut communitarian unit. But at the same time, their clear distinction between the public and private domains is inadequate for understanding the twenty-first-century city, in which these different domains now overlap.

The works of Marshall Berman and Walter Benjamin and the way they have been interpreted by René Boomkens are also of interest. For them, the public domain was not dominated by rational debates but by everyday life: it developed from the rather chaotic way in which all sorts of lifestyles overlap in the city, leading to the emergence of new publics.

These two versions of the republican ideal (one based on distance and rational debate, the other on everyday ways of life) are constantly under pressure from a libertarian urban ideal in which city dwellers actually use their parochial domains to escape the chaos of urban life. The public domain is then mainly a place where one finds the excitement of the big city, where one can be inspired by a multiplicity of lifestyles: one finds entertainment, can go shopping, see people, have a cappuccino, but real encounters no longer take place. This is, in any case, the fear that we find in the work of Hannah Arendt and Jürgen Habermas.

Hannah Arendt's and Jürgen Habermas's Rational Public Sphere

Visitors to Button's coffee house in eighteenth-century London could easily get caught up in a literary discussion about whose translation of Homer's *Iliad* was better: Alexander Pope's or Thomas Tickell's. Everyone who entered the coffee house was welcome to join in one of the many discussions that were carried on there. One of the writers might even have joined in – Pope and Tickell could often be found among the well-dressed and wigged gentlemen who visited Button's.

The debates that were held at the long wooden tables were not limited to literary themes: all sorts of political topics were also discussed. Moreover, the coffee house was one of the best places to hear the latest news. Visitors were welcomed with cries like, 'Your servant, sir, what news from Tripoli?'[6] Newspapers, a fairly new medium, played an important role in the exchange of news and opinions, and a discussion often began after someone had read aloud a newspaper article. And what if someone did indeed bring news from Tripoli or a discussion led to a new insight? Then a report was sent to the newspaper – for that purpose Button's even had a post box shaped like a lion's head, and Joseph Addison, senior editor of *The Guardian* and a regular at Button's, used it for collecting newspaper contributions. An anthology of letters to the editor appeared once a week in the newspaper's 'The roarings of the lion' section.

The seventeenth and eighteenth-century London coffee houses are often referred to as perfect examples of the modern public sphere, a place where citizens met to exchange information and discuss matters of general interest. They contained the very basis of the republican urban ideal in which citizens act in order to shape society together.[7] This version of the republican ideal was based on the rational debate that citizens held in the public sphere, which included a very clear distinction between the private and the public spheres.

The best known analysis of the coffee houses is found in Jürgen Habermas's *The Structural Transformation of the Public*

Sphere, in which the German philosopher describes how the rise of the public sphere was closely intertwined with changing socio-economic relations in the seventeenth and eighteenth centuries.[8] In that period, a new middle class in Europe gradually became more powerful and started to loosen its ties with the court. Urban practices played a significant role in this process: the new citizenry met at specific places such as the coffee houses in England, the salons in France or the *Tischgesellschaften* in Germany. At these places, a ritual way of debating gradually developed, with visitors discussing matters of general interest on the basis of equality. Habermas concluded that this led to the emergence of a modern public sphere, a sphere situated between citizens' private worlds and the state. The coffee houses functioned as a place where citizens could together form an opinion that they could subsequently present to the government.[9]

Habermas's theory has a number of similarities to the work of Hannah Arendt, the philosopher who after the Second World War was one of the first to put the theme of the public domain on the agenda. In her view the public domain consisted of the free space to speak that was necessary for a democratic society. Her source of inspiration was the Greek agora, where the citizens of the city-state physically gathered to discuss the future of the *polis*. In the work of both Habermas and Arendt, the public sphere and the private sphere of the household are diametrically opposed. In the private sphere, citizens have the freedom to organize their own matters, including both intimate and economic relations. In the public sphere, citizens shed their private identities to discuss matters of general concern in public.

For Arendt, the spatial dimensions are very important: opinions must be formed in public in places where people can look each other in the eye. The public domain then becomes a 'space of common appearances', where the similarities and differences between citizens must become clear and thus can become the subject of democratic debate. This 'space of common appearances' is at the same time an expression of a 'common world', a collection of shared protocols and institutions that binds citizens together in a political community. 'The unity in question', according to d'Entrèves in an analysis of Arendt's work, 'can be attained by sharing a public space and a set of political institutions, and engaging in the practices and activities which are characteristic of that space and those institutions.'[10] Citizens' presence on the physical platform where the exchange takes place and their acquiescence in the related protocols mean that they, as citizens, are part of the political community. Community for Arendt is not based on a common identity but on a shared general interest, which is given form in the institutions of the public domain. It is this public world as such that unites citizens.

Habermas's work shows how the coffee house functioned as a

'space of common appearances'. Customers gathered to discuss political matters. The design of the interior (long wooden tables) played a significant role, as did the protocols governing discussions ('Your servant, sir, what news from Tripoli?') that became part of the coffee houses over time. In Habermas's analysis, two aspects stand out: firstly, he pointed out the importance of the protocol that applied in the coffee houses. Participants all subscribed to a shared ideal: everyone must be able to discuss matters on the basis of equality; private identities were irrelevant - participants gathered there as citizens and rational arguments would be decisive in debates, regardless of who put them forward.

Secondly, in the seventeenth century the rise of 'new media' (novels and newspapers) made it possible for the coffee houses as public spheres to develop into social institutions. Many of the debates in the coffee houses began with reading aloud opinion articles from the newspaper. At the end, participants often wrote reports of debates that could then be published in the next edition of the newspaper, after which they could in turn be introduced as 'conversation pieces' in debates in coffee houses on the other side of the city.[11] In contemporary terms, London's coffee houses formed a networked public sphere in which 'user-generated content' played a significant role. Around a newspaper article publics could develop that then entered into debate with each other in different parts of the city. Participants could imagine that the same text was being discussed in other salons or coffee houses. And the shared protocol of rational debate without regard to person also made it possible for all participants to feel part of this larger public. Even if they disagreed about content, the newspaper article and protocol connected participants with each other in a debate.

In Habermas's view, an ideal type of public sphere developed in the seventeenth and eighteenth-century coffee houses. This did not last long, however: in the course of the eighteenth and nineteenth centuries, when the coffee houses made way for a culture of pavement cafés on the newly constructed boulevards of Paris, the ideal he described gradually faded.

The Boulevard, or the Loss of the Public Sphere

In 1852 George-Eugène Haussmann was commissioned by Napoleon III to modernize Paris, which was still largely medieval. This commission led to a huge operation that was completed around 1870. The maze of narrow streets and alleys of the old city had partly made way for the broad boulevards that have since characterized the city. In total, approximately one-fifth of all the streets in Paris were demolished; the work was carried out by twenty per cent of the working population, and 350,000 Parisians were forced to find new housing.[12]

The operation was based on a number of different motives: the broad boulevards were intended to control the urban masses that had developed as a result of industrialization; they would make it more difficult to construct broad barricades and improve access for troops called in to maintain order. Other reasons to construct the boulevards varied from improving hygiene, introducing a calmer social climate with many green areas, and improving traffic circulation.[13] The boulevards also played a role in the increase in scale of industry: mass production and the rise of the bourgeoisie led to new consumption patterns. It was easier to make deliveries to shops via the boulevards, and new types of shops developed, such as Le Bon Marché and La Samaritaine department stores. The boulevards thus formed a new infrastructure, a new platform, where all sorts of new services could develop such as a lively café culture and the new pavement cafés, and they were popular with the new bourgeois class as places to saunter.

For Habermas, these developments illustrate the loss of the public sphere that he described in the coffee houses. The rise of department stores and the economic increase in scale signalled a transition from a liberal capitalism to a monopolistic capitalism: large companies and social institutions rather than private individuals now played a central role. As a result, the nature of the public that developed also changed: the ideal of a public domain for rational debate about matters of general concern lost out to the field of forces in which groups defending their own interests opposed each other.[14] Organized collectives rather than private individuals were the most important players in this struggle. As a result, in the nineteenth century the urban public space became increasingly dominated by the masses. In a political sense, these were the masses that used demonstrations to add weight to their demands; in a social sense, the urban public space was increasingly dominated by leisure activities. Citizens were still *en public* in the public space, argued Habermas, but they no longer formed a public domain. Rather than entering into discussions with each other, they preferred to be entertained. Habermas – through his English translator – talks of the transition from a 'public' to an 'audience'.

A related critique can be found in the work of Richard Sennett. He describes the boulevards of nineteenth-century Paris with their passive public of individuals drinking coffee at a small table, absorbed in their own thoughts; or, like *flâneurs*, letting their gaze wander along the performance on the boulevard – again, mainly as a passive public: 'That is how the *flâneur* is to be appreciated', says Sennett. 'He is to be watched, not spoken to. To understand him, you must learn "the art of seeing"'.[15] At the pavement cafés on the Parisian boulevards a new public protocol slowly developed whose ideal consisted of silence in the public sphere:

There grew up the notion that strangers had no right to speak to each other, that each man possessed as a public right an invisible shield, a right to be left alone. Public behaviour was a matter of observation, of passive participation, of a certain kind of voyeurism.[16]

The café was no longer a meeting place where people with different backgrounds met for discussions but rather an extension of visitors' private spheres. This development fits in with a broader trend outlined by Sennett: urban society became more complex as a result of increases in scale and industrialization, and people had to learn to live together with strangers from various backgrounds. In a reaction against this, the ideal developed of avoiding interaction with strangers. Citizens retreated into parochial domains where they mainly met like-minded people. And social relationships became increasingly valued if there was warmth, friendship and intimacy, precisely those qualities that were lacking in the impersonal life of the big city.

Sennett regrets this parochialization of urban life. After all, the experience of variety that characterizes the public domain makes our lives as people more stratified:

A city is a place where people can learn to live with strangers, to enter into the experiences and interests of unfamiliar lives. Sameness stultifies the mind; diversity stimulates and expands it.[17]

City dwellers should actually go in search of the fault lines, the interfaces, the jolts of the city: 'These jolts,' writes Sennett, 'are necessary to a human being to give him that sense of tentativeness about his own beliefs which every civilized person must have.'[18] This is crucial for Sennett: the goal of learning to appreciate differences is not so much a contemporary ideal of individual self-realization, but the awareness that political and social circumstances are not fixed facts and can be questioned.[19]

City dwellers must learn that they do not necessarily have to be the same in order to act communally. But for this to happen, two requirements must be met: firstly, common meeting places are necessary – the worlds of different city dwellers must continue to overlap; secondly, and this is vital for Sennett, the public domain that develops from this overlap must remain protected against the intimacy that is characteristic of the private sphere. It is only when we meet each other in the public domain as citizens that we can speak freely and define a common goal or confront one another with different viewpoints in an open debate. 'The city', Sennett concludes, 'ought to be the teacher of that action, the forum in which it becomes meaningful to join with other persons without the compulsion to know them as persons.'[20] The public sphere must function as a neutral terrain where city dwellers can meet as citizens.

Taken together, the visions of Arendt, Sennett and Habermas are interesting because they show how a public can be formed from the protocols that are linked to specific locations. A place in itself is not decisive but rather the ethos governing communication, the protocol that is observed there, with participants temporarily distancing themselves from their private identities. The participants in the debate create a 'common world' that unites them in a debate. Another valuable element is that these three thinkers show that a public domain can exist thanks to the differences that clash in it; harmony is not necessarily the dominant note – there is in fact a struggle between different viewpoints. In particular, Sennett's view that city dwellers do not necessarily have to get to know each other personally to be able to cooperate or coexist is an important contribution.

Yet there is also room for criticism: the ideal of a 'common world' in which citizens shed their private identities and everyone participates in debates on the basis of equality is no more than that: an ideal. Coffee houses were not the democratic places that Habermas described – 'respectable' women, for example, did not enter.[21] And it is debatable whether the strict distinction between private, parochial and public domains that these thinkers so favour is that productive. Nancy Fraser is very critical of the idea that a neutral public sphere can exist where citizens temporarily shed their identities: 'Public spheres are not only arenas for the formation of discursive opinion', argues Fraser,

> in addition they are arenas for the formation and enactment of social identities. This means that participation is not simply a matter of being able to state propositional contents that are neutral with respect to form of expression. Rather ... participation means being able to speak in one's own voice, and thereby simultaneously to construct and express one's cultural identity through idiom and style.[22]

In other words, must the public domain necessarily be dominated by impersonal communicative interaction? Could urban publics that collectively shape the future of the city not develop from a situation in which members of the public display their own life-styles? We find this argument in the work of the next thinker who greatly influenced the formulation of theory about the public domain: Marshall Berman. With him, we look again at the nineteenth-century boulevards in Paris and St Petersburg.

Marshall Berman's Boulevards as Revolutionary Interface

The construction of the boulevards in Paris at the end of the nineteenth century made an enormous impression. They cut straight through the urban fabric of winding and twisting alleyways and their length gave Parisians the sense of being able to look infinitely far into the distance. Haussmann's plan was revolutionary because of the underlying concept of looking at the city as a unit: until the middle of the nineteenth century, most Parisians were oriented towards their own neighbourhood or district, and the city consisted of a maze of neighbourhoods;[23] with Haussmann's interventions, an overarching infrastructure was constructed that encompassed the whole city and also visually linked the different quarters of the city.[24]

Once constructed, the boulevards started to fulfil a variety of new functions. What Haussmann had not foreseen was that a new type of urban life would develop on the boulevards: their 'programming' of pavements, pavement cafés and department stores attracted all sorts of new publics. The up-and-coming bourgeoisie came to shop and stroll there; they were joined by city dwellers whose roles and professions had until recently been non-existent or unusual: shop assistants, bank clerks, bureaucrats and tourists. Workers and tradesmen of the old Paris also mixed on the boulevards. For although the boulevards had replaced some of the messy old neighbourhoods, a large part of the original urban fabric between the boulevards had survived. City dwellers on the boulevard thus became part of an extremely mixed public. According to Fierro,

As boulevards cut across the city in unrelentingly straight lines, they provided a sectional slice through quartiers that had been closed to view. Immediately behind the regulated facades of the boulevard, neighborhoods of the lower classes could be seen, and their constituents had full access to the city's major thoroughfares. Consequently, the boulevards provided an arena for the display of the bourgeoisie not only to each other, but to a wide demographic mix of economic classes and nationalities.[25]

Young and old, rich and poor thus encountered each other on the same boulevards as part of what were then the new urban masses.[26] Three elements were new in this experience: firstly, these new masses were seen as something unusual because they also provided a certain freedom from social control, despite the presence of many other people. Whereas in more traditional village societies the inhabitants knew each other personally and kept an eye on each other, the new masses of people in the big cities consisted of strangers who would remain strangers to each other. A second novelty was that the city dwellers brought together on the boulevard belonged to different groups and could take notice of each other in passing. The urban poverty in itself was not new but now different groups were spatially confronted with each other. Planning historian Peter Hall describes how, on the boulevards, the middle and upper classes were constantly confronted with members of the working class, a world that until then had been largely invisible to them.[27] A third change lay in the fact that these strangers found it more difficult to place each other. In the pre-industrial city, population groups had also mixed to a certain extent but their mutual relationships were often immediately obvious due to sumptuary laws for example. 'Haussmann's works', writes René Boomkens,

> (. . .) turned various neighbourhoods, social groups and com-munities into a large collection of city dwellers. This led to the emergence of the everyday phenomenon of the anonymous, mobile, urban masses, the permanent flow of shuffling, shopping city dwellers in overcrowded streets, but, as an unintended consequence, a new sort of urban confrontation also became possible.[28]

One important detail: all these different city dwellers did not go to the boulevards with the intention of forming a common public; that developed as a side-effect. These city dwellers came to the boule-vards for different reasons, but a mixed public developed precisely because the boulevard had various 'programmes' that attracted all these groups.

But how did this process actually work out on the boulevards? In what way did the boulevard function as an interface? In his book *All That is Solid Melts into Air*, Marshall Berman describes two social mechanisms that led to the development of a public on the boulevard: the confrontation scene and the recognition scene. To explain how this worked, Berman quotes two prose poems by Charles Baudelaire that were serialized in a Parisian newspaper in the nineteenth century. In the first poem, Baudelaire described two lovers having a drink at a pavement café on a newly constructed boulevard; the backdrop consists of the rubble of the demolished workers' houses that contrasts with the café's lighted, exuberant interior. The scene illustrates how lovers at pavement cafés on the boulevard can be *en public* in a new way: surrounded by a dream-like urban landscape of fleeting sensations – the café's lighting, the bustling masses on the pavement – they cherish a private moment in the midst of public urban life.

But not for long: suddenly, the couple is stared at by an impoverished family; they receive a look that is not so much reproachful as resigned. The paupers contemplate a world of luxury that they know will never be theirs. The lovers react differently to this brief confrontation. The man sympathizes with the poor; the woman would rather get rid of them as quickly as possible. Their different reactions also lead to a new distance between the lovers, although this is not Baudelaire's main point here. According to Berman, the poem shows how the confrontation between different classes on the boulevard led to something resembling a confrontation scene in literature: the confrontation means that the lovers must somehow relate to the family with its craving eyes:

> The setting that magically inspired the romance now works a contrary magic and pulls the lovers out of their romantic enclosure, into wider and less idyllic networks. In this new light, their personal happiness appears as class privilege. The boulevard forces them to react politically.[29]

On the boulevard, the lovers are part of an urban public in a new way. But this given also entails obligations: through these very confrontations, they are forced to constantly relate to developments around them.[30]

Berman argues that in a similar way, the boulevard also offers the less privileged classes a place where – in a recognition scene - they can become aware of their situation, and where this awareness might lead to a collective awareness and collective action. To illustrate this, he refers to a second prose poem by Baudelaire: in this poem the poet is almost killed while crossing the boulevard with its busy traffic. Berman sees this as a metaphor for modern experience: modern man is dragged into a maelstrom of movements that he must join to a certain extent in order not to be trodden underfoot. At the same time, this maelstrom of modern traffic also provides the freedom to visit new places that have been opened up by the boulevards. But Berman wonders what would happen if modern man did not have to react to the traffic on his own; what if the men and women who were continuously terrorized by the roaring traffic joined forces?

> For one luminous moment, the multitude of solitudes that make up the modern city come together in a new kind of encounter, to make a people. . . . they seize control of the city's elemental matter and make it their own. For a little while the chaotic modernism of solitary brusque moves gives way to an ordered modernism of mass movement. (. . .) This possibility is a vital flash of hope in the mind of the man in the mire of the macadam, in the moving chaos, on the run.[31]

The boulevard threatens to drag everyone into the chaotic life that takes place there, but it also offers the prospect of confrontations or recognition and the creation of a new collective awareness; the chance to take control of one's own life. This is where city dwellers can recognize other city dwellers who are struggling with the same issues and this can create a momentum that results in collective action: '[The] personal encounter in the street emerges as a political event', writes Berman, 'the modern city works as a medium in which personal and political life flow together and become one.'[32]

Berman argues that the personal identity revealed by citizens in public spaces is what leads to the development of political awareness. He elaborates this idea with the air of a romantic revolutionary: Berman envisages the new publics that he optimistically describes emerging from more or less nothing out of the masses on the boulevards, like flashmobs *avant la lettre*. Consider, for example, his description of a demonstration on Nevski Prospekt, the most important boulevard in St Petersburg:

> On the morning of December 4, 1876, several hundred of the miscellaneous people on the Nevsky will suddenly coalesce into a crowd, and converge collectively on the magnificent baroque colonnade in front of the Kazan Cathedral.[33]

One moment the boulevard is full of mere passers-by, the next moment this constellation of individuals who were apparently present by sheer coincidence has been transformed into a revolutionary public that appropriates the street. The underlying social mechanisms remain hidden from sight. Where are the leaders who had to convince the workers to leave their factory districts and cross the Neva river to demonstrate in the very heart of power? Why are these workers prepared to risk their lives? Did their families try to dissuade them or did they actually encourage them? What role was played by students and the institutions where they are educated? Where did the red flag suddenly come from that one of the demonstrators unfurled before he – again, if we are to believe Berman's description – spontaneously addressed the crowd? Berman makes it almost appear as if it was the boulevard itself that more or less created the public, but this is, of course, too naive.

This does not detract from the interesting twist Berman gives to the concept of the public domain. In his view, the public domain is no longer exclusively reserved for rational debate between individuals: personal outpourings, physical experiences and visual confrontations can also play an important role. This marks the disappearance of Arendt's and Habermas's clear distinction between the private sphere, where individual identities were formed, and the public domain, where these fully formed individuals can relate to each other. Berman shows that it is by making personal lifestyles public that new (political) identities can develop. This makes it possible for city dwellers to recognize each other in the public domain and act collectively. The public domain is the very place where city dwellers can become part of all sorts of publics that are based on collective experiences or interests.

This shift in the concept of the public domain means we also need a new way of looking at city dwellers and the way they manifest themselves there. One lead here is the figure of the *flâneur*, the mythical urban resident who saunters along the boulevards of Paris in Baudelaire's mid-nineteenth-century poems.

Walter Benjamin, René Boomkens and the *Flâneur*

During the twentieth century, the *flâneur* became a mythical figure: since the French poet Baudelaire drew his existence to the attention of his readers 150 years ago, innumerable writers have let him wander past the wares on sale in shopping arcades in Paris. We see him strolling aimlessly past the urban dream worlds that are evoked in lighted shop windows; he saunters past pavement cafés where customers are clad in the latest fashions; he picks up a newspaper at a kiosk here, overhears a conversation in a park there, lets his gaze wander over the masses that move forth over the newly constructed boulevards; effortlessly, he assimilates all these dizzying impressions and draws on them for inspiration to give his own life form.

This is the romantic image of the *flâneur* that we have been familiar with for more than a century. Consider, for example, Siegried Kracauer's 1927 comparison of *flânerie* with smoking marijuana. The *flâneur* is:

> (. . .) the aimless saunterer who sought to conceal the gaping void around him and within him by imbibing a thousand impressions. Shop-window displays, prints, new buildings, smart clothes, elegant equipages, newspaper-sellers – he indiscriminately absorbed the spectacle of life that went on all around him. (. . .) to the flaneur the sights of the city were like dreams to a hashish smoker.[34]

Yet this does not do full justice to the *flâneur*. For Walter Benjamin – and especially in René Boomkens' interpretation of his works – *flânerie* is not so much a romantic escape from reality: the *flâneur* is above all a philosophical figure, someone who must set us thinking about the way in which we can deal with the experience of modern urban society.

Boomkens links the rise of the figure of the *flâneur* to the huge growth of a number of European cities from the middle of the nineteenth century onwards. Industrialization led to migration, and for the migrants the trek to the industrial metropolises meant their arrival in a new world. The experience of the modern city, with its innumerable new impressions that overwhelm the city dweller, is radically different from the way traditional village life is experienced. To make that difference clear, Boomkens uses Benjamin's different concepts of experience: a brief (intensely felt) experience (*Erlebnis*) and meaningful experience (*Erfahrung*). An *Erfahrung* refers to the acquisition of new experiences that can be placed in the continuous flow of earlier experiences: we can link what we experience in the here and now to all sorts of conscious and unconscious personal and collective memories. This means we can place the here and now, that we can understand a situation, that we feel embedded in a larger whole. Individual experiences can thus be integrated into a series of collective experiences. In traditional societies, they even overlap to a certain extent: rituals link personal experiences to collective experiences.[35]

According to Benjamin, modern urban life hardly provides these opportunities. Modern urban life is rather the domain of the *Erlebnis*: the brief, discrete experience that is unconnected to any individual or collective memory. Benjamin refers to this as a condition of shock: an occurrence that can hardly be placed in a context any more, that cannot be assimilated into an individual or a collective framework. René Boomkens pithily summarizes the antithesis as follows:

> Whereas traditional experience was based on the integration of new events in a series of previously assimilated discrete, brief experiences in a gradual process of habituation and training, the radical novelty and the unpredictability of events in large-scale urban society prevents their being assimilated in a similar confidence-inspiring connection of meaning. The shock actually disrupts any potential connection and sustainability: the immune system reacts to the shock by isolating an event so that it remains a one-off.[36]

Benjamin did not convert his *Erlebnis – Erfahrung* antithesis into a nostalgic exposition of an orderly world that has been lost and that we must try to recover from modernization. In this new urban experience he actually saw opportunities and possibilities to be part of all sorts of collectives in a new way. The figure of the *flâneur* was the first step in this process. Benjamin built on Baudelaire's description of the *flâneur*: an artistic city dweller who lets his distant gaze wander somewhat aimlessly over the apparently nondescript urban masses. He possesses the ability to pick out exactly those few elements that inspire him to create a new poem or work of art.[37] Boomkens compares the *flâneur*'s attitude with the approach taken by the private detective and the journalist, two professions that were also coming into their own towards the end of the nineteenth century and that also fascinated society at the time. The core concept here is what Boomkens describes as 'scattered attention': a state 'between shock and a brief, discrete experience, it is directed at constructing the *flâneur*'s own story and making a meaningful selection from the indifferent and rapid succession of experiences, facts or images.'[38] It is this vast number of impressions that allow the modern city dweller to make different choices in the public domain and be absorbed in the various publics he comes across on the boulevard. This description reminds one of 'network individualism': the city dweller as an individual is part of various, partly overlapping publics; in the urban public space, all these publics come together and this in turn leads to the development of new cross-links.

Benjamin adds a critical note here: the emphasis on *flânerie* can also result in a too individualistic way of life as part of a libertarian urban ideal. The happily sauntering city dweller then cuts and pastes together his identity but otherwise pays little attention to his surroundings. This is not what Benjamin advocated. The modern city dweller's task is not only to find a place in an existing society that is disorderly by its very nature; the *flâneur* must also be able to create new publics, for instance to question existing repressive power structures. Benjamin considered it important for urban inhabitants who seek to embed their individual lives in collective experiences to also actively seek 'dialectical images' – images that illustrate the confrontation between different stories, points of view and ways of looking at things, for example the way in which different regimes are stratified in a city's architecture.[39]

Benjamin links the *flâneur* to a related development, the privatization and parochialization of urban life, which he illustrates (or rather, scoffs at) using the image of the 'cocooned human', the opposite of the *flâneur*. Benjamin describes how in the mid-nineteenth century the bourgeoisie started to withdraw into the private sphere. Around this time, economic activities disappeared from the home, which acquired an increasingly intimate nature. Precisely because the modern public domain created such a chaotic (or in Benjamin's words, labyrinthine) impression, those who had the means for it withdrew into their own enclaves, where a certain order and clarity still reigned. We saw this analysis earlier in Sennett's work. The home was perceived as a place that was diametrically opposed to the harsh outside world. The interior became a place where people could express their own identities, where dreams and illusions were cherished.

Nineteenth-century bourgeois interiors were crammed with velours, antique furniture and curiosities from all over the world. 'Above all, this interior was a haven', Boomkens writes, 'where little or nothing was allowed to remind the inhabitants of life outside.'[40] The individual's home, his dwelling, thus gradually became a segregated cocoon while at the same time public life outside the home was increasingly seen as chaotic and dangerous. So it seems that Benjamin used the figure of the *flâneur* not so much to describe a widely accepted practice but rather to intervene in this debate. He defended the public domain: it was here, amidst the masses, that the individual must shape his life, and not in the protected private sphere.

In his books *Een drempelwereld* (literally, 'A threshold world') and *De nieuwe wanorde* (literally, 'The new disorder'), Boomkens also argues that city dwellers should look for points of contact in the complexity of the public domain to shape their lives and relate to their fellow city dwellers. This is a complex affair that occurs in all sorts of domains in the urban public sphere:

> The urban public sphere is an elusive phenomenon. One can express this public sphere in strictly spatial terms, referring to the public domain, the spaces in cities that are accessible to all or many people, from city streets and squares to cafés and coffee houses and even semi-public interior spaces such as theatres, department stores and shopping centres. Beside this, the public sphere can also be understood as public life. While it is true that to an important extent this life takes place in this public space, it cannot be fully understood in purely spatial terms. Public life is reflected in a tradition of publications and in the different ways in which this tradition has become institutionalized: from the press, the world of publishing and the political pamphlet to the world of telecommunications and electronic mass media. This in turn is all based on a much less institutionalized whole (a collection of networks) of practices and habits used in public behaviour: pub conversations, encounters and exchanges on the street, market life, public events, parties, nightlife and even more everyday activities such as shopping or simply going for a walk.[41]

The urban public sphere thus consists of those places where we, in the process of doing, thinking, observing, walking and talking, acquire an identity that is part of broader collectives. Whereas Berman sees new revolutionary publics coalescing out of nothing on the boulevard, Boomkens points out that through all these subtle, semi-unconscious confrontations, encounters and even simple passing movements, we become part of a much more elusive public: the city as a community of strangers. And whereas Habermas and Arendt emphasized the importance of rational discussion and the concept of the public domain as a neutral meeting place, for Boomkens the urban public space is actually dominated by everyday life. An important concept for him is that of 'continuity': this is not – as the modernist exposition would have it – about creating *ex nihilo* a new world of experience for the city dweller; it is about letting the various worlds of experience overlap so that they can provide a foothold in a chaotic world without this leading to segregation. The republican urban ideal is thus given a more everyday interpretation.

Boomkens thus shifts the perspective to the individual perception of the public domain. How can we as city dwellers be part of different urban publics without segregating or withdrawing? He shows how the private and the public domains are intertwined. The high level of abstraction in his argument is both valuable and difficult. The public domain must be a place where the harmonization of individual and collective identities is possible, where we learn to feel at home when surrounded by strangers. But this also confronts us with a new dilemma: exactly which harmonization is desirable or necessary? Is there a specific relationship or range within which a city as, indeed, a community of strangers, can develop, and is this threatened when such relationships drop under a certain minimum or exceed a certain maximum? And where exactly does this minimum lie? And what exactly are the constituent elements from which that experience is created? The theory gives designers few practical footholds.

On the other hand, the emphasis on continuity and embedding in urban life does provide a welcome foothold regarding a number of other dominant expositions about the public domain that emerged after the Second World War. Two neo-avant-garde movements provided two contradictory perspectives on urban public spaces: Situationist artists such as Constant (Nieuwenhuys) built on the modernist body of thought in which a new world of experience was created as an alternative to the existing world, and the Archigram movement embraced a more libertarian public domain in which the latest technology would help city dwellers to harmonize their lives with their individual preferences.

New Babylon and Plug-In City: the Neo-avant-gardists' Interactive Cities

New Babylon, the artist Constant's futuristic city, was never built. But the idea of a labyrinthine city for modern man survives in innumerable sketches, scale models, ink drawings, paintings, maps and texts. People who view them see a gigantic structure, an endless network of similar passages, towers and platforms that hover fifteen metres above the surface of the earth. Underneath there is plenty of space - for through-traffic, for the factories to deliver their products without any human mediation, or for nature reserves and water. In one of the paintings, the structure of New Babylon is reminiscent of a city that unites Mondriaan's rhythms and Miró's graceful shapes. In a drawing the high derricks and other industrial elements in the design stand out; the models accentuate the endless, repetitive nature of passages and bare spaces; maps of Paris and Amsterdam on which the structure of the building project has been sketched in, emphasize its huge scale. New Babylon is not a building but a structure that is at least as big as our cities.

All in all, Constant's work was an exploration of a future in which technologies have released man from everyday chores. In Constant's post-industrial utopia, machines have taken over all the work and man is completely free to spend his time as he chooses. This new human being does this in a labyrinthine system of passages and spaces that the user himself can arrange in all sorts of ways. Light hardly penetrates into the passages; instead, an advanced technological system of 'air conditioning' regulates the climate. One can easily get lost because there are no points of recognition: 'Every space is temporary, nothing is recognizable', wrote Constant, 'everything is discovery, everything changes, nothing can serve as a landmark.'[42] If necessary, the air conditioning can also contribute to this atmosphere: 'There is no attempt to effect a faithful imitation of nature, however; on the contrary, the technical facilities are deployed as powerful, ambience-creating resources. . .'[43] Recognition points are superfluous in Constant's ideal city because, thanks to automation, life is now no work and all play and if one no longer has to work, there is also no longer any reason to live in one and the same place according to Nieuwenhuys:

(. . .) sedentary life would lose its raison d'être. Human behavior during work-free periods – holidays – provides sufficient proof of this. Without the restrictions imposed by work, moving around becomes more important than staying put: the dormitory town loses its function because residence can be temporary rather than permanent.[44]

Nieuwenhuys considered the new nomadic freedom an important achievement. In his view, existing dogmas in architecture and planning placed too much emphasis on providing spatial unity, a continuity in which the city dweller could be absorbed. Such a framework disciplines the individual far too much and is effected at the expense of the freedom to shape one's own life and world. Instead of an environment that provides points of contact, Nieuwenhuys argued for an environment that continuously summons up all sorts of situations that surprise the inhabitants of New Babylon:

If one proceeds from a conception in which life represents not continuity but a succession of moments, moments that are incessantly changing their nature and orientation, so that each successive moment disavows and erases its predecessor, if one proceeds from this dialectical view of life, one cannot continue to see the living environment as a settlement, a fixed abode.[45]

Constant's labyrinth is thus completely different from Benjamin's. Benjamin placed the *flâneur* in the limelight as an example of someone who has found a way to harmonize individual and collective identities in the labyrinth that the city is by its very nature and thus make this labyrinth 'habitable'. For Constant, the notion of habitability seemed to consist of relinquishing all forms of continuity: 'A long sojourn in New Babylon', he said, 'would surely have the effect of brainwashing, erasing all custom and routine.'[46] His city consists of large, empty halls that can be configured in all sorts of ways by its users. City dwellers would constantly be looking for new experiences there, for new 'situations', and thus feel released from the disciplining structures of the state or of capitalism. It is no wonder that the sketches of New Babylon are rather vague and incomplete: New Babylon was intended as a platform; the final interpretation was to be the result of - to use a recent buzzword from the Internet industry – 'user-generated content':[47]

> New Babylonians play a game of their own devising, against a backdrop they have designed themselves, together with their fellow townspeople. That is their life, therein lies their artistry.[48]

Constant's utopia must be seen in the light of the Situationist International, a neo-avant-garde movement centred round Guy Debord. In post-World War II Paris, Debord advocated a new vision of the city. Urban culture as it had developed until then was too heavily dominated by the lifestyle of the bourgeoisie. Emerging technologies had created a new regime of leisure time but this had mainly led to a 'battle of leisure', in which the ruling class managed to entertain the proletariat with a mind-numbing leisure industry: both spatially and on television the public domain would discipline the working class to follow the preferences of the bourgeoisie.[49] New methods such as *dérive* and *détournement* must therefore create new urban experiences that would disrupt this process, claimed Debord. Hovering in the background was the concept of psychogeography: the study of how geographical surroundings influence an individual's emotions and behaviour. This research should consist of all sorts of interventions being carried out in the city in order to study their effects.[50] The *dérive* interventions consisted of a 'passionate journey out of the ordinary through a rapid changing of ambiances'. The goal of the interventions was always to evoke 'situations' that had an alienating effect, or to playfully disrupt the unnoticed everydayness of life – the rules and agreements that are considered 'normal' in specific social and spatial constellations. Or, as Debord put it: 'Life can never be too disorienting.'[51] Gijs van Oenen wrote that 'Central to Situationism was the idea of a "unitary urbanism", aimed at wresting urban life from the private, social or political conventions that had it in their grip.'[52] Debord claimed that architects must therefore no longer design buildings that evoked a particular emotion but instead direct themselves to designing 'situations' (interfaces) that could disrupt the status quo: with their interventions the Situationists tried to constantly reprogramme the public domain in such a way that city dwellers would become aware of the repressive structures that they were part of.

New Babylon can be seen as an extreme example of the *derive* intervention, according to Van Oenen: '(...) the ramble that undermines the structure of the city by creating ephemeral surroundings that are beyond the reach of any centrally organized authority'. But while Constant hoped that this would liberate city dwellers and confer on them a new, self-constructed identity, Van Oenen mainly sees aimlessly wandering individuals:

> In the eyes of the contemporary reader, Constant's own sketches of the project give a completely different impression: that of lonely, wandering individuals who can no longer decide on a direction or goal and who are primarily all searching for themselves in the immense spaces of the project. They never seem to be really engaged with anyone or anything.[53]

What is valuable in the Situationists' thinking is the idea that architects, artists or designers can act as 'interface designers' who, through specific programming, can create situations that result in political awareness. This is how new urban publics can emerge. But in its most extreme form, as embodied in New Babylon, this approach also excludes every form of taking root, of feeling at home somewhere. Constant assumes a world that is populated by people who want to construct their own identities completely free of any sort of embedding whatsoever. The radical rejection of any form of continuity that we have seen in Constant's work means that the public domain is almost unviable in his vision.

While the Situationists in 1950s Paris linked Marxist theory to playful interventions in the public space, in the 'swinging London' of the 1960s nine editions of *Archigram* magazine appeared in which the authors actually argued for a more libertarian interpretation of the public sphere.[54]

Archigram was the mouthpiece for the group of architects of the same name whose 'design language' was clearly inspired by earlier avant-garde movements such as Dadaism.[55] Despite the ideological differences between Archigram and Situationism, their ideas about a number of issues were very similar: both movements assumed an architecture whose starting point was the 'situation' or 'event'. Archigram's concept of architecture did not revolve around buildings either; instead, it centred on the way in which a specific, dynamic spatial staging could create an experience. Architecture – in its traditional sense – was only one aspect of this staging. As prominent Archigram member Peter Cook put it in now magic words:

When it is raining in Oxford Street the architecture is no more important than the rain; in fact the weather has probably more to do with the pulsation of the Living City at that given moment.[56]

Archigram argued that new (computer) technologies should be used to chart and make visible this intangible world of experiences and social processes. Equipping buildings with modern technology such as sensors would allow the built environment to change in line with a city's social processes.[57] The architect's task would then be the 'tuning' and 'amplification' of the city's social processes: architects would design not only a ready-made environment but also the algorithms with which this environment could play along with the activities that took place there.

This idea was elaborated in innumerable drawings and sketches of one of Archigram's most famous archetypes, the Plug-In City, whose set-up is reminiscent of New Babylon. The Plug-In City consisted of a complex infrastructural network of passages and paths on which all sorts of units were hung such as shops, bedrooms and office spaces. These units could be relocated using large cranes that were part of the structure. This city would never have a permanent form: its architecture would always be fluid.[58] The Plug-In City was not self-contained: its existence would be made possible by its shadow and nerve centre, Computer City. All sorts of processes in the city would be measured and the data converted into adaptations of the physical infrastructure. To illustrate this idea, Archigram's *Living City* exhibition included a drawing of a 'punch card', the standard interface for operating computers at the time. The caption reads like a poem:

who likes it straight?
who will buy what?
who believes which?
who lives or dies?
thought, action
chain response
life forces balanced
in tension
the urban community
the city
CROWD [59]

The suggestion is that the computer is capable of mapping out individuals' lifestyles, based for example on their purchasing patterns. As we saw in chapter 3, the first experiments in this field took place in the 1960s. What was new was Archigram's proposal to use these profiles to harmonize the built environment itself: 'If only we can get to an architecture that really responded to human wish as it occurred', wrote Peter Cook, 'then we would be getting somewhere. (. . .) Man/machine interface. Information feedback results in environment change.'[60]

This was a revolutionary idea at the time. With it, Archigram embraced the rising science of 'cybernetics', the study of interactive systems:[61] It was hoped that computers could be used to orchestrate all sorts of 'feedback loops'. The Plug-In City therefore did not have a master plan; instead, it had a dynamic system that could anticipate what was happening in the city at all times. Architecture thus became a 'scene machine', according to Simon Sadler, 'a continuous creative recomposition of architecture, a lived and playful process configured by the user.'[62]

In this respect, Archigram did bear resemblances to a Situationist strategy – 'playful situations' were developed for interventions in urban life. Yet there was also a significant ideological difference between the two movements. For the Situationists, the interventions were aimed - through the tactic of playful alienation - at recapturing the city from the capitalist bourgeoisie and its sensationalist society. It aimed at a critical reflection on the social system: the interventions were intended as 'consciousness-raising interfaces'. Archigram, on the other hand, embraced the 'pop' spirit of the time, with its increasing prosperity and the world of instant pleasure. Consider, for example, the *Living City Survival Kit* installation, a collage of articles that Archigram considered necessary for an existence in the contemporary city: Coca-Cola bottles and a jar of Nescafé for during the day, cigarettes, Bell's whisky and jazz records for the evenings, and a packet of Alka-Seltzer painkillers to survive the morning after.[63] The architecture described by Archigram was intended to meet city dwellers' wishes, but its implementation was based on a libertarian individualism. Computer City would make it possible for the city to adapt to the individual, but how social relations, let alone social contrasts, were to be given shape was not addressed. The 'brave new world of systems', writes Simon Sadler, was to be placed at the service of a 'beat lifestyle'. In Archigram's city the class differences that the Situationists wanted to expose simply no longer existed. Automation would result in a city of plenty, dominated by a pleasant 'Nescafé anarchism' - a precursor of the cappuccino urbanism in the 'creative class city' in the early twenty-first century, which is discussed in more detail in the next chapter. Archigram's urban life consisted of long nights in jazz clubs and champagne openings of trendy boutiques.

This resulted in a public domain that was no longer dominated by Benjamin's 'shock' but by the 'kick': the city dweller would be stimulated and inspired by all sorts of new fashion trends and lifestyles. According to Peter Cook, the city is a place

(. . .) where so much is happening that one activity is stimulated by all the rest. It is the collection of everything and everyone into a tight space that has enabled the cross stimulus to continue. Trends originated in cities. The mood of cities is frantic. It is all happening – all the time.[64]

This concept is reminiscent of Benjamin's *flâneur*, but it also differs from this figure. After all, Benjamin also gave the *flâneur* the task of going in search of dialectical images in order to confront past and present with each other. For Archigram, the 'kick' consists of the pleasure of being part of a kaleidoscopic, anonymous urban scene. The 'other' in the public domain can be a source of inspiration for shaping one's own life but no more than that. In the context of the *Living City* exhibition Archigram argued that 'There is no desire to communicate with everybody, only with those whose thoughts and feelings are related to our own.'[65]

Viewed from the issue of the public domain, New Babylon and the Plug-In City confront us with a number of problems that are still relevant because many of today's new-media developers are inspired by both the Situationists and Archigram. They consider these movements archetypes of interactive urbanism because of their stimulating ideas of architecture as a 'scene machine' and the role of the artist as a designer of provocative situations. By designing specific programmes, both movements aimed to create new types of public. An important motive was individual autonomy and freedom: the freedom to be able to arrange one's life according to one's own insights, regardless of social conventions. In Constant's plan, disorientation and disrupting fixed collective frameworks were the beginning and the end of the project. New Babylon provided infinite freedom but hardly any new collective experiences that the individual could be part of. The Plug-In City had the opposite problem: 'The problem for those such as Archigram', argued Scott McQuire, 'was their collapse of questions of power entirely into matters of individual choice.'[66] The public domain thus became a platform where confrontations with others would provide a source of inspiration, with the aim of arranging one's own lifestyle.

We must not lose sight of the fact that both movements were progressive at the time. Each aimed to provide an alternative for what they perceived as a suffocating dominant culture. In the case of the Situationists, this was the rise of the sensationalist society and excessive consumerism. And in the case of Archigram, the movement's emphasis on the 'beat lifestyle' was a way of actually escaping the coercive communitarian 1950s feeling and opening up the prospect of individual self-realization.

But if the renewed popularity of Arendt is anything to go by, then the lack of individual freedom in the current debate is no longer the main problem. The question now is how we can ensure the continued existence of the public domain in an era of individualism and parochialization. The main issue in this regard is what this public domain should look like: should it be a neutral space where all city dwellers meet as citizens? Or will we find it in the somewhat chaotic way in which various everyday worlds of experience overlap in the modern city? The latter approach fits in best with the development of parochialization, which has partly been stimulated by the rise of urban media. But it also confronts us with a difficult challenge: what sort of programming is required to ensure that these worlds of experience do actually overlap every now and then?

The discussion about the public domain is above all a normative one. The central question is always: how are city dwellers expected to relate to all those other city dwellers, with all their different ideas, identities, expectations and so on? In the libertarian urban ideal, city dwellers are left to find the answer themselves. In the republican ideal, participation in public life is a *duty*: city dwellers may not retreat into homogeneous enclaves but are expected to be open to experiencing differences. If they are not, the continued existence of the city as a society is under threat, according to a number of the philosophers quoted here.

This duty must be fulfilled by citizens as well as designers and policymakers. They must design urban interfaces that can evoke such public domains. Whether and how that happens is discussed in the following chapter. Using Rotterdam's Schouwburgplein (literally 'theatre square') as an example, an overview is given of how the debate about and the design for this public domain in Rotterdam have developed over the last fifty years.

Schouwburgplein: the Public Domain in Practice

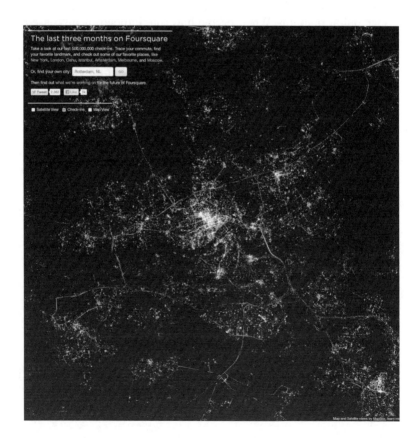

The last three months on Foursquare

Take a look at our last 500,000,000 check-ins. Trace your commute, find your favorite landmark, and check out some of our favorite places, like New York, London, Oahu, Istanbul, Amsterdam, Melbourne, and Moscow.

Or, find your own city: Rotterdam, NL | GO

Then find out what we're working on for the future of Foursquare.

Tweet 2,382   Like 1K

■ Satellite View ■ Check-ins ■ Map View

Map and Satellite views by MapBox, learn more

It was nearly midnight on Saturday 21 June 1997 when the mayor of Rotterdam Bram Peper held a short speech at the city's Schouwburgplein. Just before the Cuban Candido Fabre big band was due to start its performance to mark the inauguration of the square, he invited members of the public to toast the opening of the new 'square of the muses' - a reference to the square's location, wedged between the theatre, the De Doelen concert hall and a multiplex cinema. After decades of wrangling about the square's future and the rejection of innumerable plans – one Rotterdam architectural historian counted forty of them – the matter finally seemed resolved. The new Schouwburgplein, designed by architect Adriaan Geuze of West 8 urban designers, had been officially opened.

Earlier that day, the public had been given an informative tour of the special materials that were used to refurbish the square: a boardwalk with a seventy-metre-long bench, separated from the rest of the square by a band of rubber; steel plates have been laid next to it, with a 'mosaic floor' of acacia wood and a green epoxy floor; huge hydraulic cranes provide lighting and have been painted the same shade of red as the Willemsbrug bridge, a reference to Rotterdam's harbour. The whole square is 35 centimetres higher than its surroundings: it is to function as a 'stage' for the city, an urban public space intended to be 'colonized' by the city's inhabitants.

The design was not without its critics: architectural historian Bernard Hulsman argued that the square looked splendid when seen from the air but all these exotic materials were not particularly attractive from the perspective of the everyday pedestrian.[1] Women's stilettos got stuck in the metal grids and the rainwater on the epoxy floor did not drain properly. The square that looked so appealing on the drawing board was above all a 'designers' square', according to critics. It did well in international publications on architecture, and its idiosyncratic design provided Rotterdam with a fine icon, but as an urban public space, as a place to meet or rest, it was unusable.

Not everyone was so critical: Rotterdam architectural historian Herman Moscoviter argued in a column in the *Rotterdams Dagblad* newspaper that while Schouwburgplein was not a traditional public space with lively outdoor cafés, it did provide a platform for groups other than the usual urban middle class. Skaters, roller-skaters and wheelers, for example, exploited the square to the full.[2]

The debate that developed around Rotterdam's Schouwburgplein was a debate about the urban public sphere. In this debate, different concepts about the function of this urban public space were articulated. Should it be dominated by middle-class conviviality? Should the Schouwburgplein be a square for all Rotterdammers? Or was it in fact a positive development that a specific subculture (the skaters and wheelers) considered the square their 'home'? Should the urban public space mainly function as a meeting place? Or should it be deployed as an icon to help the city achieve international standing?

The debates about Schouwburgplein at the end of the 1990s were not the first: from the time the square first appeared in the post-war reconstruction plans for Rotterdam at the end of the 1940s there had been debates about the design and use of the square. Together, all these debates provide an insight into the way both the city council and the designers started to think differently about the best way to shape the public domain.

Two debates played a key role here as 'philosophical moments': at the end of the 1970s the architect Herman Hertzberger presented an alternative for the modernist design of the 1960s. The original square had been dominated by the modernist design principles of the separation of functions and traffic circulation, but Hertzberger (a structuralist) now proposed a plan that was closer to a republican urban ideal. However, those in power at the time did not see any value in his idea for the square as 'the city's living room'.

It was not until the beginning of the 1990s that a new design was actually approved. The debate about the design by Adriaan Geuze that was finally implemented led to a number of new developments. In the preceding years, urban policy for the public domain had become increasingly dominated by city marketing and the leisure culture of the middle-class. At the same time, it is possible to trace a change in the use of urban space, partly because city dwellers increasingly preferred the parochial domain to the public domain. This was translated into a design approach for Schouwburgplein in which the public, at least in theory, was assigned a bigger role: it was to 'colonize' the space according to its own ideas.

All these developments led to the urban public sphere functioning in a new way. It was no longer necessarily a central platform where all city dwellers met, which is not to say that interaction between city dwellers disappeared but rather that an urban network of overlapping parochial domains developed. An analysis by Hajer and Reijndorp shows that this approach also provides new leads for the design of the urban public sphere. These developments are illustrated by the case of Schouwburgplein.

Herman Hertzberger's Plan (1977)

In 1977 Herman Hertzberger presented a new (and as it quickly turned out, controversial) plan for Schouwburgplein at the request of the Rotterdam city council. Hertzberger wrote in his introduction that 'A square is (...) the symbolic living room of the city, where the feeling of somehow still belonging together should be given expression.'[3] A square, thought Hertzberger, should give city dwellers the feeling that they are part of an urban community. This should not be a clear-cut communitarian community; rather, his ideas seem to dovetail with the republican urban ideal: there should be space for several perspectives. Hertzberger considered it the architect's task to 'help broaden our world of experience'. The square should be arranged in such a way that visitors and users would be tempted into acquiring new impressions.

At the end of the 1970s, these ideas met with considerable resistance from the Rotterdamse Kunststichting (RKS), an arts advisory foundation. It considered Hertzberger's plan 'rustic' and 'quaint' and 'neither one thing nor the other'.[4] It simply did not fit in with the city council's modernist planning ideal in which urban public spaces were primarily conceived as spaces for infrastructure and traffic circulation. The debate that followed the plan and RKS's reaction to it constituted a turning point in the thinking about the urban public domain. The arts advisory foundation got its way and Hertzberger's plan was not implemented. Despite this, his design approach slowly gained ground and it was eventually the modernist perspective that faded into the background.

When Hertzberger submitted his plan, Schouwburgplein was barely three decades old. In 1946 it appeared for the first time on a map of Rotterdam in city architect Cornelis van Traa's basic plan for reconstructing the city after the Second World War, during which the city was severely damaged by an extensive bombing raid. However, it did not take shape until the middle of the 1960s, based on a design by an engineer named Fokkinga.[5] He was guided by the principles of modernist architecture, with its spatial separation of urban functions and its emphasis on traffic circulation (the square was located on several through roads, and underground parking facilities were also constructed). Fokkinga turned Schouwburgplein into an open surface flanked by three water basins on one side and by three kiosks on the other. There was no direct relationship with the square's surroundings.

Fokkinga's plan was preferred to the alternatives that had provided for more greenery, conviviality and restaurants and cafés – the Heineken beer brewery had even submitted a plan that advocated a mixture of functions: shops, recreation and culture. The square was never popular, although it was used by businessmen from nearby offices at lunchtime when the weather was fine.

When the local newspapers wrote about the square, the same words always recurred: windy, bare and inhospitable. From the 1970s onward, plans were constantly launched for the refurbishment of the square.

Herztberger's plan was the most high-profile. Hertzberger belonged to a wider movement, the structuralists, who, from the end of the 1950s, advocated the reintroduction of the human dimension as the guiding design principle in architecture. They rejected the development in which 'city-forming' (the construction of commercial districts in the heart of a city) was coupled with the development of 'centres of growth' (the construction of dormitory cities). In their view, the city should have a vibrant core. Urban design should give city dwellers a 'home' and at the same time provide space for people to meet. In a much discussed issue of *Forum* magazine, they added weight to their arguments by alternating photographs of bleak flats with photographs of pleasant squares.[6]

The design of a 'home' was echoed in a key concept in Hertzberger's plan for Schouwburgplein: 'hospitality'. A place must be capable of creating lasting meanings and associations; it must be a pleasant spot to relax and people should feel at home there. His description of the sort of sculptures that should be placed in the public space to achieve this effect clearly represents his concepts. He argued that the sculptures should not be reminiscent of

> (. . .) dentists' drills (. . .) whose only aim seems to be to achieve so-called alienating effects over and over again (in a world where alienation is one of our most urgent problems) (. . .) [Instead] we hope the city will be given sculptures that evoke tender, friendly, warm associations with which one can build an affective bond.[7]

It is easy to recognize this as a critique of the Situationist ideas that, as we have already seen, actually advocated alienating and disruptive experiences. In Hertzberger's view modern life was already confusing enough. The public domain should be designed in such a way that this chaotic world would once more be 'experienceable'. City dwellers should be able to become attached to a place; they should be able to feel part of a collective rhythm there.

To make Schouwburgplein more 'hospitable', Hertzberger proposed splitting the large, uninviting surface of Schouwburgplein in two. The new, small-scale spaces would evoke a more intimate feeling. Because various cultural institutions would be located on the square, visitors would simultaneously acquire all sorts of new experiences. In addition, there would be a number of places where people could sit and relax. To give some idea of what he had in mind, his plan included photographs of Milan's Galleria Vittorio Emanuele and Rotterdam's pre-World War II glass-covered Hoogstraatpassage shopping arcade.

It is no coincidence that Hertzberger selected two shopping arcades: they fit in with a vision of the public domain that emphasizes the sensuousness as well as the ephemeral but embedded experience of modern urban life.[8] The arcades are the territory par excellence of Walter Benjamin's *flâneur*: it is where he absorbs the masses, admires the wares on display or gazes at the wonders of modernity – the Hoogstraatpassage was the first building in Rotterdam with electric lighting. At the same time, the arcades, with their human dimension, also provide the *flâneur* with a dynamic 'home': here, he can be absorbed in modern urban life without losing himself completely in it. They are 'threshold worlds', to use Boomkens' term, or 'interfaces', where harmonization between individual and collective identities or between the new and the old can take place.

In the 1960s and 1970s the structuralists were not alone in criticizing the modernist reconstruction vision that set the tone in Rotterdam at the time. In the media, the lack of a human dimension in the centre of Rotterdam was often discussed: architecture critic and columnist Rein Blijstra wrote in the *Het Vrije Volk* newspaper that Rotterdam had deliberately been made uninviting 'because it was thought that twentieth-century man has a different lifestyle, a different way of moving around from, for example, medieval people. Was this assumption wrong?'[9] This criticism grew with the publication of R. Wentholt's 1968 book *De binnenstadsbeleving van Rotterdam* (literally, 'The inner-city experience of Rotterdam'), in which he wrote that there was an abundance of openness, too little seclusion, and altogether too little intimacy in the architecture, making it impossible for people to feel at home in inner-city Rotterdam or identify with its built environment. All these criticisms applied to Schouwburgplein in particular: 'The walls already present around the square do not lend themselves well to a satisfactory experience of the square, and the later designation of a bit of unused land as a central square that has not been taken into account in or harmonized with the overall spatial structure of the city imposes limitations.'[10] What the square needed to become a vibrant place was a 'densification' of activities, that is, bringing together all sorts of functions. Instead of an 'aesthetically sophisticated' grand square, he proposed the design of a 'loose accumulation of spaces for cultural uses'. Criticism, which gained wider support at the time, largely came down to this: the international style propagated by the CIAM on which Schouwburgplein was based, was an ineffective interface. This architecture was intended to create an 'urban interface' in which a new human would grow to full stature, but it had lost sight of the human dimension. The process of harmonization that should have taken place in these urban interfaces simply failed to get off the ground: CIAM architecture was not the solution to 'alienation' that, for example, Le Corbusier had hoped for; instead, it actually exacerbated it.

Neither Wentholt's book nor Hertzberger's plan were popular with the RKS arts advisory foundation at the time. In September 1977 the Studiecommissie Schouwburgplein (literally, 'Schouwburg-plein study committee') handed over a report of its findings to the city council.[11] In their report, the authors heavily criticize Hertz-berger's ideas about urban public spaces as places where inhabitants should feel at home. The RKS arts advisory foundation still largely supported modernist reconstruction ideals: a good square, wrote the RKS in its recommendation, 'is a communicating vessel for the surrounding areas. It is a junction from which one can head in many directions'. The rest of the report also emphasized mobility and movement in the public domain: 'Some famous city squares are used only as traffic intersections, while other squares serve mainly as parking facilities.'

Which was not saying that the square should only have a traffic function: the RKS also paid considerable attention to the social activities that took place at the square, such as 'drumming competitions, roller-skating displays, [and sailing with] model boats and dinghies.' It was just that these sorts of activities should not be elicited or planned. A square – or in a broader sense, the urban public space – must primarily provide space for all sorts of dynamic activities. This concept had parallels with Constant's New Babylon: city dwellers must be given the opportunity to organize their surroundings according to their own judgement. Every form of embedding was rejected by the RKS as 'quaint' and 'rustic'; as was to be expected, the establishment of cultural institutions on the square was also rejected by the RKS.

Hertzberger's plan and the RKS report gave rise to considerable upheaval and eventually the plan was not implemented. The humanist perspective as advocated by Hertzberger, which emphasized the feeling of being 'at home', lost out at the end of the 1970s to the emphasis on mobility and movement that the modernist reconstruc-tion plans still bespoke. But it was not long before the tide turned and the arguments put forward by Hertzberger, Wentholt and others gradually gained a foothold in urban planning policy. In 1978, the city council accepted the structural plan, 'Rotterdam binnen de Ruit' (literally, 'Rotterdam within the rhombus'), which put an end to the separation of functions and included plans for more dwellings in the city centre. This was followed in 1982 by a report by Stadsontwikkeling Rotterdam ('Rotterdam urban development') on Schouwburgplein that argued that the design of the square must take more account of the 'human dimension'.[12]

Yet it was not until the beginning of the 1990s that a final decision was made, and Adriaan Geuze of West 8 urban designers was commissioned to redesign Schouwburgplein. To put this plan in context, it is important to first briefly consider a number of broader developments that were directly related to the public domain.

The Public Domain in Rotterdam 1980-1990

In the 1980s, the Rotterdam city council's vision of the public domain changed. This shift was associated with broader developments concerning urban culture: commercialization and parochialization. The humanist development principles became generally accepted over time, but they were given a twist: instead of serving the ideal of a republican urban community; rather, they were dominated by concepts such as city marketing and the consumer society.

These developments first became noticeable at the end of the 1970s. Shops and recreation functions, including cafés and restaurants, were allocated more space in Dutch inner cities. The city dweller was increasingly seen as a consumer who enjoyed 'fun shopping'. Cities were all too willing to exploit this, partly because it became increasingly important to distinguish themselves from other cities as attractive locations for companies to establish themselves. In a service economy that is closely intertwined with the rise of global communication networks, companies are less tied than before to specific geographic locations for both their head-quarters and their production units. As a result, perhaps counter-intuitively, location has become not less but more important: people or companies that are free to establish themselves anywhere and everywhere choose the most attractive location. As a result of this development, cities find themselves in a competitive struggle in which they try to outdo each other. The organization of the public space plays an important role here: it acquires an increasingly representative character. Cities try to distinguish themselves through ambitious, high-quality designs for public spaces. Growing emphasis is placed on the iconic value of an urban public space and at the same time, this public space is increasingly dominated by leisure consumerism.[13] This means that the design of public spaces is geared more and more towards the tastes of a new group of city dwellers (the 'creative class'), whom these cities want to attract.[14]

For American scholar Don Mitchell, this transition marked an important shift in the way the public domain was conceptualized. It was no longer a platform for political representation; instead, it had become a platform for carefree leisure time. He contrasted these two visions of the public domain in an seminal article about the People's Park riots in Berkeley in the1960s. He described the concept of the urban public sphere as a free political space where publics can organize themselves free from interference from those in power. The public domain is a place for (political) representation, and different groups can enforce their political claims on it through their physical presence. This also means that public spaces can sometimes be somewhat chaotic or that they might be the scene of a political struggle. This is precisely what happened in Berkeley: homeless people occupied People's Park and stood up for their rights;

they waged a battle against a number of institutions (the university, the city council) that had a different vision of the public domain and that wanted to remove homeless people from the park so they could develop it. For them, the urban public space was a place

> (. . .) for recreation and entertainment, subject to usage by an appropriate public that is allowed in. Public space thus constituted a controlled and orderly retreat where a properly behaved public might experience the spectacle of the city.[15]

Mitchell thus described a shift in which urban public space was increasingly dominated by this latter vision.

This shift could also be traced in Rotterdam. In 1984 the city's planning department (Dienst Ruimtelijke Ordening) compiled a memorandum tellingly entitled 'Schouwburgplein: from draughty square to entertainment centre' ('Schouwburgplein: van tochtgat tot uitgaanscentrum').[16] Policy documents dating to 1985 stated that Rotterdam must become an 'attractive city'. And in the 1993 Binnenstadsprogramma (literally 'Inner-city programme'), it was emphatically argued that the public space must become the 'city's showpiece'.[17] In *Buitenruimte* (literally, 'Outdoor space'), a book in which the city council accounted for its changed policy on public space, this space is described as a 'public domain that in both a functional and an architectural sense expresses the identity of the city and its component parts'.[18] A budgeting adjustment underlined this change in policy: until the mid-1980s the construction of public spaces in Rotterdam was mainly approached 'democratically': when these spaces were constructed, the same budgetary principles applied to the construction of all these spaces. In the mid-1980s this policy changed: more money was made available for constructing public spaces with particular (representative) functions.[19]

For a while, it looked as if this vision of public open space, which was dominated by a distinguishing iconic identity and which also tried to do justice to the rise of the consumer society, would be put into practice in the redesign of Schouwburgplein. In 1987 the then new director of urban development (Stadsontwikkelinkg) Riek Bakker invited American architect Benjamin Thompson to develop a new plan. In his plan, the square would be given a diagonal glass roof to create an arcade accommodating market stalls, similar to those in an American shopping mall. The square itself would be fitted out with Las Vegas-like iconic ornaments: whimsically shaped windmills as high as the De Doelen concert hall, a pair of gigantic clogs and delft tiles. Like its many predecessors, this plan perished in the city council.[20]

Another development that became more prominent from the 1980s onwards and that influenced ideas about urban public spaces was that of privatization and parochialization. Privatization means that some activities that traditionally took place in public spaces now take place in semi-public spaces: department stores and shopping centres might indeed fulfil public functions but they are private property; the owner ultimately decides what is and what is not permitted and who may and may not enter these spaces. Parochialization means that a particular space is dominated by a particular group; even in the case of a public space that is accessible to everyone, a specific square, park or nightlife street can be dominated by a particular group of city dwellers, giving other groups the feeling that they are visitors there.[21] These sorts of parochial spaces, which are meaningful to members of specific urban groups, are gradually becoming more important in the daily lives of city dwellers than the encounters that take place in the public domain, a development that was already touched upon in the first three chapters of this book.

This development had implications for the way the public domain was to be understood, the employees at the planning and urban renewal department (Dienst Ruimtelijke Ordening en Stadsvernieuwing) explained in *Buitenruimte*. The public domain was no longer an unambiguous space where all Rotterdammers must be able to recognize themselves and be able to meet each other; instead, the urban public space consisted of a network of partly overlapping parochial spaces. In Rotterdam the city council would thus like to

> (...) create a meticulously described system of open spaces that can absorb the current reality. Within this network, specific public domains can develop, consisting of collective and public spaces that can be used and appropriated by different urban communities at different times. The inner-city outdoor space is no longer the place where the general interest is self-evident. It is the threshold zone where the sometimes sharply contrasting extremes of urban reality can meet; where differences are celebrated.[22]

On the other hand, it was also feared that the urban population would become fragmented. According to the city council in its 1998 'Actieplan Attractieve Stad' (literally, 'Action plan for an attractive city'), the public space as a whole must also function as 'the cement of the city'. The aim was to develop a public domain that 'holds everything together, creates calm and recognition, that belongs to everyone and is used by everyone'.[23]

The developments described above resulted in a vision of the public domain that contained a certain tension: on the one hand, there was the idea that the inner-city public spaces must become the city's showpiece; they must endow the city with an attractive identity and were thus dominated, to a certain extent, by 'city marketing'. On the other hand, the public spaces must also be interesting spaces for the city dwellers themselves, where they could recognize themselves and meet. Policymakers were conscious of the fact that different groups appropriated and sometimes dominated different places in the city. At the same time, the public space as a whole was to function as 'the cement of the city'. It is against this background that Adriaan Geuze's plans for Schouwburgplein were approved.

Adriaan Geuze's Schouwburgplein (1997)

The theme of the 1992 Christmas issue of *Grafisch Nederland* was the urban public sphere. One of the writers was the young architect Adriaan Geuze. Together with Herman Moscoviter and Paul van Beek, he contributed an article that, in hindsight, could be read as a manifesto for his design for Schouwburgplein. This manifesto began by stating that the traditional urban public space had lost its most important functions: encounters and exchanges mainly took place in media networks and no longer in physical spaces. The city dweller of the 1990s greatly valued his privacy but was also very mobile, so that he was no longer found every day in archetypal urban public spaces such as the city centre square. He was more like a 'nomad', with the whole world at his disposal. He was not found sauntering on the boulevard but on the spaghetti junctions on the motorways; not shopping in the heart of the city but enjoying his holidays in sunny or snowy destinations opened up by tour operators and cheap flights: 'Traditional public life on the streets, boulevards and squares has largely been elbowed out by the world behind the front door, television, motorway culture and package holidays.'[24]

According to the authors, this shift required a new vision of the public domain. They sought inspiration in neither the type of public domain that developed on the metropolitan boulevards at the end of the nineteenth century, nor in the concepts of the modernist avant-gardes. The nineteenth-century ideal was too limited for the authors because this form of public space was dominated by the rising bourgeoisie. It was their norms that applied there and in the course of time they developed into new protocols; anything that deviated from these protocols was forbidden: 'Even the slightest chaos quickly tended to smack of an attack on the achievements of the well-off.'[25] In other words, the boulevard and its successors such as the high street are actually not public domains at all, but rather the parochial domains of the bourgeoisie. The authors also rejected the public space of the modernist avant-gardes because they found the separation of functions too rigid.

A new notion of the public domain must be based on the principle of the 'emancipated citizen': he no longer lets himself be bossed around but decides for himself what is best for him. He is no longer part of a mass culture that he shares with all his fellow urban citizens but is part of a niche culture with its own standards, values and habits. Coupled with increasing mobility, this means that city dwellers 'annex' spaces for their own use but these spaces are no longer necessarily located in the city centre. The authors give the example of the Delta works dykes: they were constructed as dams but are now very popular among Rotterdammers for recreational purposes. Such developments mean that designers of public spaces should no longer strive to develop a public domain with a predetermined programme that will be used simultaneously by all city dwellers:

> It [is] time to admit that large sections of public space are not always equally public and it is also time to consider the consequences this has for their design. Subcultures have appropriated specific places to such an extent that it can be stated that the universal and everyday public space is in the minority. The modern city is a rainforest of subcultures that constantly write and adapt their own scripts.[26]

Geuze elaborated on this concept in a later article: architects and planners should provide the public with the opportunity to 'colonize' the public space. Geuze found the public spaces of the time too prescriptive: they reflected the bureaucratic urban planning approach in which all sorts of rules determined what could and could not take place there. In this article, he also discussed the way in which he had converted these principles into a design for Schouwburgplein. The huge empty surface and the unusual materials were intended to 'confuse' the user. The way the square was fitted out and the mood it could create were flexible: the hydraulic cranes could be placed in different positions; the fountains, intended to encourage children to play, would spout with a force that depended on the weather; and the material itself would be affected by the passing of time. Events would leave their traces in the metal floor,[27] and in a lecture Geuze also expressed his hope that the wooden floors would invite visitors to carve in their declarations of love.[28]

Schouwburgplein was thus intended to become a stage, and in this, Geuze distanced himself from the earlier plans of other architects and policymakers who, in his eyes, tried to breathe new life into the Italian idea of a piazza, surrounding the square with beautiful façades. Geuze, by contrast, was inspired by the different groups that appropriated the square at different times of the day: in the evenings, Surinamese boys playing football, at midday local office workers eating lunch, and shoppers during the rest of the day.[29] Schouwburgplein was thus also a 'scenario of emptiness' that would challenge visitors to become engaged; it was to be a place they could use according to their own judgement.[30] Geuze's design seemed to combine two ideals for the public domain: on the one hand, the ideal of 'interactivity', which is related to Constant's ideal and allows the city dweller himself to shape a public space that has largely been developed as 'emptiness'; on the other hand, this space must also provide the possibility for a certain 'continuism' as described by René Boomkens;[31] the square must acquire character with the passing of time through all sorts of events and activities leaving their traces there.

Several architecture critics embraced Adriaan Geuze's ideas. In *Archis*, for example, Arthur Wortmann described developments in urban culture in a similar way: he also referred to the 'collectivization' of the city – his term for parochialization. Traditional public spaces where all sorts of urban functions and different groups met as they used to at the traditional agora or the Roman forum no longer existed. Wortmann made clear that cities did not need 'nostalgic spaces', yet they did need places for interaction and confrontation and planners should therefore elicit 'hitches' and 'disruptive moments'. Planners must take advantage of parochialization but also attempt to confront different subcultures with each other. In his critique, prompted by the 1993 design, Wortmann expressed the hope that this would also happen at Schouwburgplein. After all, the square opened up different parochial domains: that of the classical music lovers and people attending conferences at the De Doelen concert hall, that of visitors to the mega cinema that was planned for the square and those of people shopping or going out. The square could therefore be colonized by different groups of users simultaneously, and precisely herein lay its strength.[32]

When Schouwburgplein was inaugurated in 1997, opinion was divided, as we saw earlier. While some people praised the innovative design, others distanced themselves from it. Just as with the first design in 1966, people found it an unattractive square: popular as it might be in international architecture magazines, Rotterdammers would rather walk around it than across it. *NRC* newspaper critic Bernard Hulsman was extremely critical: the unusual materials made it impossible to 'colonize' the square, he wrote. But a week later letters to the editor claimed the opposite: the square was being exploited to the full: by football players, frisbee players and skaters.[33]

The issue at stake here is not whether the new Schouwburgplein design was a success or not. Instead, it is much more interesting to consider how the debate about the public domain has shifted over recent decades. The importance that was attached to the public domain as a platform where political publics could gather has declined, and the debate has become increasingly dominated by city marketing and by how various subcultures use the public domain. These developments fit into broader social developments and have consequences for the way urban publics develop.

The Twenty-First-Century Urban Public Space: towards a Network of Parochial Domains?

The debate about Rotterdam's Schouwburgplein is part of a wider debate about the public domain and the question of how it should function as an urban community interface. Geuze linked his design to a broader development: over the last few decades, cities have gradually acquired a different spatial character. This view closely resembles what Arnold Reijndorp has described in various books as 'network urbanism': the contrast between centre and periphery has become less clear. All sorts of 'centre functions' such as cinemas, shopping centres and offices can now be found in the former periphery.[34] This has contributed to the development of a fragmented urban landscape that is no longer dominated by a single clear centre. The contemporary city dweller - who has also become increasingly mobile – uses all these places in his own way: he 'cuts and pastes' together his own city according to his own needs. In the process, he prefers to look for like-minded people and avoids others as much as possible. This process was discussed in depth in chapter 2; the repercussions for the public domain are discussed below.

Several critics think the public domain is being eroded by these developments: to an increasing extent, urban spaces are spatially fragmented and largely consist of interchangeable 'non-places' as a result of growing commercialization.[35] Colourful local cafés hardly exist any more; the city dweller is at the mercy of Starbucks, which has the same menu, the same interior and the same music all over the world. They lack any reference to a local identity, and metaphors to describe the twenty-first-century city tend to have their origins in the shopping mall and the airport. City dwellers withdraw as much as possible into homogeneous zones – the often-cited gated communities in the United States are the critics' worst nightmare. This development is all the worse because the new urban spaces are completely dominated by consumption; they are not places for meeting or confrontation – in fact, everything about the architecture is aimed at ensuring consumption proceeds as efficiently and friction-free as possible. Moreover, these spaces are not public spaces either: the owners can decide who is allowed access to these consumption zones. In a seminal volume Michael Sorkin argued that the city has become a sort of Disneyland as a result:[36] long live fun, smiling is mandatory, and whoever cannot purchase a ticket is not allowed in. In his book *The Capsular Civilization*, Belgian philosopher Lieven De Cauter is strongly critical of this development. Under the influence of a neoliberal economic wind, a new kind of city is developing that is very fragmented and that mainly consists of 'capsules':

> Capsular architecture is architecture that functions like a space capsule, creating an artificial ambiance, minimizing communication with the outside world and creating its own hermetically sealed environment.[37]

De Cauter sees the rise of capsular architecture as the ultimate consequence of the libertarian urban ideal; it eventually leads to an 'evacuation of the urban space'. The new city is a party city with a vibrant outdoor-café culture, where everyone permanently lives the life of a tourist. This development also has a darker side. Besides 'Disneyfication' (the process in which all sorts of urban areas, with the aid of smartly designed themes, are becoming increasingly dominated by consumption) there is also a process of 'Bronxification': not all parts of a city are themed; large parts are also left to fate - the authorities retreat, there is hardly any investment, gangs and criminals take control. This contrast also leads to an increasing militarization of urban life: the border between Disneyland and the Bronx is characterized by physical barriers, walls and all sorts of control regimes that are intended to keep undesirable groups out. De Cauter sees the city as an interface that has a powerful filtering effect: anything that does not fit in with the ideal urbanism of Mediterranean cafés is excluded from reality - by force if necessary. A public domain no longer exists; the city is either arranged according to the ideal image of the shopping middle class or utterly neglected.

De Cauter's Mayday message must be taken seriously: there are certainly developments that point towards his capsular society. The frightening force of his book, which can be read as a dystopian manifesto, results from the magnification of a number of social developments. This is also its weakness: there is little room for nuance or for seeking new types of public domains that are developing in the twenty-first-century city. Surely it is precisely this changed urban typology that calls for new ways to in turn create new urban publics?

A more optimistic view is provided by Maarten Hajer and Arnold Reijndorp in their book *In Search of New Public Domain*. They also present a picture of the city that has become dominated by a consumer middle-class society and that consists of spatial archipelagos of different urban groups or 'tribes':[38]

Society has become an archipelago of enclaves with people from different backgrounds developing increasingly effective spatial strategies in order to meet the people they want to meet and to avoid the people they want to avoid. (. . .) [the balance is tipping in favour of] a city of individuals that consists as much as

possible of a combination of carefully chosen, safe, socially homogeneous places that can be easily, safely and comfortably reached
by car.[39]

However, these writers prefer to look forwards instead of
backwards. Hajer and Reijndorp argue that it makes little sense to
compare our urban society with the idealized urban public spaces
of Vienna or Paris two centuries ago. The question is not how to
prevent this development but rather how to use the opportunities
presented by this new landscape. First of all, Hajer and Reijndorp
argue that in all critiques, the modern city dweller is far too easily
dismissed as a conflict-evading 'cocooned human being'. Reality is
more complex: while most city dwellers do indeed show a
preference for surroundings where they feel at home and where
they are surrounded by like-minded people, this preference is not
without its ambiguities. People who work in industrial zones next
to the motorway certainly find it easy to work there because they
can reach these zones more quickly by car than the inner city, but
they also miss the urban feeling of the inner city. The suburbs are
popular because residents find them pleasant and a good place for
children to grow up but again, this does not mean they no longer
yearn for a more urban life.[40] Despite their selective spatial use,
city dwellers are certainly interested in acquiring new experiences.

This is precisely where the core of the public domain lies,
according to Hajer and Reijndorp. They define the public domain as
'places where people acquire new experiences, where a change of
perspective is possible.'[41] This is best done – and here they make an
interesting mental leap – by visiting the parochial domain of a
different group. The public domain is not a neutral platform where
all city dwellers despite their differences still come together, as in
Arendt's vision. It is exactly the opposite: different urban groups
have their own network of parochial domains. An experience of the
public domain occurs when we visit the domain of another group:

> Perhaps it is not parochialization that hinders the creation of a
> public domain but in fact an over-expectation of the public space
> as a neutral meeting place for all social groups.[42]

The task for designers is thus not to design a space that is attractive
for every city dweller but to ensure that the different parochial
domains partly overlap or in some way become involved with each
other, for example, because they are located near each other so that
different groups meet each other in passing.

This is an interesting thought that partly fits in with the
philosophy behind Adriaan Geuze's Schouwburgplein. The
parentheses that hold society together are no longer placed around
the public space but around a long series of parochial domains. It is
a concept of the public domain that also fits in with the theories of

thinkers such as Berman, Boomkens and Benjamin, who already saw the various urban spheres as porous and overlapping. A public domain is not so much a fixed place but rather an experience that can be given shape at different moments.

One criticism is that this approach to the public domain is somewhat free of commitment: does this notion of the urban public space go any further than attending a cultural festival or a quick visit to an exotic part of a city for lunch? In other words, is there, as in Arendt's vision, also a necessity for confrontation, for finding a way of living with the other? On the other hand, in a society that highly values individual freedom it is perhaps simply not possible to expect more of the modern city dweller. The republican ideal may be too demanding, while the libertarian ideal is too free of commitment. The possibility of arranging one's life according to one's own judgement can also be seen as freedom. This freedom can get out of hand if city dwellers no longer have any shared frameworks, as in De Cauter's doom scenario. Hajer and Reijndorp prefer to reason the other way around: as long as parochial domains continue to overlap and city dwellers are prepared to occasionally leave their own comfort zones, it will still be possible to refer to the city as a community of strangers. It might be a minimal community but also one whose members allow each other a certain freedom to live their lives as they see fit.

How then does the emergence of digital media exploit these developments? Do they reinforce the increasing privatization and parochialization of the public domain? Or do they in fact provide citizens with the possibility of withdrawing from these developments? Or, continuing Hajer and Reijndorp's line of argument, do they make it possible to create new cross links between a city's different parochial domains within a development of collectivization? These questions will be addressed in the last chapter using a number of test cases.

Digital Media and the Public Domain

Plastic Container of Liquid Soap

Disposed at

457 Madison Ave New York, NY 10022

Traveled

18.3 Miles

Category

Plastic

Leonia
Ridgefield Park
Fort Lee
Little Ferry
Palisades Park
Ridgefield
Rutherford
East Rutherford
Edgewater
North Bergen
North Arlington
Secaucus
Union City
New York
Hoboken
Green Point

Sep 5th, 2009, 07:22 AM
Sep 5th, 2009, 09:02 AM

Deployment
Sep 4th, 2009, 2:00 PM
457 Madison Ave
New York, NY 10022

Sep 5th, 2009, 05:19 AM
Sep 8th, 2009, 07:26 AM
Sep 8th, 2009, 04:13 AM
Sep 5th, 2009, 05:02 AM
Sep 5th, 2009, 04:34 AM
Sep 5th, 2009, 04:21 AM

En Route
Plastic Container
of Liquid Soap
Last seen from:
786-798 Bellevue Turnpike
Kearny, NJ 07032

senseable city lab

From the 'executive apartment' on the sixty-second floor of the First World Towers complex you usually have a splendid view of New Songdo, the brand new city that is being built from scratch on a reclaimed sandbank in the Yellow Sea just off the coast of South Korea. But unfortunately, apologizes Jonathan Thorpe, vice-president of project developer Gale International, an easterly wind is blowing a storm front from Japan across the Korean peninsula today. The new city's special design remains blanketed by thick clouds.

Thorpe and his colleague Scott Summers compensate for the lack of view with an enthusiastic power-point presentation that they show on a large television screen in the living room. The master plan for their new city is ambitious, and is intended to combine the best of all worlds: a Venetian canal, a park modelled after New York's Central Park, a golf course designed by top golf player Jack Nicklaus, and a private school whose curriculum is based on Chadwick School's, one of Los Angeles' most famous schools and loved by Hollywood stars.

But Songdo is primarily known as one of the world's first smart cities to be constructed on a large scale. The latest technologies will soon be closely interwoven with everyday life, sometimes without people even noticing it. A central computer system collects all sorts of data from the city, from the energy that buildings use to the number of occupied parking spaces; from traffic conditions on the roads to the current location of all buses and metros; it will even be possible to record who throws how much rubbish away and when – in order to access rubbish containers you must identify yourself with a smart card. The hope for the smart city is that when all these data are combined and analyzed, life in the city can be optimized: buildings will be more economical and life more efficient, more agreeable and safer. The 'magic of software' that Bill Gates spoke of is intended to be given concrete form here, in a city that is seen by many as a model for the future. Will Archigram's dream be realized here: a city that will fully meet human needs automatically?

This question has sparked worldwide debate. And, although most smart-city technologies have not been implemented yet, Songdo, as an icon for the smart city, plays a significant role in the debate. Is this the city of the future? And if it is, do we want to live in such a city? Its supporters point out that the new technologies will lead to greater ease, comfort and economic growth, turning Songdo into a globally competitive and attractive place for companies to establish themselves. As such, it is a city that comes close to the libertarian urban ideal: the city is primarily a marketplace, a platform for economic growth, and it is well organized; it must be a pleasant place to live for the internationally oriented creative class. But it is this libertarian principle that a global chorus of critics most object to. They fear that technology will turn Songdo into a closed city where digital infrastructure is managed by commercial companies and citizens are mainly consumers who can make use of services if they pay. This would be the nail in the coffin for the republican ideal of a society of citizens who can act of their own accord.

It is too early to say who is right. Many of the smart-city technologies are potential rather than actual technologies. For the moment we will have to make do with the marketing films that have been placed on the Internet by Cisco and ULife Solutions, the companies that are developing the infrastructure and services for Songdo. Their main themes are convenience and safety: soon you will no longer have to go to the relevant authority to renew your driver's licence – you can do this online via a special system; children will be given special wristbands equipped with a chip so that parents receive a message when their child has arrived at school safely; images recorded by security cameras – ubiquitous on Songdo's streets – will be monitored using computer algorithms so that if something untoward happens, the hospital or police will automatically receive an emergency signal. 'Now, you can have a 100 per cent safe life', promises one of the promotion film clips. Sustainability and efficiency are other important spearheads: closely monitoring energy use should produce considerable savings. In the smart city, the road or the pavement will 'know' if someone is coming and adjust the streetlighting accordingly, and office buildings themselves will be able to switch off all the computers and lights when the last person leaves the building.

Cisco wishes to make the data generated by the smart city sensors available to other companies so they can also develop new services. For example, an app that enables parking spaces to communicate with a car's navigation system: the TomTom would then guide you to an available parking space. Songdo is seen as a model city, a pilot where these sorts of technologies can be developed and tested. And if they work, the aim is to export them globally, with or without an accompanying master plan. China has already expressed interest in ordering two Songdos, including the school and Central Park.

Greg Lindsay, author of *Aerotropolis*, says it is remarkable that in the smart city scenario it is the technology companies that share in the responsibility for shaping the city of the future: 'They are entering the fields of architecture and planning but these are disciplines they know very little about.' And it is remarkable that so much confidence has been placed in technology to solve urban problems: 'Planners once thought that society was makeable,' says Lindsay. They thought it was possible to capture all sorts of social processes in complex calculations and then convert these into an overall master plan. The Paris *banlieue* and the Amsterdam Bijlmer housing estate are the result. Just as we are abandoning this approach, technology companies are making their entrance, along with their algorithms that will supposedly make life more intelligent, more convenient and more efficient.[1]

This is the wrong starting point, says urban media researcher and designer Adam Greenfield. The modernist approach is geared towards managers who want to make urban processes more efficient, or towards institutions like the state that want to control what happens:

> It's an aesthetic with a distaste for the messiness and complexity of metropolitan life, and, equally, with clear political implications: the Corbusian city is one consecrated to administration, where the potential for any organic development is subordinated to the needs of managers.[2]

Greenfield argues that this vision does not do justice to the city and its inhabitants. The ideal should not be efficient management but providing space to the 'spontaneous order from below': the unpredictable, at times chaotic, everyday behaviours that Jane Jacobs and others have described as the very essence of urban life.

Richard Sennett, too, is critical of the smart city ideal. In an opinion article tellingly entitled 'No One Likes a City That's Too Smart', which appeared in *The Guardian* newspaper at the end of 2012, he wrote that of course it is pleasant if everything in a city is well organized, but the way this is happening in Songdo is too premeditated, too top down: citizens are primarily seen as consumers and have little to say about the way life is organized there. He has this to say about Masdar, a smart city under construction in the United Arab Emirates:

> Urbanites become consumers of choices laid out for them by prior calculations of where to shop, or to get a doctor, most efficiently. There's no stimulation through trial and error; people learn their city passively. 'User-friendly' in Masdar means choosing menu options rather than creating the menu.[3]

Sennett's criticism is based on his vision of the public domain, which should be shaped through citizens acting of their own accord and determining the rules for society together. People who are different should be able to run into each other and learn to empathize with each other without necessarily becoming part of a clear-cut communitarian community. This is exactly what comes under threat when a city is reduced to a series of convenient services for consumers: 'We want cities that work well enough, but are open to shifts, uncertainties, and mess which are real life', writes Sennett.

Cisco top man Wim Elfrink understands some of the criticism. But, he argues, the smart city is not intended to replace the city as we know it. What Cisco has in mind is the development of a number of additional services to make life more pleasant. And this is important, he thinks: 'You can see that cities worldwide are increasingly competing with each other, for example to attract highly educated workers. The city with the most attractive environment will win this battle.'[4] Cisco launches its new technologies on the market using the label 'Smart and Connected Communities'. But Cisco's definition of 'community' mainly highlights the economic perspective: 'Thanks to our data platform, everyone can develop new services,' replies a Cisco employee when asked how the new technology can be of use to citizens. 'This means: new jobs, new business models, economic growth and thus also improved social relations.'[5]

In Songdo, Cisco's vision is gradually taking shape: broad boulevards are lined with skyscrapers, and the small street-level shops, which preferably have English or French names like Tous les Jours (an 'authentic French bakery') and the Zoo Coffee Shop, also include a take-away pizzeria, a supermarket and of course a Korean barbecue restaurant. It certainly is not a capsular society like the one described by Lieven De Cauter. Public spaces are open to everyone and wandering through Songdo is a pleasant experience. The city has been designed for pedestrians and many small parks with playgrounds have been laid out between all residential tower blocks. The city is also popular with Korean pop stars: its modernist decor regularly features in their video clips, and the clip for the worldwide YouTube hit Gangnam Style was partly filmed in Songdo.

But Songdo does not have the vibrant street life of Seoul's Gangnam nightlife district. Despite all the cosmopolitan references and sophisticated urban architecture, the city actually feels rather suburban. 'We like to compare ourselves to New York', says Jonathan Thorpe, 'but perhaps this is more like Orange County' (the endless series of suburbs south of Los Angeles). Do not misunderstand him - this is not necessarily a negative comparison: a neat and tidy 'master-planned community' has its own advantages, even if it is sometimes rather dull.

Thorpe hopes that the TelePresence (a Cisco invention that is to be installed in every flat) will compensate for Songdo's suburban character. This large television screen with an inbuilt camera connected to a super-fast Internet connection enables you to watch and send high-quality video images. Residents will be able to use this screen to order all sorts of services: cookery lessons with a famous French chef; English or mathematics tutoring for the children – a market with great potential in Korea: middle-class families spend more than one-third of their income on their children's education; or consulting a doctor, another growth market, in view of the aging population. Residents themselves will also be able to develop new services, says Thorpe: he hopes people might start giving concerts or organizing poetry evenings via the system. This is how the city must come alive, from the comfort of people's living rooms.

The TelePresence resembles the App Store that Apple developed for the mobile phone: a screen environment where consumers can purchase all sorts of services. And, just as with Apple, it will not be an open system: it is true that a variety of parties will be allowed to develop new services, but the final decision as to whether they will be admitted lies with the technology company.

It is this aspect that is targeted by critics of the smart city scenario: what will this platform of services actually look like? Will it actually be a closed environment in which commercial companies offer services to consumers? Or can citizens themselves also play an active role in the development of the platform? Will Songdo acquire the character of a parochial domain in both the physical and the virtual senses? Or can citizens also use platforms such as TelePresence and the data that the city collects in order to organize urban publics in a new way? And will this also be possible without their first having to ask permission from the controlling party, whether this is the state or a commercial party? Can citizens use the technology to organize themselves around a specific issue such as environmental pollution? Might they even be allowed to commonly manage certain matters? In that case, instead of a company supplying a commercial service, city dwellers would develop a communal service together, for instance the sharing of a car or the development of a vegetable garden. Might new ways develop in which citizens can relate to each other through technology? Who has what agency in this scenario? Will the smart cities of the future actually be modelled on a libertarian ideal of individual freedom? Is the design of smart cities based on the management ideal, in which efficiency and control are central? Or will alternatives also develop?

To answer these questions, we must leave Songdo and again consider a number of test cases. These provide different scenarios for the way the public domain might develop in the twenty-first-century media city. First, we will look at an influential blogpost in which urbanist Dan Hill minutely exposes the dilemmas concerning the design of the street in the future.

Test case 4 'The Street as Platform' and 'The City as a Service'

On 11 February 2008, Australian urban media expert Dan Hill posted a new article on his City of Sound weblog entitled 'The Street as Platform'. At the request of an NGO, he ventured to describe the street of the future. This turned out to be a difficult task because many new technologies that interfere with life on the street are largely invisible:

> We can't see how the street is immersed in a twitching, pulsing cloud of data. This over and above the well-established electro- magnetic radiation, crackles of static, radio waves conveying radio and television broadcasts in digital and analogue forms, police voice traffic. This is a new kind of data, collective and individual, aggregated and discrete, open and closed, constantly logging impossibly detailed patterns of behaviour. The behaviour of the street.[6]

Hill argued that the street increasingly functions as an 'experience marker', to use the terminology in this book. Many activities that we undertake leave a trail of data and these are invisibly communicated via different networks and stored in a variety of databases. Together, all these data form a new platform for the development of all sorts of services.

But Hill wondered where all these data came from, and what sorts of services they lead to. A long list follows: joggers have a device in their shoes that measures their speed and distance; their iPods then adjust the music selection to their pace. A BMW that has stopped at the traffic lights sends details about the engine's performance to the dealer's maintenance department. The street itself has sensors that measure traffic volumes, information that is used to automatically adjust traffic lights. Passers-by ring via Skype or their mobile network and thus indicate their location to their providers. The Wi-Fi network in a café keeps track of how much data are sent and which websites are visited. A customer scans his customer-loyalty smart card and his order is added to his 'record' in the customer database. An electricity meter in one of the houses registers the inhabitants' use of electricity and compares it with that of the neighbours. A man uses his smartphone to alert the council, via a special information service, of a pothole in the road. A bus shelter recognizes the waiting passengers' mobile phones and adjusts the advertisements to match their profiles. Another digital billboard shows the number of burglaries that have taken place in the neighbourhood recently – a police awareness campaign that uses live data from their own databases.

And so it goes on, although not all technologies in Hill's

scenario always work as promised: the street has not been properly indicated on the map database of one of the GPS navigation providers, so drivers get lost; the scanner in one of the street's shops does not work, so a client cannot purchase a pair of shoes.[7] Hill uses all this information to sketch a dizzying picture of various networks in which data are collected, exchanged and aggregated. These data are then used to personalize the advertisements at a bus shelter, regulate traffic, or adjust the music on joggers' iPods.

The development of the street as a platform is vaguely reminiscent of the construction of Haussmann's boulevards. As with the boulevards, motives such as improving safety and logistical efficiency play a role in the construction of new infrastructure – consider the example of New Songdo. Once this infrastructure is in place, all sorts of new services can develop such as pavement cafés and department stores. The data collection that Hill gathers under 'The Street as Platform' similarly makes new services possible.

But at the same time, something else also happened in nineteenth-century Paris: a new type of urban public developed on the boulevards. The city dwellers who used the new infrastructure and related services formed a new public for and with each other. Will the rise of the 'street as a platform' again lead to the development of new types of urban publics?

Hill sketches two contrasting scenarios that might lead to new publics in different ways: 'Locked Down Street' and 'Open Source Street'. In the Locked Down Street scenario, commercial parties organize the recording and analysis of data in closed systems and use them in programmes aimed at marketing and the provision of specific, often personalized services. In this scenario, users can exercise little influence. This process could lead to what Stephen Graham calls 'software-sorted geographies': computer software compiles customer profiles and uses them to make places in a city attractive for different publics. This could eventually lead to considerable social fragmentation and the capsulization of society.

In contrast, in the Open Source Street scenario a data platform with its details about urban life is made accessible. Citizens, institutions and commercial parties can then add data to the system and use the data in the system to access information or develop services. Hill considers the contrast between Locked Down Street and Open Source Street a caricature, and aspects of both examples will probably be realized simultaneously. They are mainly useful for outlining the possible extremes of a number of developments. These extremes also provide a good springboard to study the way the public domain in the city does or does not come to life.

We will therefore take a closer look at the Locked Down Street scenario. This scenario is mainly characterized by a service-oriented approach: companies develop all sorts of often closed, or in any case controlled, platforms where they can offer services to consumers –

think of the various examples in New Songdo. A completely new branch of business has developed that concerns itself with the collection of data and the development of services: 'reality mining'. Some 'evangelists' claim that 'reality mining' could even result in a utopian future in which the world around us will adapt to meet our individual needs before we have even become aware of those needs ourselves. Alex Pentland, a researcher at MIT Media Lab and also one of the initiators of the CitySense app referred to in chapter 3 writes,

> For individuals, the attraction is the possibility of a world where everything is arranged for your convenience – your health checkup is magically scheduled just as you begin to get sick, the bus comes just as you get to the bus stop, and there is never a line of waiting people at city hall.[8]

Some governments also embrace this approach. For example, the South Korean government has set up a major programme called 'u-City' aimed at stimulating national businesses to develop new urban ICT services. The letter 'u' is a reference to the term 'ubiquitous computing', a design approach for computer systems in which the computer literally disappears from the picture. The ideal consists of a system that is present in the background and does its work unnoticed by the user. Such a computer system could then operate 'seamlessly': it would gather data about and silently intervene in all sorts of everyday social and economic processes. This is why the u-City programme's central slogan is based on 'the city as a service': in this design approach the city is conceptualized as a collection of 'infrastructural services' such as transport, safety, housing or finding entertainment. In u-Cities such as New Songdo, it is promised, these services will be managed more efficiently and they will be adjusted to meet individual needs.

This 'city as a service' approach fits in with a wider shift in the way designers, governments and project developers think about urban infrastructure. More than a century ago, urban infrastructure was mainly seen as common property, as networks to which all citizens should be connected as equals. From the 1950s onwards this approach has given way to the idea that infrastructure is primarily a tailored service that can be supplied to individual consumers. This development has been described well in *Splintering Urbanism* by British geographers Stephen Graham and Simon Marvin. They show how most of our modern urban infrastructure (electricity cables, water pipes, sewerage and railways) originated in the second half of the nineteenth century. This was also the time when nation states developed in Europe and positivism reached its peak in the sciences. The construction of infrastructure was closely connected with these developments. Railways were constructed to unite the entire territory of a nation state by connecting all its regions to the same system. Boulevards, electricity networks and sewerage were similarly intended to weld together cities such as Paris into a united whole. The new infrastructure integrated the inhabitants of a region into a greater whole: according to Graham and Marvin, '[Technological infrastructures] are believed to bind cities, regions and nations into functioning geographical or political wholes'.[9] Here, the positivist idea of progress played a role: 'universal access' became an important goal in the construction of new infrastructure, which was to elevate the lives of all citizens in the new states to a higher plane.

From the 1950s onwards, this ideal gradually faded away. Increasing commercialization, individualization and growing criticism of the universal ambitions of modernist planners played a role in this development. Gradually, the city came to be seen as a complex system that could not be subjected to any specific order: it was what Graham and Marvin call an 'urban soup', consisting of 'complex patchworks of growth and decline, concentration and deconcentration, poverty and extreme wealth'.[10] Planners, engineers and policymakers aimed less and less at integrating this fragmented landscape into a universal whole. Instead, new technologies were developed and exploited to open up this landscape to a variety of customers. The privatization of a great deal of urban infrastructure was part of this development. The expectation was that the market would be better equipped to meet consumers' requirements than the state.

Digital media are the next step in this development. They create an extra information layer over the chaos that the city is by its very nature. Apps and other services help city dwellers pick out the things that are important to them. The mobile phone is a compass or filter, making habitable the enormous accumulation of diversity that the city is. The aim is no longer to integrate the individual in the larger whole but rather the exact opposite: the starting point is the 'networked individual's' world of experience. How can his needs, which are related to the different roles he plays in various networks, be tailored to the extremely complex supply of people, services, markets and institutions that criss-cross the city?

It is interesting to see how Graham and Marvin constantly link these different design approaches to particular notions of urban publics: in the ideal of 'universal access', the users are conceived of as citizens who, on the basis of equality, are connected to systems that hold the city together as a whole; in the case of 'the city as a service', the system 'appeals to' individual consumers who purchase tailored services and pay according to their measured use.

This shift is not only metaphoric or instinctive. The emergence of 'the city as a service' does actually lead to other mechanisms of inclusion and exclusion and new ways in which urban publics are formed. Graham elaborates on this theme in his article 'Software-Sorted Geographies'.[11] New technologies make it possible to electronically measure individual use of infrastructure and make customers pay accordingly. The price can also be dynamically adjusted; users do not pay a fixed price per unit consumed but an amount that is determined by circumstances. On toll roads, for example, the amount charged can be adjusted according to traffic volumes: the busier it becomes, the higher the charge; this higher charge will lead to fewer people using the road, thus ensuring the uninterrupted flow of traffic.

Graham sees similar systems appearing in other places. Amsterdam's Schiphol airport has systems that provide passengers who pay for them with faster access to the departures hall: an iris scanner confirms their identity and permits or prohibits access to the exclusive lounge and the departures hall. Another example: telecommunications companies and banks keep up-to-date profiles of their customers. When 'good' customers ring a call centre, they are given priority and do not have to wait so long in the queue; they often get better offers as well.[12]

These examples have one thing in common: software systems are deployed to distinguish between different users. Graham speaks of 'a politics of differential speed'. Users who are trusted by the system (because they have disclosed their credit card details and/or iris profile) and who are tagged as 'good' users are given access to the fast channel. Others, who are unable or unwilling to pay extra, must wait in the queue or the traffic jam.

The data collected from 'the street as platform' can also be used to literally admit or exclude 'undesirables'. Graham calls this a dream of 'securitized urban omniscience': the idea that digital technologies can make urban spaces safer and more pleasant, thus excluding undesirable behaviour, ranging from terrorists to loitering juveniles. Based on this design approach, digital media are deployed to make it easier to control urban spaces and filter out possibly unwelcome elements. Software is used to analyze pictures from security cameras at, for example, shopping centres or city squares: if the filmed pattern of movements deviates from what the software recognizes as 'normal behaviour', a security guard or the police are alerted. In this context, a concept of 'normal' or 'good' behaviour is converted into a software algorithm that analyzes the public. This might mean that types of people who are 'suspect' according to a specific norm are denied access. Graham fears that similar algorithms will be deployed to exclude 'failed consumers' (loitering juveniles, minorities, the homeless) from specific parts of the city:

> [T]here are grave dangers that algorithmically controlled CCTV systems might work to deepen already establish[ed] ecologies of normalization, and demonization, within neoliberal urban

landscapes of power. Exaggerating logics of exclusion against 'failed consumers', the young, refugees/asylum seekers, or other demonized minorities, within the increasingly polarized landscapes of contemporary cities, these very logics could, conceivably, be embedded in biases within the very code that makes facial recognition CCTV systems work.[13]

The above examples show how certain protocols of what is considered 'normal behaviour' are laid down in software algorithms. Furthermore, the way cultural protocols are laid down in software codes partly determine how urban life is shaped. The geographers Nigel Thrift and Shaun French argue that:

> These orderings – written down as software – are becoming one of the chief ways of animating space. . . . Software challenges us to understand new forms of technological politics and new practices of political invention, legibility and intervention that we are only just beginning to comprehend as political at all: politics of standards, classifications, metrics, and readings.[14]

Graham refers to this development as 'software-sorting geographies'. Whereas Haussmann's boulevards unintentionally created a mixed urban public because city dwellers with diverse backgrounds came together there, the opposite now threatens: in Graham's scenario, the combination of a neoliberal service economy, governments' emphasis on 'safety paradigms' and the use of complex software can lead to city dwellers being spatially sorted so that they are no longer confronted with each other. This development could reinforce the development of the capsulization of society described by Lieven De Cauter.

What are we to make of this theory? Must we indeed fear 'software sorting', and if so, what are the implications for the public domain? Graham and Marvin's studies are particularly interesting if they are read as a dystopian manifesto. They are a warning against the possible effects of digital technology on how the public domain functions if this technology is deployed solely on the basis of the design approach they describe. The Locked Down Street scenario is, however, not an absolutist scenario. Graham himself has indicated that reality is less totalitarian than the myth of complete control associated with this scenario. It is difficult from a practical point of view to link up all sorts of computer systems and databases in order to subject them to an unambiguous software analysis. Thus, instead of a big system that organizes the whole of society according to a neoliberal ideology,

> (. . .) we may find the production of myriads of little stories – a messy infinity of 'Little Brothers' rather than one omniscient 'Big'

Brother. Some of these may be commercial, some personal, maybe some militarized.[15]

The 'street as platform' is thus unlikely to become a completely closed system; there will always be niches and small openings.

However, this does not dispel the concern expressed by Graham and Marvin. One objection is that their approach, despite all its nuances, is primarily an ideological critique of neoliberalism rather than a critique of the design approach itself, with its emphasis on efficiency, personalization and controllability. In their view, a dynamically priced toll road leads to inequality and a 'sorting' of citizens into different classes and related geographies: the toll road for the rich, the ordinary road with its traffic congestion for the ordinary mortal. Yet this is mainly the result of underlying socio-economic inequalities, which means a higher price is a major problem for some citizens and not for others.

But what if motorists could pay for the toll road not with their credit cards but with 'mobility points' - points that were allocated equally to every citizen to be used at their own discretion? Would such a system be an honest way to share scarce resources such as mobility? This alternative scenario is largely missing in Graham's work: he describes the alarming emergence of a jumble of new systems that can use the data generated by 'the street as platform' in order to geographically 'sort' city dwellers. The examples are convincing and his concern is justified. But is the logic of these systems also unstoppable? Do city dwellers limply comply with the systems described by Graham? Or can citizens also use the digital platform of the street in alternative ways and actually organize themselves as urban publics in new ways? Hill's second scenario, the Open Source Street, explores this possibility. To study this in greater depth, we now travel to Rome, where the MIT SENSEable City Lab tested a new, open platform during the 2007 Notte Bianca.

Test case 5: 'The City as Platform' and the WikiCity

During the evening of the 2007 Notte Bianca, a large cultural festival that is organized in cities around the world at the beginning of summer, large screens appeared in different places in Rome. They had been put there by the SENSEable City Lab, a research institute at the Massachusetts Institute of Technology. During the evening and night, the American researchers projected a dynamic map of Rome onto the screens. Light blue areas on the map showed the busiest parts of the city based on the real-time collection of mobile phone users' location details. Visitors to the event could thus see at a glance which platforms in the city were crowded and adjust their routes accordingly – something that was made even easier by the fact that it was also possible to follow

Rome's city buses on the same map: yellow lines indicated their updated positions. In addition, journalists reported live from the event and their contributions also appeared on the map.[16]

The researchers called the experiment WikiCity Rome. That evening, they wanted to research if it was technologically possible to develop a data platform that would bring together different data from different providers in real time. But the installation was not only intended as a technological 'test case': the researchers mainly wanted to raise a number of political questions. Can such a data platform be developed in an 'open-source' way? That is, can citizens themselves add data to the platform and use them according to their own judgement? The initiators thought this was important: the Internet's power lies in the fact that it is an open system; there is no central, hierarchical authority that determines what users are and are not allowed to do with the technological infrastructure. WikiCity must therefore also become a network of different datasets supplied by different parties. The ideal is 'universal access': just as a city's road system is an open infrastructural system that can be used by all city dwellers, the collection of data sets all over the city should also be common property. Yet it is not certain whether this will also apply to the digital media systems of the future: all sorts of companies are actually trying to set up (partly) closed systems that they themselves control, from Apple's App Store to Cisco's TelePresence.

The enthusiasm for open systems such as WikiCity gradually attracted political attention in the five years following the experiment in Rome. A number of cities have now embraced the idea of 'open data'. Local authorities try to make as many data as possible publicly accessible, partly in the hope that this openness with the public will lead to a new 'public domain'. Consider, for example the way the Rotterdam Open Data initiative describes its aims:

> Rotterdam Open Data is an initiative in which the Rotterdam University of Applied Sciences, companies in Rotterdam and the Rotterdam City Government will together organize access to information from, about and for the city of Rotterdam and make this information clear and comprehensible. This will contribute to the right of Rotterdam's citizens to receive information in order to make decisions, it will reinforce the sense of solidarity that Rotterdam's citizens share with the city and with each other, and it will enable them to better contribute to the city we live in.[17]

It is questionable whether this will happen all by itself. As we saw earlier, an urban public space does not automatically become a public domain; it can also develop into a specific group's parochial domain. Similarly, making data public says nothing about the way these data will be used: an open platform can also lead to the emergence of personalized services that contribute to the 'sorting' of a city into different lifestyles.

The question is therefore: how can a platform such as Wiki-City or an 'open data' initiative actually contribute to the way in which a public domain develops? There are at least three possible answers. Firstly, the data can be used to spatially bring city dwellers together in new ways. Secondly, the data can form a basis around which new publics are formed, as happened around the newspapers in Habermas's coffee houses. Thirdly, such a platform might also make new forms of communal control possible and breathe new life into the idea of a 'common', where a public develops that is collectively responsible for shared property.

The initiators of WikiCity see the most potential in the first answer. They point to the possibility of using data for designing 'discovery' services as described in chapter 3. But the SENSEable City Lab researchers reverse the logic of these systems: the algorithms in the software would not be used to bring people together who already have many things in common, but to tempt users to try something new for a change. Calabrese, Kloeckl and Ratti wondered 'What elements of a city contribute to constructive new discoveries by its citizens?'[18] It is an approach that is reminiscent of Kevin Lynch's work. Lynch was one of the first theorists to focus on how city dwellers themselves attribute meanings to the spaces around them. This could lead to a process of parochialization, with a specific group's symbolic meanings being coupled with specific places. Lynch considered it the designer's task to break through this dynamic:

> (. . .) the function of a good visual environment may not be simply to facilitate routine trips, nor to support meanings and feelings already possessed. Quite as important may be its role as a guide and a stimulus for new exploration. In a complex society, there are many interrelations to be mastered. In a democracy, we deplore isolation, extol individual development, hope for ever-widening communication between groups. If an environment has a strong visible framework and highly characteristic parts, then exploration of new sectors is both easier and more inviting. If strategic links in communication (such as museums or libraries or meeting places) are clearly set forth, then those who might otherwise neglect them may be tempted to enter.[19]

Lynch argued that a well-designed city invites city dwellers to become acquainted with the lives of others. Visual design plays a decisive role here. At the beginning of the twenty-first century this means that not only the physical but also the virtual environment should meet this requirement. An algorithm or interface design will be needed that actually invites city dwellers to explore new parts of a city or alternative points of view. The data collected by WikiCity types of systems should be able to supply the input for such designs.

One of the first prototypes to explore this possibility was the Urban Tapestries project, which was implemented by Proboscis in London between 2002 and 2004. Proboscis described Urban Tapestries as a study of the possible 'public authoring' of the city: its inhabitants' collective rhythms and routines determine how the city is experienced. Urban Tapestries was intended to make these experiences visible, and so Proboscis developed a digital media platform where inhabitants could leave messages that were related to a particular location. People who were interested could then open these messages, for example using the computer or the smartphone.

In an interview with Anne Galloway, the project's initiator Giles Lane said he hoped that different annotations made at the same place would serve as a catalyst, for example, for action groups that wanted to organize themselves around a local issue. If city dwellers annotated their surroundings and coupled issues they considered important with the places where these issues were relevant, then other citizens would be able to use them to advantage. At times it concerned personal memories, at other times it involved political issues. The exchanges via the map could thus set a process in motion that also had consequences outside the Urban Tapestries communication system. For example, it could lead to events, demonstrations or street parties. According to Lane:

> Urban Tapestries is designed to create asynchronous interactions that are essentially anonymous centred on places. (. . .) offering opportunities for people to animate their environment through shared knowledge building. Outcomes of this might well have other manifestations such as demonstrations, community parties, etc.[20]

Urban Tapestries users would thus be able to discover new perspectives and be brought into contact with a variety of people and organizations. This is again reminiscent of Benjamin's ideal in which city dwellers' diverse worlds of experience overlap, or Berman's ideal in which the boulevard serves as a recognition scene, when city dwellers recognize themselves in each other. But twenty-first-century *flâneurs* do not only pick up these experiences while sauntering through shopping arcades; they also pick them up through digital systems. This makes the design of an interface with conspicuous 'landmarks' more important than ever: whereas one automatically sees Kevin Lynch's striking architecture of libraries or urban landmarks when walking through a city, there is a very real risk that all these online doublings of urban experiences will remain invisible.

In a different way, the data collected in a WikiCity system can also lead to the development of new urban publics: by collecting, analyzing and visualizing data, specific social processes such as environmental pollution, vacant housing or social inequality can be clarified. A public can then develop around a particular visualization that deals with the issue at hand. This is a process reminiscent of the role of the newspaper in Habermas's coffee houses: because participants in a debate made their opinions public, the debate could continue in another coffee house; the newspaper facilitated the development of a protocol that made debate possible and a public that participated in this debate. Now it is not the participants in a debate who publish news or developments in the platform 'newspaper' but rather sensors, which collect data from all over the city and publicize these on a data platform.

The Spanish In the Air project is a case in point. In Madrid, data on air pollution are collected and visualized in different ways: there is an online map of the Spanish capital with a projection of the concentration of different gases in the air.[21] The initiators also developed a fountain whose colour and height make the current air quality in the physical public space visible.

The visualizations have several aims. The initiators hope that the visualization of information about air quality will lead to an increased involvement of people in environmental issues; the information collected can be used in the public debate and lead to 'political action'. An app might also be developed that combines data from In the Air with a travel planner: it would provide users with information about how much their journey will contribute to pollution and how they can increase or decrease their carbon footprint by choosing a different means of transport. The designers hope this will not only inform the public about a problem but really get them involved in the issue of air pollution. Another plan for the future is to ask people to help collect details about air pollution: currently, the data still come from a government database, but it is also technically possible to equip participants' mobile phones with a small sensor or install measuring instruments on their balconies and share the information via a WikiCity type of system.

This aspect of the project brings to mind a movement in political philosophy that emphasizes the importance of publics that organize themselves around specific issues.[22] In two essays published by the Architectural League of New York in its *Situated Technologies Pamphlets*, the authors link this vision to the rise of the 'internet of things': all sorts of objects are linked to the Internet and can either collect and distribute data, such as In the Air's air pollution sensors, or they can receive an instruction, such as In the Air's fountain.[23] In their 'MicroPublicPlaces' essay, Hans Frei and Marc Böhlen link this development to the theories of two different thinkers: Hannah Arendt and Bruno Latour. They adopt Arendt's notion of a 'public realm' that brings together people with different backgrounds and interests. As we saw earlier, Arendt's public sphere was a physical environment par excellence, an urban public space based on the ideal of the classical agora. Frei and Böhler argue that in our era, however, we need new 'parentheses' that can bring together the differences, and they look for these in Bruno Latour's *Dingpolitiek*. In Latour's theory, a thing is 'an issue of concern' around which a public can gather. Like Arendt's 'public realm', Latour's public does not consist of a unanimous mass but of people with different opinions and interests who must somehow reach an accommodation with each other.[24] Can a data flow that charts the processes of urban life function as such a 'thing', as an object around which city dwellers with different ideas can organize themselves in order to take action? Can a project such as In the Air create a public domain in a new way? Can data visualizations take over the role of the newspaper in Habermas's coffee house as a central 'conversation piece', as a medium that puts new issues on the agenda, elicits debate and thus links together publics in different locations around the debate?

Benjamin Bratton and Natalie Jeremijenko express this hope in a second essay in the *Situated Technologies Pamphlets* . They see a possible future in which projects such as In the Air lead to new political practices, to a transition from a 'representative democracy' to a 'democracy of representations'.[25] The representations of data flows generated in everyday urban life can play a role in public debates and political processes: 'If objects come alive with information in new ways', Benjamin Bratton argues, 'the possibility of their very public voice seems not only possible but in some ways inevitable.'[26] Visualizations of aggregated data can, for example, also make visible and tangible all sorts of processes that were invisible until now. However, Bratton and Jeremijenko consider the current projects inadequate to achieve this because while they provide insights into important issues, they ultimately do no more than that. How can the public really become involved with important issues through such information flows? How can protocols be developed around data flows that really lead to action? These are open questions to which they do not have ready answers yet.

There is a third way in which platforms such as WikiCity can play a role in creating a public domain. Meticulously monitoring the use of all sorts of urban services also makes a new communal management of those services possible. In the previous test case we saw how digital media make it possible to monitor an individual's use of a motorway and introduce a 'pay-as-you-use' system. Stephen Graham warns that this can lead to what he calls 'software sorting'. But what if that software were not used to market a service – in this case, mobility – and then offer it to those who pay most? What if, instead, this service were managed collectively? To stick with this example, mobility could also be seen as a shared resource, a 'common' that could be communally managed using digital media. The term 'common' refers to the common grazing fields that English farmers were allowed to use for their grazing livestock. In economic theory, the common is often referred to as an interesting but no longer viable form of organization. The often quoted American ecologist Garett Hardin even talks of 'the tragedy of the commons': it was attractive for individual farmers to let as much livestock as possible graze on a common - after all, the increased yield of every extra sheep benefited him personally; but, it was disastrous for the community as a whole if every farmer followed his instinct for profit maximization because the common would be overgrazed and become a victim of its own success. Can the rise of digital technologies change such processes? Imagine that every sheep were equipped with a sensor that registered exactly how much grass it had eaten. At a collective level it would then be possible to set up a profit and loss account that made visible which farmers had used more than their fair share of the common. Can mobility, like a common, be similarly divided between city dwellers, for example, through a system of mobility points that they could use to pay for the use of dynamically priced toll roads?

Can digital media thus lead to the creation of reputation systems and forms of collective management? And can new publics or perhaps moments of overlap be created around this collective management? And what sorts of programming and ownership relations would this require? There are currently a number of ongoing experiments whose outcomes cannot be predicted yet: websites where car owners can share their car with neighbourhood residents; other platforms where city dwellers have the opportunity to lend tools to their neighbours or collect meals from home cooks. Very functional, everyday practices can lead to new practices so that city dwellers with different backgrounds meet. This may vary from short, informal meetings when borrowing a drill to more structured forms of cooperation in the communal management of a neighbourhood garden or cultural centre. These are forms of cooperation that fit in with the small scale of neighbourhood or village societies, where people often know each other because they regularly meet or are involved with each other through schools, clubs or churches. These platforms are often absent in the large-scale, individualized urban environment. Can digital media, with their reputation systems, breathe new life into such mechanisms? Can ownership, which has increasingly become a private matter, again become something communal? Or can it be made accessible to others in new ways?

A good - albeit light-hearted – example of this is the rise of 'couch surfing': an online platform where individual city dwellers offer tourists a sofa bed in their house. And when they themselves travel, they can also make use of the overnight accommodation offered by others. It offers tourists the opportunity to become acquainted with city dwellers and their way of life instead of staying at an anonymous hotel. This creates new moments of overlap, the traditional private sphere temporarily becoming a public domain where city dwellers and visitors can become acquainted. Host and visitor can also evaluate each other on the platform, gradually building up a reputation that others can refer to. Thanks to Couchsurfing.com's programming, the 'global collection of sofa beds' becomes a 'common' that can be controlled by the owners and be made available to use by others, thus potentially creating new moments of overlap.

All three examples – Urban Tapestries, In the Air and the idea of the city as a digitally managed common, are still experimental explorations of how the city as a platform can create a public domain in a new way. It is theoretically possible to design systems that tempt city dwellers to leave their well-trodden paths. It is also theoretically possible that urban publics will start to organize themselves around issues that are made visible by data flows - or, to go one step further, that urban publics will find themselves in communal management structures. But such systems also have their problems: are reputation systems indeed a solution for the 'tragedy of the commons'? Is the transparency that they require in fact desirable? And what about users' privacy? And do we actually want to capture the whole world in mathematical profit and loss accounts? Does this not undermine a form of solidarity that is based on human trust? These are very important questions associated with the development of the 'city as platform', and they need to be answered.

For the time being, it is mainly artists who are experimenting with these sorts of examples and their impact is still limited. Projects such as Urban Tapestries and In the Air are also subject to criticism: they are often short term and reach only a small public; some critics wonder whether there is a public at all for the maps with their annotated memories and emotions. How is it possible to ensure that exchange does indeed take place and that the media layer also becomes visible?[27] These criticisms are relevant, but these art projects show that there are alternatives for the Locked Down Street scenario. However, only providing a data *platform* does not in itself lead to the creation of a public domain in the republican sense; this also requires programming that is relevant for different city dwellers. On the one hand, this provides opportunities for designers to create these programmes. On the other hand, digital media also offer citizens tools to programme public spaces in new ways, as the following test case shows.

Test case 6 Flashmobs: International Pillow Fight Day

In the afternoon of 3 April 2010, dozens of mostly young people gathered at Rotterdam's Schouwburgplein. Some of them were wearing orange capes, others were wearing white T-shirts with a blue cross. A strikingly large number of those present were carrying plastic bags from which they all – in a more or less synchronized movement – pulled out a pillow at about three o'clock. Suddenly the people in the crowd attacked each other in a massive pillow fight. Pillows flew through the air and feathers floated down onto Schouwburgplein. Most of those present became completely absorbed in the fight; a few individuals filmed or photographed the events with their mobile phones. Later, these images appeared on websites such as Hyves, Facebook and YouTube. The event on Schouwburgplein that day was part of a global event: International Pillow Fight Day. Pillow fights took place in dozens of cities all over the world, from Accra in Ghana to Izmir in Turkey to Boston in the United States and Sydney in Australia. Via websites such as Flickr and YouTube all these events were linked together, photographs and film clips from the various cities were placed next to each other.

The pillow fight at Schouwburgplein was a 'flashmob', defined by one dictionary as a 'group of people convened via the Internet, who gather at a specific location more or less unexpectedly and without knowing each other in order to do something frivolous'. According to some cultural critics, although flashmobs are often concerned with frivolous actions, the way they are created is an indication that city dwellers can use digital media to create new bottom-up urban publics and determine the programming of urban spaces. The organization of a flashmob is a collective process that usually does not originate in a central institution. The public creates itself, as it were, using networked media such as text messages and social networks. This could have major political implications – consider, for example, the recent uprisings in the Arab world. It is an interesting claim. But is it true? And if it is, is it necessarily a positive development? Is there not also a real danger of social chaos – think of the London riots in the summer of 2011? The pillow fight at Schouwburgplein might seem a trivial example, but it provides a number of leads for studying the underlying mechanism of the flashmob more closely.

The aim of International Pillow Fight Day was to breathe new life into the urban public space at the expense of 'non-social, branded consumption experiences like watching television'.[28] International Pillow Fight Day was intended to turn passive consumers into a community of active citizens and reclaim the urban public space from commercialization, individualization and parochialization. Flashmobs such as International Pillow Fight Day are therefore also compared with the Situationists' interventions: Andrea Mubi Brighenti and Cristina Mattiucci wrote that 'Their aim is precisely to transform the nature of urban space, gathering people together in an out-of-the-ordinary interaction regime.'[29]

A significant point that is constantly emphasized in discussions about flashmobs is that the flashmob public is not created on the orders of an institution or leader (think of the union that organizes a protest march or state-organized Mayday parades in the former Soviet bloc). Of course there is an ultimate initiator who draws up the invitation but in the end, the public is created through the net-worked structure of the social media. The way the public is formed corresponds with the development of 'networked individualism'. City dwellers are part of various, partly overlapping networks. If people from these networks recognize themselves in a message or feel that an issue concerns them, they will also publicize the message in their other networks. The call to convene for a flashmob can thus 'leapfrog' from one network to another, and the public creates itself, as it were. The social network rather than the boulevard functions as a 'recognition scene' as described by Berman: people recognize themselves in the messages that circulate there and maintain their circulation through 'likes', 'twitters' and 'reblogging'. They then use the network to coordinate collective action.

This process can be traced in the way the call to convene for the pillow fight was issued: the website that announced the event, www.pillowfight.com, did not ascribe the idea to any organization or person; the only person who was named was the website's webmaster. It referred to 'a collaboration of many people who comprise a loose, decentralized network of urban playground event organizers all over the world'.[30] Anyone who wanted to organize a pillow fight in his or her city could register at the site and was encouraged to use social networks, mailing lists and other digital media in order to bring the event to people's attention.[31]

Can this type of social organization be used for more than just frivolous events? A broader consideration of flashmobs can be found in Howard Rheingold's influential book *Smart Mobs*, in which he describes different examples of city dwellers organizing them-selves using their mobile phones. He defines smart mobs as follows:

> Smart mobs consist of people who are able to act in concert even if they don't know each other. The people who make up smart mobs cooperate in ways never before possible because they carry devices that possess both communication and computing capabilities. Their mobile devices connect them with other information devices in the environment as well as with other people's telephones.[32]

Thus, thanks to the combination of software and mobile media, it is now possible for people who do not know each other to collaborate or meet in new ways. In Rheingold's view this does not necessarily lead to a better democracy or a new interpretation of the public domain. Football hooligans who use their mobile phones to mobilize and to coordinate fights are also examples of smart mobs. Seen from this point of view, the skirmish between supporters of the Dutch football clubs Feyenoord and Ajax in a field next to a motorway in Beverwijk might well have been the first Dutch smart mob.[33] Despite these negative aspects, Rheingold is optimistic: the new means of decentralized communication and coordination that are made possible by digital media might lead to new interpretations of the public domain.

In order to study this claim, a comparison is made between two of the earliest smart mobs that play an important role in Rheingold's work and that should be seen as precursors of the Arab uprisings: the two 'revolutions' that took place at exactly the same place, the Epifano de los Santos Avenue (EDSA) in Manila, with a fifteen-year interval between events. In 1986, President Marcos fled the Philippines after angry crowds had protested against his regime for four days; in 2001 four days of demonstrations were again held on this boulevard in the centre of Manila, this time forcing President Estrada from office. Virtually every article that discusses the possible democratizing effect of digital media in the public domain refers to these historic events. In 2001, so it is claimed, the revolution was partly made possible by the formation of a 'smart mob'.

During the first People Power movement, as the events were later called, the radio and a hierarchical social organization still played an important role in the mobilization of the public. Radio Veritas, a Catholic station that was not under direct government control, broadcast a press conference on 22 February 1986 in which two military leaders declared that Marcos had committed fraud in recent presidential elections. The radio station used the popular archbishop Jaime Cardinal Sin to appeal to listeners to mobilize that very day to support resistance to the president and gather at EDSA. Listeners heeded the call on a massive scale; at the square, the demonstrators held radios close to their ears. The authorities tried to stem the unrest by going straight to its source: members of the military who remained loyal to the president disconnected the radio mast that broadcast Radio Veritas's signal through the ether. An alternative, albeit less powerful, transmitting station was quickly installed and the station continued to broadcast reports about the military's latest troop movements.

Descriptions of People Power II in 2001 usually attribute a central role to the mobile phone and the decentralized peer-to-peer networks that it helped create. This time, President Estrada was the target because impeachment proceedings against him had suddenly been halted. Consider, for example, how Howard Rheingold describes the events of that year in his book *Smart Mobs*:

> Opposition leaders broadcast text messages and within seventy-five minutes of the abrupt halt of the impeachment proceedings 20,000 people showed up.

(. . .) Over 1 million Manila residents [were] mobilized and coordinated by waves of text messages (. . .) On January 20, 2001 President Joseph Estrada of the Philippines became the first head of state in history to lose power to a smart mob.[34]

The uprising rapidly developed into a mass movement because, according to Rheingold, those involved sent text messages such as 'Go 2 EDSA, Wear Black 2 mourn d death f democracy. Noise barrage at 11 pm' to the entire address book in their mobile phones.[35] Globe Telecom sent 45 million text messages that day, nearly twice as many as normal.[36] The network quickly became so overloaded that telephone companies placed extra mobile transmission masts in the vicinity of EDSA. Other decentralized 'grassroots media' also played a role: criticism of Estrada, often in the form of caricatures, was sent by email and the online forum E-lagada is said to have collected 91,000 signatures against the president's rule.[37]

But Castells, Fernández-Ardèvol and Qiu rightly question whether it really was 'invincible technology' that made the uprising succeed. Was this smart mob facilitated by new processes of valorization, so that the isolated actions of individuals rather than the appeal from an authority through the mass media led to mobilization? Did individual participants become 'broadcasting stations' that kept the message in circulation without the state being able to exercise any influence over this process?[38]

Many participants in the demonstrations agree with this description. In his article 'The Cell Phone and the Crowd: Messianic Politics in the Contemporary Philippines', Vicente Rafael chronicled a number of participants' accounts in newspapers and online discussions: 'The mobile telephone is our weapon', said one jobless construction worker; 'The mobile telephone was like the fuse of the powder keg, kindling the uprising.' And another one, in the same upbeat prose: 'As long as your battery's not empty, you're "in the groove", and you feel militant.' And: 'The information and calls that reached us by way of text and e-mail were what brought together both organized and unorganized protests. From our homes, schools, dormitories, factories, churches, we poured onto the streets there to continue the trial [against Estrada].'[39]

Rafael considers these statements in a broader cultural context. At the end of the 1990s the mobile phone became immensely popular in the Philippines, especially after the Global provider introduced prepaid subscriptions with options for cheap text messaging. Owners referred to the telephone as a 'new limb' with one crucial quality: wherever they were, they could always simultaneously be somewhere else. In every social setting they could communicate with members of a self-selected group that was not present on the spot. The reverse was also true- the telephone could be used during mass gatherings as a binding instrument: 'While telecommunication allows one to escape the crowd, it also opens up the possibility of finding oneself moving in concert with it, filled with its desire and consumed by its energy.'[40] Text messaging became a symbolic practice: it was presented as the expression of an 'imagined community' referred to as 'Generation TXT'. Text messaging can be seen as the contemporary equivalent of waving a revolutionary banner. Rafael's descriptions are reminiscent of Marshall Berman's depiction of the publics on St Petersburg's Nevski Prospekt that spontaneously coalesced out of the masses of individuals who suddenly recognized themselves in each other. This recognition no longer takes place on the boulevard but through the media networks of text messages and social networks.

But did the mobile phone also signal a shift in authority structures, as Rheingold and others claim? Was this a public that created itself? We must be wary of technological determinism here. As Castells et al. also showed, the claim that the mobile phone alone was responsible for deposing Estrada is highly questionable. Many other factors played a role as well: traditional authorities such as the army and the church also led opposition against Estrada, and a number of the original text messages originated from opposition leaders. Furthermore, the power of the state was already weakened and, as a result, the government could not react effectively against the uprising. In countries where the state is more powerful, political smart mobs are far less successful. In Iran the 2009 'Twitter revolution' was violently suppressed by a strong state that still had the security services on its side. In China, too, the authorities still manage to limit protests: in Urumqi in 2009, for example, mobile phone communications were closed down during clashes between Han Chinese and Uighurs, and smart mobs could no longer organize themselves. A stronger state in the Philippines might also have been able to shut down the text-message network, just as it blocked Radio Veritas's transmission in 1986. Instead, the telecommunications companies, whose profits from text messages doubled that day, actually set up extra mobile transmissions masts at EDSA.

It is therefore going too far to say that the revolution took place solely thanks to the mobile phone and the cultural practice of text messaging. Nevertheless, the type of social networks made possible by the mobile phone in the cultural, political and economic circumstances in the Philippines certainly played a role. Rafael's analysis of writer Bart Guingona's contribution to a discussion forum is interesting: Guingona belonged to a group that organized one of the first protest meetings. He was initially sceptical about the use of the mobile phone as a mobilization tool. When someone proposed sending an appeal via text message, he did not expect it to be effective without such a message being validated by an authority. A priest who was involved in the preparations suggested using Radio Veritas, just as in 1986.

But it was decided that a test text message should be sent. When Guingona switched on his mobile phone the following morning, it turned out that friends and friends of friends had forwarded the message en masse, to his inbox as well: he had indirectly received back his own text message but now augmented three-fold.[41] According to Rafael's analysis, Guingona had little faith in the power of text messages: in his view they only had the status of a rumour, and for an appeal to be credible, it have to be endorsed by a traditional authority. This proved to be a misconception. A text message is not an unconnected message from an unknown and dubious source; it is a message from a known sender with his or her own social network that remains unchanged, regardless of how many times the message is forwarded. A message is not validated by an authority but through an accumulation of individual decisions to forward or not forward it within a network. Rafael:

> The power of texting here has less to do with the capacity to open interpretation and stir public debate than it does with compelling others to keep the message in circulation. Receiving a message, one responds by repeating it. One forwards it to others who, it is expected, will do the same. Repeatedly forwarding messages, one gets back one's exact message, mechanically augmented but semantically unaltered.[42]

Rheingold reaches a similar conclusion. Contrary to writing a text message, forwarding a message is extremely simple: only a couple of actions are required to make it circulate quickly. The downside is that this also applies to rumours - Rheingold writes that panic broke out in the Philippines after a false report was forwarded via a text message announcing the death of Pope John Paul II.

The People Power movement is one of the most frequently cited examples of political protest movements that were organized as smart mobs, but it is certainly not the only one. The mobile phone played an important role during the WTO protests in Seattle. In 2002 mobilization via the mobile phone and via user-generated content websites such as Ohmynews contributed to the election of the political outsider Roh Moo-hyun in South Korea. In Spain, text messaging was used as to coordinate demonstrations against the government following terrorist attacks in March 2004. In 2011 social networks also played a significant role in the organization of the *indignados* protest camps at central public places in several Spanish cities.[43] Recent examples that appeal most to the imagination are undoubtedly from the Middle East – we now speak of 'Facebook revolutions', in which not only the network but also the symbolic role of Facebook may have played a role. Just as young people in the Philippines and the emerging middle class embraced the mobile phone and text messaging as a symbolic practice that distinguished them from other groups, Facebook developed into the symbolic expression of young Arabs' protests against those in power. It was not only a means of communication but also the banner under which the public became united.[44]

The example of People Power II shows that peer-to-peer networks played a role in the process of validation and mobilization in Manila's public spaces centring on a political issue. It also shows that in order to fully understand such phenomena, we must not become fixated on technology or the processes of networked communication alone: we must consider the whole context of an event and the related components of an ecosystem.[45] In this case, it was the interaction between different media scales - mass media, niche media and peer-to-peer networks - that created an instant public around the issue of the suddenly halted impeachment proceedings. Validation of a message – whether anyone will respond to an appeal, for example – can be influenced by network effects: if someone suddenly receives the same appeal from different people in his network, this can be a significant factor. But validation remains a complex process based on several factors, including personal relationships, the possible repercussions of taking action, the importance someone attaches to a specific issue, and so on.

However, text messaging and Facebook do play a role in mobilization. Mobile phone and Internet networks open up new ways for publics to organize themselves. These media can be used as 'territory devices' to take possession of an urban public space. This involves a two-fold dynamic: members of a public recognize a common issue in the media network and use this to organize themselves. The political action itself takes place in the physical urban space. Spatially bringing together bodies is still the most meaningful way to make a political claim. This claim then acquires a broader meaning because it is filmed and given a second life on Twitter, Facebook or YouTube, which can in turn promote mobilization.

The effects of flashmobs should not be idealized, but this analysis does show that city dwellers are not completely powerless in the face of the software-sorting logic of digital technologies. In the first case, we saw how Stephen Graham positioned agency at the moment when the software for digital technologies is written:

this 'coding' is the process of establishing cultural codes, laws, ideals and/or concepts in the software and algorithms of the services that are developed on the platform of the street. In this example, a number of writers place agency on the side of the users, who can deploy the technology to organize themselves in urban publics. This is perhaps too utopian, but in certain circumstances digital technologies do make it possible to organize urban publics in new ways, although these are certainly not always publics whose intentions are 'good', as the London riots in the summer of 2011 showed.

The examples cited here show that digital and mobile media have indeed given citizens a new means to mobilize publics. Yet this is only the start of a political process. The challenge for the public domain is more than a question of mobilization: after all, a smart mob that develops as a phenomenon out of the total sum of innumerable individual acts of communication has little structure; there is no clear leader, nor is there an institution that can influence the direction in which the masses move. How can a political process arising from such a movement be given direction? How can the energy of the masses be converted into structures and institutions? How can the demands of the mobilized public (which largely consists of a collection of individuals without clear leaders) be transformed into an enduring political process of change? Perhaps the answer can be found in some of the examples given in the previous test case, in which city dwellers used new media to organize themselves around a collective interest or to gain collective control over a shared resource. But whether, and how, these sorts of examples can also be used on a larger scale is still unclear.

Test case 7 *Body Movies*

In September 2001, when Rotterdam was the Cultural Capital of Europe, Schouwburgplein hosted a special interactive video installation: *Body Movies – Relational Architecture 6* by Mexican artist Rafael Lozano-Hemmer. He projected gigantic slides of people shopping onto the side wall of the Pathé cinema. The images were not particularly clear because at the same time the beams from two bright xenon lights were shone at the wall. It was only when people happened to walk through the beams of one of the xenon lights that his or her shadow made part of the projected slide visible again.

As soon as passers-by realized that they could 'expose' photographs with their shadows, they began to experiment with them. Soon a number of passers-by started playing traditional shadow games: by assuming all sorts of shapes with their bodies or by going closer to or further away from the lights, they created shadows in a variety of shapes, each time revealing a different part of the original photograph. If several people simultaneously walked through the beams, more and more of the projected photograph became visible.

Lozano-Hemmer included an interactive, playful element in his installation: when the shadows of passers-by exactly matched the profiles of the people on the projected photograph, a new photograph would appear - a camera with image-recognition software was constantly analyzing the shadow play. Passers-by were thus encouraged to work together with the aim of together assuming exactly that one position in front of the xenon lights that matched the composition on the cinema wall. In Rotterdam this led to 'often comical and sometimes moving performances', the *Algemeen Dagblad* newspaper wrote afterwards. 'Shadows of unsuspecting passers-by were lovingly embraced or mercilessly trampled by huge giants. They turned out to be little boys who believed for a moment that they were big and powerful.'[46]

In recent years, *Body Movies* has become a canonical work in the branch of art criticism that is concerned with digital and interactive media. The work denounces in particular the influence of the ever-larger 'urban screens' in urban public spaces that mainly display advertisements. Lozano-Hemmer used *Body Movies* to provide an alternative to this in terms not only of content but also of form: his screen is not a passive but an interactive medium. Spectators play an active role, and the design of *Body Movies* also challenges passers-by to enter into brief social relationships with each other. The existing protocol – strangers do not disturb each other in public spaces – is thus disrupted. According to a number of critics, it is this aspect that makes Lozano-Hemmer's work so important. Sennett argues that the protocol of silence threatens the continued existence of the urban public domain, and a project such as *Body Movies* shows that digital media can lead to new forms of social interaction.

The emergence of 'urban screens' fits in with a long tradition in which architecture is embellished with inscriptions, whether these are statues on temples, frescoes and stained-glass windows in cathedrals or flashing neon advertisements in Tokyo's Shibuya or New York's Times Square.[47] What is new is that the content of the media layer has become flexible. Frescoes and stained-glass windows have been part of the buildings they adorn for centuries; the content of a digital screen or neon installation is largely unrelated to its physical support. In some cases, this media layer can also be influenced by passers-by or users of the location. *Architectural Design* magazine considers *Body Movies* a forerunner of an architecture whose form and content constantly change: by annotating the physical environment with media, Lozano-Hemmer shows how the 'dominant narratives of a specific building or urban setting'[48] are becoming increasingly fluid.

With the emergence of urban screens we seem to have come nearly full circle: as described earlier, a number of critics think the advent of the television combined with increasing suburbanization contributed to the rise of privatization and the erosion of the urban public space. The significance of the spatial urban public space lost out to the exchange of messages via the television screen. According to Paul Virilio, 'The screen became the city square',[49] and publics developed around the television screen. The development we are now seeing seems to be the opposite of this: 'urban screens' are once again at the centre of public spaces. The exact significance of the emergence of urban screens for the experience of the public domain obviously depends on how the screen is used: on the one hand, there are examples of urban screens around which publics form, for example to collectively watch a concert, political event or football match. This way, urban publics are formed around media contents in the public domain with both the fact of physically being together at a location and the content on the screen playing a role in the way the public is created.

But the emergence of urban screens can also easily be linked with the commercialization of the public domain. Many 'urban screens' mainly show advertisements and appeal to the shopping public as consumers. The latest generation of screens can even adapt their messages to the public present in a space.

Lozano-Hemmer uses projects such as *Body Movies* to denounce this increasing commercialization. He aims to provide an alternative to the rise of a worldwide popular and commercial culture, one of whose consequences is that all over the world, everything is starting to look the same, whether it is a branch of Starbucks or McDonald's or the design of shopping malls and airports. According to Lozano-Hemmer, billboard images also contribute to this trend: they are often part of global advertising campaigns and thus partly strip a city of its local identity. He argues that 'Cities are saturated with images and messages but they rarely show diversity and do not relate with the public on an intimate level'; they mainly evoke a sense of distance.[50] Lozano-Hemmer uses *Body Movies* to reverse this feeling - his spectacular installations are in fact intended to arouse a sense of intimacy and involvement.[51]

The Situationists' body of thought is an important source of inspiration for Lozano-Hemmer. Like this group of artists who centred around Guy Debord in the 1950s and 1060s, his aim is to enable city dwellers to look at themselves and the city around them in a new way, to 'liberate' them or at least provide an alternative to the disciplining mechanisms of consumer society; to temporarily ease them out of their everyday routines and invite them to make their own 'readings' and 'interpretations' of the city.[52] Lozano-Hemmer is particularly charmed by the Situationist practice of the 'virtual appointment': someone would be instructed to appear at a pre-arranged time at a specific location, where he would meet someone who had received similar instructions. This would greatly intensify the way the participants perceived their surroundings:

Every person walking by might be about to step into your life. The slightest of gestures amplifies into an emergent sign of recognition. The space around is no longer a neutral frame. It is charged with anticipated gazes leading to potential approaches.[53]

Urban art interventions should have a similar quality, according to Lozano-Hemmers: the motto is 'To exceed the expected', a task inspired by the Situationists' *dérive* and *détournement*.[54]

Body Movies shows how digital media can be deployed to endow the public domain with new meanings. Instead of advertising campaigns showing life-size depictions of international celebrities and sports heroes, *Body Movies* consists of a collection of images of 'ordinary' people who have been photographed going about their everyday urban routines such as shopping or going out for a walk. The interactive projections are an added layer in physical urban locations, providing them with a local context and identity that might have been eroded by their physical design and designation.

Lozano-Hemmer is not only concerned with the content of the projections but also with the social interaction that his project elicits. For example, the element of play in *Body Movies* invites city dwellers to briefly work together to make the system jump to the next photograph. This leads us to a second aspect of the way the project intervenes in the urban public space: the role of the media interface to encourage or prevent all sorts of social relationships. What sorts of social protocols are made possible by Lozano-Hemmer's specific concept of interactivity? According to Scott McQuire, *Body Movies* is so special because a temporary public forms around the installation out of what until shortly before were total strangers; they briefly share a frivolous experience, discovering that by performing a collective choreography, they can influence the atmosphere of their surroundings.[55] Lozano-Hemmer's work is also placed in the context of 'relational aesthetics', a concept developed by the influential French curator and art critic Nicolas Bourriaud: the aim of a work of art is not to express an artistic experience but to somehow create new social relationships.[56] This spontaneous choreography partly comes about as a result of Lozano-Hemmer's specific interactive approach. An interactive system in a public space is usually developed in such a way that only one interaction at a time is possible: someone or something supplies the input, after which the installation produces an outcome. This includes two possibilities: either members of the public take turns in using the installation, in which case each person can influence the interactive system in his or her own way; or the system measures the participants' average and uses this average to produce the outcome. Lozano-Hemmer finds both possibilities unsatisfactory, which is why he considers it important that for *Body Movies*, several people can simultaneously participate in the installation and their mutual interaction plays a role in the overall outcome. On the one hand, each participant can participate in his own way without his input disappearing in a democratic average, and on the other all sorts of collective patterns develop.[57] Lozano-Hemmer therefore refers to 'relational architecture' rather than interactivity, which has become a hackneyed term that can mean anything and therefore could just as well mean nothing. All too often, 'interactive' is used to mean 'reactive': the user presses a button and then something happens according to a pre-set pattern. The term 'relational' is intended to express the multiplicity of relationships that can develop as a result of his work: '"Relational" has a more horizontal quality; it is more collective. Events happen in fields of activity that may have resonances in several places in the network.'[58]

A number of critics see a connection between the way Lozano-Hemmer uses his digital interface in an attempt to elicit fleeting social relationships and theories about urban public spaces developed by thinkers such as Richard Sennett. As we saw earlier, Sennett outlined a development in which the public domain was increasingly dominated by silence. City dwellers no longer addressed each other to have a chat or even a debate based on an impersonal role-play. City dwellers had a growing sense that they did not have the right to speak to each other. Since the rise of the pavement-café culture on the nineteenth-century boulevards, people look at each other at best, and even this visual confrontation is under pressure as city dwellers continue to retreat to geographical zones where they feel at ease and where they mainly meet like-minded others.[59]

Can a hybrid interface such as *Body Movies* be deployed to stop this development? Can a similar intervention nudge city dwellers to interact with each other again, however briefly? Can interactive design tempt citizens to break the public silence? An installation such as *Body Movies* could play a vital role here, according to McQuire:

> Through mutual participation, people discover they are able to intervene – albeit ephemerally – in the look and feel of central city public space. In short, they are platforms encouraging creative public behaviour, enabling the city to become an experimental public space.[60]

The repercussions of this insight reach beyond this specific artistic intervention. Sennett's work, argues McQuire, shows us that his ideal interpretation of urban culture is not a natural condition: it is an acquired attitude. What Sennett emphasizes is that city dwellers should accept a number of protocols that are connected with all sorts of everyday settings such as the coffee house. Can the interface of mobile media stimulate or even impose a similar protocol?

Body Movies can be placed in the context of a broader development in which artists, using digital media, try to breathe new life into the urban public space. For example, at the beginning of the twenty-first century a broader group of artists embraced the term 'locative media': 'locative' was used to distinguish an artistic practice from the commercial applications of location technologies that emerged at the time, often under the name 'location-based services'. These same technologies were often used to make the urban experience more personal or efficient. Locative-media artists and their successors, who work in the same spirit, emphatically argued for a different application of this technology. It was no coincidence that on the centenary of the Futurist Manifesto, American researcher Eric Paulos called for digital technologies to be used for urban ideals such as frivolity, serendipity and curiosity. In his *Manifesto of Open Disruption and Participation*, he wrote:

> (. . .) we claim that the successful ubiquitous computing tools, the ones we really want to cohabitate with, will be those that incorporate the full range of life experiences. We want our tools to sing of not just productivity but of our love of curiosity, the joy of wonderment, and the freshness of the unknown.[61]

Can works of art such as *Body Movies* breathe new life into the public domain? Can they bring back the Situationists' sense of wonder? Or breathe new life into social contacts between city dwellers and perhaps even contribute to the development of new protocols? Perhaps this is asking too much of artists. Nevertheless, these questions do express the importance of interventions such as Lozano-Hemmer's: they show that an alternative interface design can stimulate brief encounters as part of everyday urban life. They also show the importance of an open notion of 'interactivity' in the design.

This brings us back to the question that was raised at the beginning of the last three chapters: does the emergence of digital media threaten the republican notion of a public domain? Will common meeting places disappear? Will citizens be reduced to consumers – a fear expressed by several critics, prompted by the construction of the Korean smart city New Songdo? Or will citizens retain the initiative in the digital world? And can publics that include city dwellers from different backgrounds develop in new ways?

There is still no clear-cut answer to these questions. It is becoming more difficult to point to places that function as public domains where the whole urban community is held together in the way advocated by Hannah Arendt. But this does not mean that the urban public sphere is doomed to disappear: it might develop through new platforms and at unexpected places. Private, parochial and public domains overlap. Besides, urban media make it easier than ever for us to retreat to our parochial domain. But these parochial domains are hardly ever completely unambiguous. They often show an overlap with the parochial and private domains of others. And it is this overlap that creates the potential for public domains to be created in new ways - by making this overlap visible in digital media layers, or when installations such as Lozano-Hemmer's invite us to briefly step out of our private cocoons and start brief relationships with other passers-by. Digital media can also make new common issues visible and provide city dwellers with the opportunity to organize themselves around them. What the examples from these test cases have in common is that they do not attempt to reanimate a nineteenth-century idea of a central public space. The idea of a collective *space* is not central: the starting point is a shared interest, or a shared practice. And the question is always: how can a public consisting of city dwellers from different backgrounds be temporarily united in a larger whole around such an interest or practice?

Here, agency seems to have partly shifted to individual city dwellers: they can use technology to shape their world. Open data movements and the organization of flashmobs show that citizens can use the platforms themselves in order to actively shape their lives. Yet this fact is far from self-evident. There are all sorts of developments through which 'the city as platform' functions as a closed system in which the city dweller is mainly approached as a consumer. Interactivity is then often reduced to 'reactivity', and citizens actually have little or no opportunity to question the rules of the service offered.

The City of the Future, the Future of the City

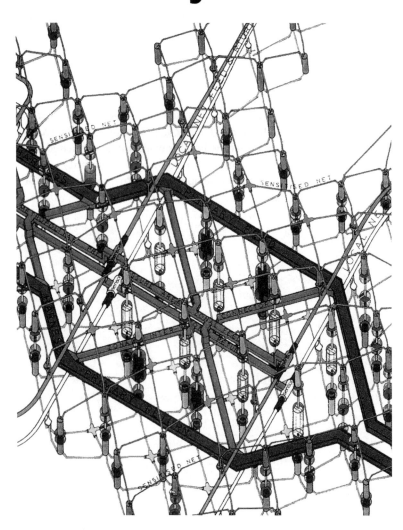

Can our large cities still be called urban communities? Have they not in fact gradually become large agglomerations of people living separate lives, who indeed feel connected with the social group they are part of yet outside this group feel lost in the masses?[1]

These were the words used in 1946 by the mayor of Rotterdam Pieter Oud to express his concern about the future of his city. As a result of the increase in scale in the port and industry, and the migration from far-off parts of the country such as Brabant, Zeeland and Friesland, Rotterdam had rapidly expanded in the decades before the Second World War. But had this changed the city into a 'brick desert' where 'harmonious life' could no longer flourish? Had modernization also led to alienation and the fragmentation of urban society? Or, in the most optimistic scenario, to the development of a series of divergent, isolated groups?

Since the beginning of the twenty-first century, a number of critics and artists have again raised questions about the future of the city. What are the implications for the city of urban media? Will the emergence of digital media technologies in everyday life lead to a far-reaching parochialization of urban society? Is there a renewed risk that, to use Mayor Pieter Oud's words, the city will consist of 'large agglomerations of people living separate lives' who only 'feel connected with the social group of which they are part?

That exactly the same questions have been posed half a century after they were first raised is hardly surprising. They are, after all, the same questions that have been raised continuously since the rise of the modern industrial metropolis at the end of the nineteenth century. At the beginning of the twentieth century Chicago School sociologists argued that the essence of the modern city was its combination of density and differentiation. Most modern cities combined a high population density with a great diversity of lifestyles. It is this very combination that is the power of the modern city: the city is a marketplace for goods, services, ideas and identities, and thanks to the high density and variety of people there is a real probability that supply and demand in whatever field will meet. But this also gives rise to a complex social question: how are we to live together with all these people whom we not only do not know personally but who are also different from us? From Walter Benjamin to Richard Sennett, from Hannah Arendt to Jane Jacobs, from Archigram to Lozano-Hemmer, in the various debates I have referred to, this question was always central.

The tram, the train, the car, the television, and now the mobile phone: new technological, economic and cultural developments enable citizens to organize themselves spatially and socially into different publics in new ways. Each time this happens, it changes the way in which parochial and public domains are shaped. What remains unchanged is the issue of harmonization between these two domains: how does the city function as an interface where citizens can organize themselves in publics of like-minded people while also relating in some way or other to all those people whom they do not include in their own parochial domains? And what should the ideal relationship between these two domains be?

Mayor Pieter Oud expressed his concern in the foreword to a book entitled *De stad der toekomst, de toekomst der stad* (literally, 'The city of the future, the future of the city'), in which the Bos committee unfolded its 'neighbourhood concept', a new design philosophy for the post-war reconstruction of Rotterdam. The book concluded with a number of design principles that, if applied correctly, would ensure that the city functioned as an 'interface' where individual city dwellers could be absorbed into a number of local, communitarian communities.

The book before you can also be seen as a philosophical exploration of the city of the future as well as the future of the city. I have discussed a number of design approaches that designers, policymakers, architects, programmers, new-media designers, artists and other parties can use to contemplate the design and organization of urban life. This is not an indisputable set of guidelines that can be used to impose a predetermined, top-down design on urban life. Rather, it is an attempt, in the spirit of Jane Jacobs, to name 'catalysts' that might help a number of social processes to gain momentum.

My principle throughout has been the republican ideal of the city as a 'community of strangers': urban society must provide people with the freedom to arrange life according to their own views, but this freedom must not result in a complete lack of commitment or social fragmentation. City dwellers are first and foremost citizens who can act of their own accord, and they can certainly be expected to bear the common good in mind and feel some involvement with society as a whole. On an axis between communitarian and libertarian visions of the city, this republican ideal can be located halfway: it is not diametrically opposed to these other two ideals but successfully combines elements from both. The central question is always the difficult task of finding a balance between individual freedom and mutual involvement.

In the words of Lotte Stam-Beese, the architect behind the urban design plan for Pendrecht that was based on the neighbourhood concept: 'The modern city (. . .) should be spatially organized in such a way that diversity and alteration [are] present to the human being who is moving and present in it the feeling that he has the freedom to choose from many possibilities.' But she also set an important precondition: 'not being part of', according to Stam-Beese, must be excluded: 'We stand in a space, and are part of it.'

It is this last aspect that highlights the unusual character of current discussions about the future of the city: at the beginning of the twenty-first century, whoever is 'in a space' is – thanks to urban media – no longer automatically part of it. The way urban media are used as 'experience trackers' and 'territory devices' changes not only the experience of places in a city itself but also which places city dwellers visit and which other city dwellers they meet there. This could have major consequences for the way urban publics develop.

A series of test cases showed that urban media can stimulate the parochialization of a city: city dwellers use urban media to find or create their own parochial or private spheres. These media help us to find exactly those things in the relative chaos of urban life that are relevant to us. This is both an active and a passive process: sometimes city dwellers use urban media actively to create their own parochial domains, for example when they use their smartphones as 'experience trackers' and show who they are on different sorts of social networks. This can stimulate a broader development, with symbolic spatial use becoming more important to mark social status. The reverse is also true: research by Mimi Ito and Rich Ling indicates that city dwellers also use their mobile phones to create their own parochial domains within a public domain: city dwellers can use their mobile phones to stay in contact with people from their network throughout the day. The mobile phone is a membrane with which they allow or deny absent others access to their world of experience. 'Closeness' is thus no longer necessarily that which is physically nearby but that which can quickly be accessed or found.

Yet, this process of parochialization does not always happen by choice: the digital traces we leave behind when we use our mobile phones or social networks and search machines are deployed to create profiles of us that are used to personalize our experience of the city, even if we are not aware of this. Just as different people who use Google get different search results when they type in the same search term, different city dwellers can also be shown different maps of a city, showing the places that are of interest to them according to some (probably secret) algorithm. The objective city map thus becomes a subjective 'living map'. From now on, we will always be at the centre of our cartographic universe, a flashing blue light surrounded by neatly arranged 'useful places' that might be of specific interest to us.

All these new interfaces that we can use to organize our lives in new ways emerge against the backdrop of a number of spatial and social developments that had already started before the advent of urban media. The use of urban media matches a broader development that researchers like Barry Wellman, Jan-Willem Duyvendak and Menno Hurenkamp call 'light communities' and 'networked individualism': their research shows that individualization does not mean that people become lonelier but that they have more choice between the groups they consider themselves part of. People join different groups that are connected with different social and societal roles. These groups do not form close communities; instead, contacts tend to be non-committal, although this naturally varies from one group to the next.

Spatially, this leads to a pattern of what Arnold Reijndorp calls 'network urbanism': the city can no longer be understood with the aid of a concentric model in which the most important functions are clustered in the centre, with housing areas in the periphery. Rather, an 'urban field' has developed in which different functions and the parochial domains of various publics appear at different locations. To use a computing metaphor, the city dweller 'cuts and pastes' together his own city. As a result, the inner city's central role is becoming less important: it is no longer the central place where the most important functions of urban life come together. This means there are fewer places that function as traditional public domains, that is, places where all city dwellers come together and take notice of each other.

This public domain is also under pressure as a result of another development: the privatization and commercialization of the public domain. Traditional concepts of the public domain such as Hannah Arendt's and Richard Sennett's emphasize that this domain is a space where citizens can act of their own accord and where they themselves can also establish the rules and protocols. But in the city, public spaces are increasingly dominated by leisure activities such as 'fun shopping' and they are sometimes even managed by commercial parties. Security camera surveillance and all sorts of local protocols discourage deviant behaviour: above all, the public space must remain a pleasant and representative space. Moreover, public spaces are increasingly acquiring an iconic function with which cities try to distinguish themselves from other cities. To an increasing extent, the urban infrastructure is seen as a commercial service that can be sold to consumers. This commodification is also found in the digital domain, which consists of commercial and private platforms that function as urban media. Facebook, TomTom, Google, Cisco – these companies ultimately decide what is and is not allowed on their platforms and, in turn, which protocols apply to communication there. Of course, as commercial companies they cannot completely ignore the wishes of the paying customer, but it is anything but a democratic process.

Spatially, all these developments can lead to two different scenarios that can occur simultaneously. On the one hand, urban media can be deployed to reinforce the spatial boundaries of a parochial domain: electronic access gates, dynamic pricing mechanisms or camera monitoring can exclude or, more subtly, make a place less attractive for those who are not considered part of a parochial district or do not comply with the applicable protocol. Digital media can thus strengthen the clear boundaries between the domains of different urban groups. Stephen Graham referred in this context to 'software-sorting geographies': using software that analyzes behaviour to spatially sort people according to their different backgrounds.

A contrasting scenario can be found in Antony Townsend's work. He actually predicted the rise of urban locations where different protocols simultaneously apply to different users. Different publics might use the same spaces yet mainly maintain contact with the 'members' of their own public. A software layer then helps to make clear exactly who belongs to a user's public and which locations in the neighbourhood are considered suitable meeting places. This can stimulate a broader urban development that is referred to in urban research as 'living together apart': different parochial domains in a city might be right next door to each other, but their symbolic distance is huge. Indeed, this can be very convenient for the networked city dweller: after all, he is part of various publics and the spatial overlap of all these networks makes it easy to constantly switch between the different roles he fulfils in these various publics. The city of the future might thus become even more heterogeneous and complex than it already is. Smart-phone interfaces rather than physical spatial planning will introduce order to the chaos.

All these developments lead to two worrying tendencies. The first issue is whether the development of urban publics that unite city dwellers from different backgrounds will still be possible; after all, city dwellers can now use the interfaces of urban media to filter the perception of their surroundings so that anything that does not fit in with their preferences simply disappears from view. Second, the fear that citizens will no longer have any agency: companies and the state establish the protocols that determine what is and is not permitted, and this is increasingly true for both the physical environment and for the software interfaces that guide us through the city.

My aim has been to show that the fears expressed above are well founded. However, they will not inevitably become reality. Urban media can actually create a public domain in new ways but to see this, we must distance ourselves from traditional notions of this domain. It is no longer necessarily a central, more or less neutral meeting place where all city dwellers come together on the basis of equality. The public domain materializes when city dwellers from different backgrounds organize themselves for shorter or longer periods in a mixed public with a common protocol or goal.

Reijndorp and Hajer have found that it is not parochialization itself that is the problem, but rather the unrealistic ideal of an urban public domain as a neutral meeting place for all citizens. We must not become fixated on the idea of the city as it was in nineteenth-century Vienna or Paris but instead be open to contemporary developments. The rise of network urbanism and 'networked individualism' does not mean that there will no longer be occasions for encounters or confrontations: the spatial sorting of worlds of experience is not complete, and most citizens do not want to isolate themselves entirely in homogeneous zones in which they only meet like-minded people. The social and spatial networks of city dwellers continue to partly overlap.

The experience of a public domain can therefore be found when we visit the parochial domains of publics that we do not belong to at all or of which we are only partly members. Public domains develop when parochial domains briefly overlap. As long as this continues to happen, city dwellers will still be able to take notice of each other. This is precisely the crux of the republican urban ideal as I have outlined it here: the aim is not to build a harmonious, clear-cut community; the ideal is 'minimal cohesion' rather than 'maximum community'. The variety of urban life and the freedom that this leads to are actually the great strengths of the city. This means we must also accept that there will always be friction between groups – it is a dynamic that is also part of the city.

The public domain should thus be understood as a layered whole. The basis consists of those places in a city or moments during which the parochial domains of various city dwellers overlap. This first layer consists of those places in a city or moments during which the parochial domains of various city dwellers overlap, for example in brief, everyday and perhaps even trivial encounters. These are the moments when city dwellers can take notice of each other and mutual trust can develop. This is the public domain as Jane Jacobs described it and it mainly consists of superficial contacts.

The next layer of the public domain requires slightly more intensive involvement. The issue is whether new publics can develop out of all those moments of temporary overlap. Will new protocols, new collective rhythms and new ways of doing things develop in the course of time that allow people to behave collectively despite their differences? One step further is the question whether there are themes that concern the urban community as a whole: can we organize publics around common concerns such as the environment, schools, healthcare and the quality of everyday life? Can we clarify the common interest of these issues and get different city dwellers involved in them in some way or other? Non-commitment then makes way for involvement and a sense of collective 'ownership'. These processes need not necessarily take place at a central level; they are more likely to occur in a network structure.

Urban media can play an important role at all these levels. These media deployed as 'territory devices' make it easier for different worlds to overlap spatially. They can reinforce the 'living together apart' scenario, creating new opportunities for these different worlds to occasionally overlap. The 'doubling' of the city through urban media also makes city dwellers' different worlds of experience visible, although it is still unclear how these worlds can be made accessible through urban media. How can city dwellers actually be tempted to take notice of the digitally stored worlds of their fellow city dwellers? A digital platform alone is probably insufficient to achieve this. Programming is needed that actually encourages interaction, such as an interface design that, in the spirit of Kevin Lynch, rouses curiosity. This means the designer's task is not the development of the 'seamless design' of the smart city in which the experience of the city is adapted to the personal preferences or requirements of the city dweller, preferably without his or her noticing it; instead, the designer's task is the development of a 'seamful design': a design approach that actually makes the city dweller aware of the fault lines in and the interfaces with their surroundings.[2] Another way to make the overlap visible is through programming that, as in the example of Mario Bosch's neighbourhood blog, addresses different groups simultaneously; or through interventions in the physical space, such as Lozano-Hemmer's *Body Movies*. Playful elements can play an important role here, temporarily suspending existing protocols and creating the basis for new interactions.

At the next level, digital media can play a role in making collective rhythms or issues visible. Data visualizations of air quality, movement patterns, traffic rhythms, the collective use of resources and so on can make common patterns visible or provide insights into issues that concern the community as a whole: the collective level can be made visible as well the role played by individual city dwellers in creating or solving a problem. Publics can develop around these issues in new ways, and people's level of involvement can vary: from the minimal Facebook 'like' to initiating collective actions. The flashmob case study shows that new means for mobilizing publics are available.

Yet one step further is the emergence of publics that collectively manage urban resources, from sharing cars to neighbourhood gardens, from borrowing tools from the neighbours to setting up a collective electricity company. In that case, digital media function as a marketplace where supply and demand meet around very practical issues. It is the reputation systems of digital media that makes this sort of collective exchange possible. As a result, some matters can be managed as a 'common' again. Here, too, the level of involvement can vary, from the one-off hiring of a hammer-drill from the neighbour to the communal management of a neighbourhood utility – which includes dealing with all the disputes that are often associated with this.

The three examples have one thing in common: they fit in with the emergence of 'networked individualism'. The very fact that city dwellers are part of diverse publics means that new publics can develop out of the overlap between all these networks. It is because of this overlap that collective issues in one network 'leapfrog' to the next. This means that the public domain does not develop as a result of the simultaneous sharing of a single central urban space but rather as a result of city dwellers organizing themselves around a public issue. Very practical matters can be the catalysts in this process: the example of the boulevards in Paris demonstrates that a public domain does not develop because it has been created from above but because urban infrastructure has been programmed in such a way that different groups simultaneously find this domain attractive or important. In the 'living together apart' scenario, different parochial domains criss-cross in a physical neighbourhood. Very practical matters can lead to brief moments of overlap – everyone occasionally needs a car or a particular tool. The idea of a smart city (making urban infrastructure more efficient) can thus also lead to the development of a social city (the common management of this infrastructure).

But this depends on one condition: citizens must retain agency. The design of a platform must be genuinely interactive: this gives participants the opportunity to establish or change protocols instead of being forced to comply with rules laid down by companies. Magical software automatically arranging everything for us sounds very attractive, and the services provided by commercial parties will undoubtedly make life more pleasant and agreeable. There is nothing wrong with that, but, ultimately, we are better off when platforms for such services are accessible and citizens themselves can appropriate the related data and protocols in their own way.

These conclusions also lead us to the limitations of this book: I have tried to explore the latent possibilities of urban media for influencing the way urban publics develop. I have shown that in the first place they can stimulate the development of parochialization and can thus also reinforce the libertarian urban ideal. However, this is not an unambiguous development. All sorts of alternative urban media are emerging that might actually breathe new life into the republican urban ideal.

'Might' is the operative word here, because we are in the middle of a technological revolution in which the computer is not only on our desks but has become an integral part of life in the city. The emergence of urban media is changing everyday urban life, and this process is still in full swing. My hope is that this book will provide leads for everyone who is concerned with the design of the city, from architects and urban planners to interface designers and hackers, from citizens to planning officials, from companies to consumers; leads that will provide new ways of thinking about how we can develop catalysts that might also breathe new life into the republican ideal: an ideal whose starting point is no longer the public *space* but rather the way in which urban *publics* develop from the combined action of spatial and mediated practices.

As Paola Antonelli writes, 'Designers stand between revolutions and everyday life.'[3] It is the interfaces of urban media that make the technological revolution in urban media manageable. And it is the hidden possibilities of these interfaces that play a role in the way they ultimately interfere in everyday urban life. Design – as well as policy – is thus not only the invention of practical solutions but also a philosophical exercise. My aim here has been to make a start on this philosophical exercise. What we now need is a new generation of test cases that can translate the design approaches that have been discussed here into practice.

Notes
Blogs
Bibliography
Acknowledge-
ments

Introduction

1   Bill Gates, 'The Enduring Magic of Software', *Information Week* 18
       October 2000, http://www.informationweek.com/the-enduring-magic-
       of-software/49901115 (accessed 18 October 2012).

2   Cited in: P. Dourish, *Where the Action Is: The Foundations of*
       Embedded Interaction (Cambridge, MA 2004), viii.

3   P. Goldberger, 'Disconnected Urbanism', *Metropolismag.com*, 22
       February 2007, http://www.metropolismag.com/story/20070222/
       disconnected-urbanism (accessed 28 February 2013).

4   A. Blum, 'Local Cities, Global Problems: Jane Jacobs in an Age of
       Global Change', in : T. Mennel, J. Steffens and C. Klemek (eds), *Block*
       by Block: Jane Jacobs and the Future of New York (New York:
       Princeton Architectural Press, 2007), 51-53, 53

5   See Danah Boyd in: D. Boyd, 'Taken out of Context' (UC Berkeley,
       2008), 17. See also S. Livingstone, *Audiences and Publics: When*
       Cultural Engagement Matters for the Public Sphere (Portland, OR:
       Intellect, 2005).

6   See also L.H. Lofland, *The Public Realm: Exploring the City's*
       Quintessential Social Territory (Piscataway, NJ: Transaction
       Publishers, 1998), 31. On urbanism, theatre and roles, see also S.
       Lennard and H. Lennard, *Public Life in Urban Places* (Southampton,
       NY: Gondolier, 1984).

7   M. Berman, *All That is Solid Melts into Air: The Experience of*
       Modernity (New York: Verso, 1987), 196.

8   J. Jacobs, *The Death and Life of Great American Cities* (London:
       Pimlico, 2000 [1961]), 40.

9   Wirth, 'Urbanism as a Way of Life'.

10   L. Lofland, *A World of Strangers: Order and Action in Urban Public*
       Space (New York: Basic Books, 1973), 10.

11   Ibid., 9.

12   Cited in A. Blum, 'Local Cities, Global Problems', 53.

13   See also M. de Lange, 'Moving Circles: Mobile Media and Playful
       Identities' (PhD thesis Rotterdam: Erasmus Universiteit, 2010) and
       A. Galloway, 'A Brief History of the Future of Urban Computing and
       Locative Media' (PhD thesis Ottawa: Carleton University, 2008) for
       an extensive overview of different technologies.

14   See also: Tuters and Varnelis, who refer to 'annotation' and 'tracing'
       as qualities of what they call 'locative media'. M. Tuters and K.
       Varnelis, 'Beyond Locative Media: Giving Shape to the Internet of
       Things', *Leonardo* 39 (2006) no. 4, 357-363.

15   M. Ito, D. Okabe and M. Matsuda, *Personal, Portable, Pedestrian:*
       Mobile Phones in Japanese Life (Cambridge, MA: MIT Press, 2006),
       15.

16   K. Fujimoto, 'The Third-Stage Paradigm: Territory Machines from
       the Grils' Pager Revolution to Mobile Aesthetics', in: M. Ito, D. Okabe
       and M. Matsuda (eds), *Personal, Portable, Pedestrian: Mobile Phones*
       in Japanese Life (Cambridge, MA: MIT Press, 2006), 77-102, 98.

17   M. Castells, 'The Culture of Cities in the Information Age', in: I.
       Susser (ed), *The Castells Reader on Cities and Social Theory* (Malden,
       MA: Blackwell Publishers, 2002) 382. See also S. McQuire, *The Media*
       City: Media Architecture and Urban Space (Thousand Oaks: Sage,

2008); Stephen Johnson popularized the 'interface' concept as a cultural metaphor in his book *Interface Culture*. In the Netherlands, Marianne van den Boomen published an essay entitled 'De stad als interface' (literally, 'The city as interface') as early as 1996, *De Helling* no. 1 (spring 1996), http://boom.home.xs4all.nl/artikel/stad. html (accessed 28 February 2013); S. Johnson, *Interface Culture* (San Francisco: HarperEdge, 1997).

18   E. Kluitenberg, 'The Network of Waves', *Open* 11 (2007), 6-16,14
19   Galloway, 'A Brief History of the Future of Urban Computing and Locative Media', 41. Galloway also uses 'cultural probes' in her research, based on of Gaver's theory; B. Gaver, T. Dunne and E. Pacenti, 'Design: Cultural Probes', *ACM Interactions*, January – February 1999, 21-29.
20   Dourish, *Where the Action Is*, viii.
21   See also: M. de Waal, 'The Ideas and Ideals in Urban Media', in: M. Foth et al. (eds), *From Social Butterfly to Engaged Citizen* (Cambridge, MA: MIT Press, 2012), 5-20.

Chapter 1

1   D. van der Ree, 'Een deel van je leven', in: *Project Zuidelijke Tuinsteden* (Rotterdam: Dienst Stedenbouw + Volkshuisvesting, 1992), 10; D. van der Ree, 'Van boerenzij naar stadswijk', in A. Reijndorp and H. van der Ven (eds), *Een reuze vooruitgang: Utopie en praktijk in de zuidelijke tuinsteden van Rotterdam* (Rotterdam: Uitgeverij 010, 1994), 105-118.
2   R. Bijhouwer, 'Ruimtewerking en ritmiek: Een analyse van het stedenbouwkundige oeuvre van Lotte Stam-Beese', in: H. Damen and A. Devolder (eds), *Lotte Stam-Beese 1903-1988: Dessau, Brno, Charkow, Moskou, Amsterdam, Rotterdam* (Rotterdam: De Hef, 1993), 94-95.
3   A. Bos, *De stad der toekomst, de toekomst der stad: Een stedebouw-kundige en sociaal-culturele studie over de groeiende stadsgemeen-schap* (Rotterdam: Voorhoeve, 1946), 18.
4   W.F. Geyl and S. Bakema-Van Borssum Waalkes, *Wij en de Wijkgedachte* (Utrecht: V. en S., 1948).
5   Ibid.
6   Ibid.
7   Bos, *De stad der toekomst, de toekomst der stad: Een stedebouwkundige en sociaal-culturele studie over de groeiende stadsgemeenschap*, 18.
8   Ibid., 95
9   Ibid., 98.
10   Bos, *De stad der toekomst, de toekomst der stad*, 362.
11   See also: C.A. Perry, 'The neighborhood unit' (1929), in R. LeGates and F. Stour (eds), *Early Urban Planning* (London: Routledge, 1998), 22.
12   He unfolds this theory in C.A. Perry, *Housing for the Mechanical Age* (New York: Russell Sage Foundation, 1939).
13   Cited in P. Hall, *Cities of Tomorrow* (Oxford: Blackwell, 2002), 130.
14   Bos, *De stad der toekomst, de toekomst der stad*, 45.
15   Ibid., 53.

16   T. Idsinga, 'Het Nieuwe Bouwen in Rotterdam 1940-1960: Wat is stedelijk wonen in een open stad?', in: W. Beeren et al. (ed.), *Het Nieuwe Bouwen in Rotterdam 1920-1960* (Delft: Delft University Press, 1982), 108-138, 123.

17   See A. Reijndorp and H. van der Ven (eds), *Een reuze vooruitgang: Utopie en praktijk in de zuidelijke tuindsteden van Rotterdam* (Rotterdam: Uitgeverij 010, 1994), 42; A. Hebly, 'Op het ritme van de Horsten: Een stedenbouwkundig plan voor een buurt in Zuidwijk', in: A. Reijndorp and H. van der Ven (eds), *Een reuze vooruitgang: Utopie en praktijk in de zuidelijke tuinsteden van Rotterdam* (Rotterdam: Uitgeverij 010, 1994), 196; B. Jansen, 'De ideale woongemeenschap in naoorlogs Rotterdam', in: K. Hage and K. Zweerink (eds), *Van Pendrecht tot Ommoord: Geschiedenis en toekomst van de naoorlogse wijken in Rotterdam* (Bussum: Thoth, 2005), 20-25; Blum, 'Local Cities, Global Problems', 23.

18   L. Stam-Beese, 'De stad als wooncentrum', in: *Studium Generale*, March 1959, 72.

19   Cited in Bijhouwer, 'Ruimtewerking en ritmiek', 92

20   L. Stam-Beese, 'Aantekeningen over Pendrecht', archive NAi Rotterdam STAB #17.

21   Ibid.

22   Cited in E. Velzen, 'Pendrecht opnieuw bezien: Ontwerpstudies voor de vernieuwing van Pendrecht', in: A. Reijndorp and H. van der Ven (eds), *Een reuze vooruitgang: Utopie en praktijk in de zuidelijke tuinsteden van Rotterdam* (Rotterdam: Uitgeverij 010, 1994), 212.

23   Cited in R. Blijstra, *Rotterdam, stad in beweging* (Amsterdam: Arbeiderspers, 1965), 220.

24   Cited in Velzen, 'Pendrecht opnieuw bezien', 212.

25   See also: J. Schilt, '1947-1957: Tien jaar "Opbouw"', in R. Dettingmeijer, R. Beeren and P. Wardle (eds), *Het Nieuwe Bouwen In Rotterdam 1920-1960* (Delft: Delft University Press, 1982), 148-149.

26   R. Grünfeld and L. Weima, *Wonen in de nieuwe wijk Pendrecht (Rotterdam)*, (Rotterdam: Wetenschappelijk Bureau Dienst van Volkshuisvesting Rotterdam, 1958).

27   Stam-Beese, 'Aantekeningen over Pendrecht', 122.

28   G. Anderiesen and M. Martens, 'Continuïteit en verandering: Oude en nieuwe bewoners van de zuidelijke tuinsteden', in: A. Reijndorp and H. van der Ven (eds), *Een reuze vooruitgang: Utopie en praktijk in de zuidelijke tuinsteden van Rotterdam* (Rotterdam: Uitgeverij 010, 1994).

29   Dienst Volkshuisvesting, 'Onderzoek in tuinstad Zuidwijk (Rotterdam) naar het oordeel van de bewoners over de nieuwe wijk', (1954).

30   Barends en De Pree, cited in: Jansen, 'De ideale woongemeenschap in naoorlogs Rotterdam', 25.

31   See also: J. Schilt and H. Selier, 'Van de oevers van de Oder tot Krimpen aan den Ijssel', in: H. Damen and A. Devolder (eds), *Lotte Stam-Beese 1903-1988: Dessau, Brno, Charkow, Moskou, Amsterdam, Rotterdam* (Rotterdam: De Hef, 1993), 10-37, 32; Bijhouwer, 'Ruimtewerking en ritmiek', 93.

32   Grünfeld and Weima, 'Wonen in de nieuwe wijk Pendrecht (Rotterdam)'.

33 T. Lupi, *Buurtbinding* (Amsterdam: Aksant, 2005); H. van der Horst, J. Kullberg and L. Deben, *Wat wijken maakt: De wording van functionele, sociale en expressieve kwaliteiten van Vreewijk, Zuidwijk en Ommoord* (Utrecht: NETHUR, 2002); M.J. van Doorn-Jansen, *Groei en gestalte van een nieuwe stadswijk: Verslag van een sociologische verkenning in Rotterdam-Zuidwijk anno 1955* (Utrecht: Rijksuniversiteit Utrecht, 1965).

34 Van-Doorn-Jansen, *Groei en gestalte van een nieuwe stadswijk*; Lupi, *Buurtbinding*, 48.

35 See E. van Es, 'Plannen Pendrecht 1948-1965', in: G. Van den Brink et al. (ed), *Prachtwijken?!: De mogelijkheden en beperkingen van Nederlandse probleemwijken*(Amsterdam: Bert Bakker, 2007).

36 Cited in Anderiesen and Martens, 'Continuïteit en verandering', 116.

37 See for criticism of community studies J. Eade, *Living the Global City* (New York: Routledge, 1996) and B. Wellman, 'The Community Question: The Intimate Networks of East Yorkers', *The American Journal of Sociology* 84 (1979) no. 5, 1201-1231. See also: Lupi, *Buurtbinding*, 55.

38 H.P. Bahrdt, *Die moderne Grossstadt: Soziologische Überlegungen zum Städtebau* (Reinbeck bei Hamburg: Rowohlt, 1967); see also: R.E. van Engelsdorp Gastelaars and D. Hamers, *De nieuwe stad: Stedelijke centra als brandpunten van interactie* (Rotterdam: NAi Uitgevers, 2006).

39 S. Groenman, 'Goede kanten van kleine gemeenten', *Intermediair* (1971), cited in: R.E. van Engelsdorp Gastelaars, *Veertig jaar territoriale binding* (Amsterdam: Vossiuspers UvA, 2003), 12.

40 See also Ulrich Beck, who later wrote: 'Our antennas are our roots'. U. Beck, *Cosmopolitan Vision* (Cambridge, UK: Polity Press, 2006), 103.

41 See also WRR (Scientific Council for Government Policy), *Vertrouwen in de buurt* (Rapporten aan de Regering no. 72), (Amsterdam: Amsterdam University Press, 2005), 29.

42 See: Engelsdorp Gastelaars, *Veertig jaar territoriale binding*.

43 G.D. Suttles, *The Social Construction of Communities* (Chicago: University of Chicago Press, 1972); see also Lupi, *Buurtbinding* and Engelsdorp Gastelaars, *Veertig jaar territoriale binding*.

44 See 'Straatagenda van de Sint-Annalandstraat' http://www. vitaalpendrecht.nl/pendrechtnieuws2007-2/publish/news_2269.html, (accessed 14 May 2011).

45 College van Burgemeester en Wethouders, 'Het nieuwe elan van Rotterdam…en zo gaan we dat doen: Collegeprogramma 2002-2006' (Rotterdam: Gemeente Rotterdam, 2002).

46 WRR (Scientific Council for Government Policy), *Vertrouwen in de buurt*, 11; see also SCP, *Zekere banden: Sociale cohesie, veiligheid en leefbaarheid* (The Hague: SCP, 2002).

47 WRR (Scientific Council for Government Policy), *Vertrouwen in de buurt*, 11.

48 See among others: Anderiesen and Martens, 'Continuïteit en verandering'; A. Ouwehand, 'Wonen in de wijken van de vooruitgang: Bewoners als dragers van de identiteit van de tuinsteden', in K. Hage and K. Zweerink (eds), *Van Pendrecht tot Ommoord: Geschiedenis en toekomst van de naoorlogse wijken in Rotterdam* (Bussum: Thoth, 2005), 26-33; Reijndorp and Van der Ven, *Een reuze vooruitgang*; F.

Hendriks and T. van de Wijdeven, 'Real-Life Expressions of Vital Citizenship: Present-day Community Participation in Dutch City Neighbourhoods', paper presented at the Vital City Conference (Glasgow 2007); Gemeente Rotterdam, 'Rotterdam Zuid Zuidelijke Tuindsteden Wijkactieplan'; Van den Brink et al. (ed.), *Prachtwijken?!*.

49   Pendrecht is not included as an example in *Stadswijk*, but there are clear parallels with the developments that Reijndorp describes in his book.

50   A. Reijndorp, *Stadswijk: Stedenbouw en dagelijks leven* (Rotterdam: NAi Uitgevers, 2004), 146.

51   Van der Ree, 'Een deel van je leven', 48; see also Talja Blokland on a similar process in Hillesluis: T. Blokland, *Goeie buren houden zich op d'r eigen: Buurt, gemeenschap en sociale relaties in de stad* (The Hague: Dr. Gradus Hendriks Stichting, 2005).

52   Van der Ree, 'Een deel van je leven', 48.

53   Van der Ree, 'Van boerenzij naar stadswijk', 115.

54   E. Vogelaar, *Actieplan krachtwijken: Van aandachtswijk naar krachtwijk*, Ministerie van Wonen, Wijken en Integratie (Den Haag 2007), 8.

55   WRR (Scientific Council for Government Policy), *Vertrouwen in de buurt*, 11.

56   J. Uitermark and J.W. Duyvendak, *Sociale integratie: … Straataanpak in de praktijk: Ruimte maken voor straatburgerschap* (Essay Mensen Maken de Stad), (Rotterdam: Gemeente Rotterdam, 2006), 23.

57   See among others Lupi, *Buurtbinding*; S. Musterd and R. van Kampen (eds), *De stadsbuurt: Ontwikkeling en betekenis* (Assen: Van Gorcum 2007); F. Pinkster, 'Je bent wie je kent?: Buurtgebonden sociale contacten, socialisering en sociale moiliteit in een Haagse achterstandswijk', in: S. Musterd and R. Van Kampen (eds), *De stadsbuurt: Ontwikkeling en betekenis*, (Assen: Van Gorcum 2007).

58   See for example, Musterd en Kampen (eds), *De stadsbuurt: ontwikkeling en betekenis*; S. Musterd, 'Ruimtelijk Beleid bevordert maatschappelijke integratie niet', *Geografie* 9 (2000) no. 4, 12-13; S. Musterd, W. Ostendorf and S. de Vos 'Neighborhood Effects and Social Mobility: A Longitudinal Analysis', *Housing Studies* 18 (2003) no. 6, 877-892; W. Ostendorf, S. Musterd and S. de Vos, 'Social Mix and the Neighourhood Effect: Policy Ambitions and Empirical Evidence', *Housing Studies* 16 (2001) no. 3, 371-380.

59   A. Reijndorp and E. Mik, *Stad in conflict* (Groningen: Platform Gras, 2005), 21.

Chapter 2

1   J. Epstein, 'New York: The Prophet', *The New York Review of Books*, 56, no. 13 (13 August 2009).

2   J. Jacobs, 'Downtown is for People', *Fortune* 57 (1958) no. 4, cited in ibid.

3   See for example Lofland, *The Public Realm* and Lennard and Lennard, *Public Life in Urban Places*.

4   For similar observations in Brooklyn see: Blum, 'Local Cities, Global Problems'.

5   Jacobs, *The Death and Life of Great American Cities*, 67.

6   Her vision fits in with a wider movement of ideas about urbanism, in which the city is considered as a grid that is intended to maximize opportunities for meetings. See for example C. Alexander, 'A City is not a Tree', *Architectural Forum* 122 (1965) no. 1, 58-61; L. Martin, 'The Grid as a Generator', in L. March and L. Martin (eds), *Urban Space and Structures* (Cambridge: Cambridge University Press, 1972), 6-27. See also: K. Christiaanse, 'Een smeulend vuur dat oplicht in de duisternis', in: S. Franke and G.-J. Hospers (eds), *De levende stad: Over de hedendaagse betekenis van Jane Jacobs* (Amsterdam: SUN//Trancity, 2009), 21-30.

7   Jacobs, *The Death and Life of Great American Cities*, 49.

8   Ibid., 73, 75-76.

9   Ibid., 388; see also 73.

10   See for example Blokland, *Goeie buren houden zich op d'r eigen*; T. Blokland, *Het sociaal weefsel van de stad: Cohesie, netwerken en korte contacten* (The Hague: Dr. Gradus Hendriks Stichting, 2006): T. Blokland, 'Van ogen op straat naar oog voor elkaar; Jacobs these en sociale veiligheid', in S. Franke and G.-J. Hospers (eds), *De levende stad: Over de hedendaagse betekenis van Jane Jacobs* (Amsterdam: SUN/Trancity, 2009), 95-106; T. Blokland and D. Ray, 'The End of Urbanism: How the Changing Spatial Structure of Cities Affected its Social Capital Potentials', in: T. Blokland and M. Savage (eds), *Networked Urbanism: Social Capital in the City* (Burlington: Ashgate, 2008), 23-40; T. Blokland and M Savage, 'Social Capital and Networked Urbanism', in: T Blokland and M. Savage (eds), *Networked Urbanism: Social Capital in the City* (Burlington: Ashgate, 2008), 1-22..

11   R. Jenkins, *Social Identity* (London: Routledge, 1996), cited in Blokland, *Goeie buren houden zich op d'r eigen*, 67.

12   See also: A. Reijndorp, I. Nio and W. Veldhuis, *Atlas Westelijke Tuinsteden Amsterdam: De geplande en de geleefde stad* (Haarlem/The Hague: Trancity, 2008).

13   See also M. Castells, *The Power of Identity* (Oxford: Blackwell, 1997), 60; Blokland, *Goeie buren houden zich op d'r eigen*, 17.

14   Blokland, *Goeie buren houden zich op d'r eigen*, 109-110.

15   K. Lynch, *The Image of the City* (Cambridge, MA: MIT Press, 1960), 6. See also: H. Gans, 'The Potential Environment and the Effective Environment' (1968), in: H. Gans (ed.), *People, Plans and Politics: Essays on Poverty, Racism and Other National Urban Problems* (New York: Columbia University Press, 1994), 24-32, 27. See also: Reijndorp, Nio and Veldhuis, *Atlas Westelijke Tuinsteden Amsterdam*.

16   For more on 'sense of place' see also: T. Cresswell, *Place: A Short Introduction* (Malden, MA: Blackwell, 2004), cited in T. Lindgren, *Place Blogging: Local Economies of Attention in the Network* (Boston College, 2009), 28.

17   E. Gordon, 'Towards a Theory of Networked Locality', *First Monday* 13, no. 10 (2008), 6 October 2008, http://firstmonday.org/htbin/cgiwrap/bin/ojs/index.php/fm/article/viewArticle/2157/2035 (accessed 2 March 2012.

18   See also the Chicago School sociologists. See H. Zorbaugh, 'The Natural Areas of the City', in: E. Burgess (ed.), *The Urban*

Community (1926), cited in J. Lin and C. Mele (eds), *The Urban Sociology Reader* (London: Routledge, 2005).

19 Lofland, *A World of Strangers*, 122.

20 Ibid., 135.

21 Ibid., 67.

22 Ibid., 74.

23 See also: Engelsdorp Gastelaars, *Veertig jaar territoriale binding*, 25; A. Buys and J. van der Schaar, 'De woonplaats als gemeenplaats', in: J.W. Duyvendak and M. Hurenkamp (eds), *Kiezen voor de Kudde: Lichte gemeenschappen en de nieuwe meerderheid* (Amsterdam: Van Gennep, 2004), 116-131.

24 Lupi, *Buurtbinding*, 101;see also: R.P. Hortelanus, *Stadsbuurten: Een studie over bewoners en beheerders in buurten met uiteenlopende reputaties* (The Hague: Vuga, 1995); E. de Wijs-Mulkens, *Wonen op stand: Lifestyles en landschappen van de culturele en economische elite* (Amsterdam: Het Spinhuis, 1999).

25 Although this relationship varies from case to case; residents respect each other's privacy but do 'want to know who their nearest neighbour is and preferably have something in common with them', Lupi, *Buurtbinding*, 102.

26 See for example, M. van der Land, *Vluchtige verbondenheid: Stedelijke bindingen van de Rotterdamse nieuwe middenklasse* (Amsterdam: Amsterdam University Press, 2004).

27 Blokland, *Goeie buren houden zich op d'r eigen*, 204.

28 F. Grünfeld, *Habitat and Habitation: A Pilot Study* (Alphen a/d Rijn: Samson, 1970).

29 Wijs-Mulkens, *Wonen op stand*; Buys and Van der Schaar, 'De woonplaats also gemeenplaats'.

30 See also: A. Reijndorp and S. Lohof, *Privé-terrein: Privaat beheerde woondomeinen in Nederland* (Rotterdam: NAi Uitgevers, 2006); E. McKenzie, *Privatopia* (New Haven: Yale University Press, 1996); N. Ellin (ed.), *Architecture of Fear* (New York: Princeton Architectural Press, 1997).

31 Reijndorp, *Stadswijk*, 187; see also: A. Reijndorp et al., *Buitenwijk: Stedelijkheid op afstand* (Rotterdam: NAi Uitgevers, 1998).

32 Ray and Blokland's term 'network urbanism' is comparable. Blokland and Ray, 'The End of Urbanism', 36.

33 Reijndorp, *Stadswijk*; Lupi, *Buurtbinding, 119*.

34 B. Wellman et al., 'The Social Affordances of the Internet for Networked Individualism', *Journal of Computer-Mediated Communication* 8 (2003) no. 3, doi:10.1111/j.1083-6101.2003.tb00216.x.

35 J.W. Duyvendak and M. Hurenkamp, (eds), *Kiezen voor de kudde: Lichte gemeenschappen en de nieuwe meerderheid* (Amsterdam: Van Gennep, 2004), 16.

36 Blokland and Ray, 'The End of Urbanism'.

Chapter 3

1 W.J. Mitchell, *Me++: The Cyborg Self and the Networked City* (Cambridge, MA: MIT Press, 2003), 112.

2 L. Shirvanee, 'Locative Viscosity: Traces of Social Histories in Public

Space', *Leonardo Electronic Almanac* 14 (2006) no. 3, http://
leoalmanac.org/journal/vol_14/lea_v14_n03-04/toc.asp.

3   K. Hampton and B. Wellman, 'Neighboring in Netville: How the
    Internet Supports Community and Social Capital in a Wired Suburb',
    City & Community 2 (2003) no. 3, 277-311.

4   See for example also: G.S. Mesch and Y. Levanon, 'Community
    Networking and Locally Based Social Ties in Two Suburban
    Locations', *City & Community* 2 (2003) no. 5.

5   We find similar conclusions in ibid.

6   Ibid..; K. Hampton and B. Wellman, 'Neighboring in Netville: How
    the Internet Supports Community and Social Capital in a Wired
    Suburb'.

7   http://pendrecht.hyves.nl/address/ (accessed 22 June 2011).

8   http://pendrecht.hyves.nl/forum/2122412/jOaU/snackbar_De_
    Paddestoel/ (accessed 22 June 2011).

9   http://pendrecht.hyves.nl/forum/4970290/BZNf/oud_bewoner_van_
    Pendrecht/ (accessed 22 June 2011).

10 http://pendrecht.hyves.nl/forum/4477112/B-Nd/Geweldig/ (accessed
    22 June 2011).

11 Goffman, *The Presentation of Self in Everyday Life*. New York: The
    Overlook Press, 1959.

12 Boyd, 'Taken Out of Context', 108.

13 http://naturalact.hyves.nl/profile/?ga_campaign=profileDetails_
    ProfileBox (accessed 22 June 2011).

14 E. Gordon and A. De Souza e Silva, *Net Locality: Why Location
    Matters in a Networked World* (Malden, MA: Wiley-Blackwell, 2011).

15 A similar concept can be found in C. Aguiton, D. Cardon and Z.
    Smoreda, 'Living Maps: New Data, New Uses, New Problems', lecture
    for Engaging Data conference (Cambridge, MA: SENSEable City
    Lab, 12-13 October 2009), http://senseable.mit.ed/engagingdata/
    papers/ED_SI_Living_Maps.pdf.

16 'Useful Place' is the term used by the TomTom navigation system to
    indicate locations such as petrol stations, museums, parking facilities
    and restaurants.

17 C. van 't Hof, F. Daemen and R. van Est, *Check in / Check uit: De
    digitalisering van de openbare ruimte* (Rotterdam: NAi Uitgevers,
    2010), 213.

18 Gordon, 'Towards a Theory of Networked Locality'.

19 Ito, Okabe and Matsuda, *Personal, Portable, Pedestrian*, 15.

20 D. Okabe en M. Ito, 'Technosocial Situations: Emergent Structuring
    of Mobile E-mail Use', in: M. Ito, D. Okabe en M. Matsuda (red.),
    Personal, Portable, Pedestrian: Mobile Phones in Japanese Life
    (Cambridge, MA: MIT Press, 2006) 257-273. 271.

21 D. Okabe and M. Ito, 'Technosocial Situations: Emergent Structuring
    of Mobile E-mail Use', in: M. Ito, D. Okabe and M. Matsuda (eds)
    Personal, Portable, Pedestrian: Mobile Phones in Japanese Life
    (Cambridge, MA: MIT Press, 2006), 257-273, 264.

22 M. Matsuda, 'Mobile Communication and Selective Sociality', 133; we
    also come across this phenomenon in the work of other researchers.
    For example, Licoppe refers to 'Connected Presence'. C. Licoppe,
    '"Connected" Presence: The Emergence of a New Repertoire for
    Managing Social Relationships in a Changing Communication

Technoscape', *Environment and Planning D: Society and Space* 22 (2004), 135-156.

23   Matsuda, 'Mobile Communication and Selective Sociality'.

24   R. Ling, *New Tech New Ties* (Cambridge, MA: MIT Press, 2009), 160.

25   See also: Gordon and De Souza e Silva, *Net Locality*.

26   http://grindr.com/Grindr_iPhone_App/What_is_Grindr.html (accessed 5 March 2011).

27   A. Townsend, 'Life in the Real-time City: Mobile Telephones and Urban Metabolism', *Journal of Urban Technology* 7 (2000) no. 2, 85-104, 101.

28   Funda.nl, page with house for sale in Tholenstraat, (accessed 22 October 2007). When accessed on 31 May 2010, the lifestyle profiles seemed to have been made more austere.

29   www.dimo.nl (accessed 22 October 2007). On 31 May 2010 it was apparently no longer possible for private individuals to access such profile description on the basis of postcodes.

30   See also: S. Baker, *The Numerati* (New York: Houghton Mifflin, 2008) and Dowd, *Applebee's America. New York: Simon & Schuster, 2006.*

31   R. Burrows and N. Gane, 'Geodemographics, Software and Class', *Sociology* 40 (2006) no. 5, 793-812, 804.

32   Hall, *Cities of Tomorrow*, 13-48.

33   http://citysense.com/citysense/php (accessed 22 June 2011).

34   http://citysense.com/citysense.php (accessed 22 June 2011).

35   Aguiton, Cardon and Smoreda, 'Living Maps'.

36   Including Microsoft, IBM and Google.

37   Baker, *The Numerati*, 13; similar themes are also found in D. Conley, *Elsewhere, U.S.A.: How We Got from the Company Man, Family Dinners, and the Affluent Society to the Home Office, BlackBerry Moms, and Economic Anxiety* (New York: Pantheon, 2009).

38   Conley, *Elsewhere, U.S.A.*

39   http://arch-os.com/

40   P. Thomas, 'The Chemist as Flâneur in Intelligent Architecture' (paper presented at the International Symposium of Electronic Arts, Singapore, 2008), 499.

41   See: http://www.d-toren.nl/site/

42   K. Oosterhuis, *Architecture Goes Wild* (Rotterdam: NAi Uitgevers, 2002).

Chapter 4

1   J. Seijdel, 'Redactioneel', *Open* 11 (2006), 4.

2   M. Schuilenberg and A. de Jong, *Mediapolis* (Rotterdam: Uitgeverij 010, 2006), 61.

3   See http://www.situatedtechnologies.net/?q=node/75.

4   M. Shepard and A. Greenfield, *Situated Technologies Pamphlet 1: Urban Computing and its Discontents*, in: M. Shepard, O. Khan and T. Scholz (eds), *Situated Technologies Pamphlets* (New York: The Architectural League of New York, 2007), 40.

5   H. Frei and M. Böhlen, *MicroPublicPlaces* (Situated Technologies Pamphlet 6), O. Khan, T. Scholz and M. Shepard (eds) (New York: The Architectural League of New York, 2010), 14.

6   See Matthew Green, London Cafes: the Surprising History of London's Lost Coffeehouses', *The Telegraph* 20 March 2012.

7   See for example R. Boomkens, 'De continuïteit van de plek: Van de maakbare naar de mondiale stad', *Open* 15 (2008), 6-17.

8   The original German version, *Strukturwandel der Öffentlichheit*, appeared in 1962 and was not translated into English until 1991.

9   J. Habermas, 'The Public Sphere: An Encyclopedia Article' (1964), in: M.G. Durham and D.M. Kellner (eds), *Media and Cultural Studies* (Malden, MA: Blackwell 2001), 102-108; J. Habermas, *The Structural Transformation of the Public Sphere: An Inquiry into a Category of Bourgeois Society* (Cambridge, MA: MIT Press, 1991).

10 M.P. d'Entrèves, 'Hannah Arendt', http://plato.stanford.edu/archives/fall2008/entries/arendt/.

11 Habermas, *The Structural Transformation of the Public Sphere*, 37.

12 McQuire, S., *The Media City: Media Architecture and Urban Space*, Thousand Oaks: Sage, 2008, 35.

13 Boomkens, 'De continuïteit van de plek', 64; see also: Giedion, *Space, Time and Architecture*, 739 ff.

14 C. Calhoun, 'Introduction: Habermas and the Public Sphere', in: C. Calhoun (ed.), *Habermas and the Public Sphere* (Cambridge, MA: MIT Press, 1992), 1-50.

15 R. Sennett, *The Fall of Public Man* (New York: Knopff, 1977), 213.

16 Ibid., 27.

17 R. Sennett, 'A Flexible City of Strangers', *Le Monde Diplomatique*, February 2001, http://mondediplo.com/2001/02/16cities (accessed 2 March 2012).

18 Sennett, R., *The Fall of Public Man*, New York: Knopff, 1977, 296.

19 Sennett, *The Uses of Disorder*, 296.

20 Sennett, *The Fall of Public Man*, 340.

21 Criticism of Habermas's ideal of the public sphere can be found in, for example, N. Fraser, 'Rethinking the Public Sphere: A Contribution to the Critique of Actually Existing Democracy', in: C. Calhoun (ed.), *Habermas and the Public Sphere* (Cambridge, MA: MIT Press, 1992), 56-80.

22 Fraser, 'Rethinking the Public Sphere', 125-126.

23 A. Vidler, 'The Scenes of the Street: Transformations in Ideal and Reality 1750-1871', in: S. Anderson (ed.), *On Streets* (Cambridge MA: MIT Press, 1978); McQuire, *The Media City*, 52.

24 McQuire, *The Media City*.

25 A. Fierro, *The Glass State: The Technology of the Spectacle, Paris, 1981-1998* (Cambridge, MA: MIT Press, 2003), 24, cited in McQuire, *The Media City*, 133.

26 R. Boomkens, *Een drempelwereld: Moderne ervaring en stedelijke openbaarheid* (Rotterdam: NAi Uitgevers, 1998).

27 Hall, *Cities of Tomorrow*, 13-87.

28 Boomkens, *Een drempelwereld*, 67.

29 Berman, *All That is Solid Melts into Air*, 154.

30 Ibid.; see also: Boomkens, *Een drempelwereld* and McQuire, *The Media City*.

31 Berman, *All That is Solid Melts into Air*, 164.

32 Ibid., 229.

33 Ibid., 232.

34 S. Kracauer, *Orpheus in Paris: Offenbach and the Paris of His Time* (New York: Vienna House, 1972), cited in McQuire, *The Media City*, 40.

35   McQuire, *The Media City*, 67.
36   Boomkens, *Een drempelwereld*, 56.
37   Ibid., 111.
38   Ibid., 101.
39   McQuire, *The Media City*, 69.
40   R. Boomkens, *De nieuwe wanorde: Globalisering en het einde van de maakbare samenleving* (Amsterdam: Van Gennep, 2006), 97.
41   Boomkens, *Een drempelwereld*, 277.
42   Cited in McQuire, *The Media City*, 94.
43   Constant, 'Unitary Urbanism', in: M. Wigley (ed.), *Constant's New Babylon: The Hyper-Architecture of Desire* (Rotterdam: Witte de With, 1960), cited in McQuire, *The Media City*, 93.
44   Constant, 'New Babylon – Ten Years On', lecture at Delft University of Technology, 23 May 1980, included in Wigley, *Constant's New Babylon: The Hyper-Architecture of Desire*, 232-236, 234.
45   Ibid., 232.
46   Constant, cited in McQuire, *The Media City*, 95.
47   See also: ibid., 94.
48   Constant, 'Unitary Urbanism', cited in McQuire, *The Media City*, 94.
49   G. Debord, 'Report on the Construction of Situations and on the International Situationist Tendency's Conditions of Organization and Action' (1957), http://www.cddc.vt.edu/sionline///si/report.html (accessed 3 February 2012).
50   Ibid.
51   McQuire, *The Media City*, 96.
52   G. van Oenen, 'Babylonische maakbaarheid', *Open* 15 (2008); Constant 'New Babylon –Ten Years On'.
53   Van Oenen, 'Babylonische maakbaarheid', 52.
54   The first edition appeared in 1961, the last in 1970.
55   See also: S. Sadler, *Archigram: Architecture without Architecture* 9Cambridge, MA: MIT Press, 2005).
56   Peter Cook, cited in ibid., 55.
57   Ibid., 55.
58   P. Cook (ed.), *Archigram* (New York: Princeton Architectural Press, 1999), 39.
59   Ibid., 39.
60   Sadler, *Archigram*, 123.
61   See for example, N. Wiener, *The Human Use of Human Beings: Cybernetics and Society* (London: Sphere Books, 1968) and N. Wiener, *Cybernetics or Control and Communication in the Animal and the Machine*, second edition, (Cambridge, MA: MIT Press, 1965).
62   Sadler, *Archigram*, 93.
63   Ibid., 73.
64   Ibid., 61.
65   Ibid., 69.
66   McQuire, *The Media City*, 104.

Chapter 5

1   B. Hulsman, 'Verleid door het vliegtuigperspectief', *NRC Handels-blad* (Cultureel Supplement) 7 March 1997.
2   H. Moscoviter, 'Leve de controverses over het Schouwburgplein',

Rotterdams Dagblad 24 June 1997.

3   M. Kloos, 'Het Rotterdamse Schouwburgplein: Voorbeeld van een uitdaging', H. Hertzberger (ed.) (1977) (project documents Hertzberger practice).

4   H. Moscoviter, *Een podium tussen de hoogbouw: Een halve eeuw hunkeren naar een intiem Schouwburgplein* (Rotterdam: City Informatiecentrum, 1977), 41.

5   Ibid., 21-25.

6   H. Ovink, E. Wieringa and M. Dings, *Ontwerp en politiek* (Rotterdam: Uitgeverij 010, 2009).

7   In: Kloos, 'Het Rotterdamse Schouwburgplein'.

8   See also: H. Mommaas, 'Tussen verwording en wederopstanding: Het postmoderne plein', in R.V. Maarschalkerwaart and H. Mommaas (eds), *Het Pleinenboek* (Utrecht: Hogeschool voor de Kunsten, 2003).

9   Moscoviter, *Een podium tussen de hoogbouw*, 27.

10 R. Wentholt, *De binnenstadsbeleving van Rotterdam* (Rotterdam: Ad Donker, 1968), 133.

11 Rotterdamse Kunststichting, 'Rapport Schouwburgplein'.

12 'Schouwburgplein en Weena Oost' (Rotterdam: Stadsontwikkeling Rotterdam, 1982).

13 I. van Aalst and E. Ennen, *Openbare ruimten: Tussen activiteit en attractiviteit* (Utrecht: DGVH/NETHUR, 2002).

14 R. Florida, *The Rise of the Creative Class: And How It's Transforming Work, Leisure, Community and Everyday Life* (New York: Basic Books, 2002).

15 D. Mitchell, 'The End of Public Space? People's Park, Definitions of the Public and Democracy', *Annals of the Association of American Geographers* 851 (1995) no. 1, 115.

16 DROS, 'Schouwburgplein: van tochtgat tot uitgaanscentrum' (Rotterdam: Dienstenstructuur Ruimtelijke Ordening en Stadsvernieuwing, 1984).

17 Van Aalst and Ennen, *Openbare Ruimten*, 20.

18 J. Goossens, A. Guinée and W. Oosterhoff (eds), *Buitenruimte: Ontwerp, aanleg en beheer van de openbare ruimte in Rotterdam* (Rotterdam: Uitgeverij 010, 1995), 12.

19 Ibid., 13-14.

20 Moscoviter, *Een podium tussen de hoogbouw*, 59.

21 Goossens, Guinée and Oosterhoff (eds), *Buitenruimte*, 80; Aalst and Ennen, *Openbare ruimten*, 12.

22 Goossens, Guinée and Oosterhoff (eds), *Buitenruimte*, 80.

23 Gemeente Rotterdam *Actieplan Attractieve Stad* (Rotterdam: OBR, 1998), cited in: Van Aalst and Ennen, *Openbare ruimten*, 20.

24 H. Moscoviter, A. Geuze and P. van Beek, 'Het genot van leegte', *Grafisch Nederland*, Christmas edition 1992, 35.

25 Ibid., 42.

26 Ibid., 47.

27 See A. Geuze, 'Accelerating Darwin', in T. Avermaete, K. Havik and H. Teerds (eds), *Architectural Positions: Architecture, Modernity and the Public Sphere* (Amsterdam: SUN, 2009), 108.

28 Adriaan Geuze, lecture during 'Doors of Perception 3', Amsterdam 1995, http://museum.doorsofperception.com/doors3/transcripts/Geuze.html.

29   Ibid.
30   Geuze, 'Accelerating Darwin', 108.
31   Boomkens, *De nieuwe wandorde*, 166.
32   A. Wortmann, 'Tweesporenbeleid op het Rotterdamse
      Schouwburgplein', *Archis* 1993, no. 4, 70-76.
33   B. Hulsman, 'Herzien', *NRC Handelsblad* 17 October 2000.
34   Engelsdorp Gastelaars and Hamers, *De nieuwe stad*; M. Hajer and A.
      Reijndorp, *Op zoek naar nieuw publiek domein* (Rotterdam: NAi
      Uitgevers, 2001).
35   M. Auge, *Non-places: Introduction to an Anthropology of
      Supermodernity* (London: Verso, 1995).
36   M. Sorkin (ed.), *Variations on a Theme Park: The New American City
      and the End of Public Space* (New York: Hill and Wang, 1992).
37   L. De Cauter, *De capsulaire beschaving: Over de stad in het tijdperk
      van de angst* (Rotterdam: NAi Uitgevers, 2004), 29.
38   The idea of 'urban tribes' is borrowed from M. de Sola-Morales,
      'Openbare en collectieve ruimte: De verstedelijking van het prive
      domein als nieuwe uitdaging', *Oase* 33 (1992), 3-8.
39   Hajer and Reijndorp, *Op zoek naar nieuw publiek domain*, 57.
40   Ibid., 84.
41   Hajer and Reijndorp, *Op zoek naar nieuw publiek domein*, 13.
42   Ibid., 88.

Chapter 6

1   Skype interview with Greg Lindsay, 30 November 2012.
2   http://speedbird.wordpress.com/2011/11/13/wired-change-
      accelerator-posts-in-convenient-single-dose-form/
3   R. Sennett, 'No One Likes a City That's Too Smart', *The Guardian* 4
      December 2012.
4   Telephone interview with Wim Elfrink, Executive Vice President,
      Industry Solutions & Chief Globalization Officer Cisco, 18 December
      2012.
5   Interview with Munish Khetrapal, Managing Director Cisco via
      TelePresence, 14 December 2012.
6   D. Hill, 'The Street as Platform', *City of Sound* (2008), weblog.
7   Ibid.
8   A. Pentland, 'Reality Mining of Mobile Communications: Toward a
      New Deal on Data', in: S. Dutta and I. Mia (eds), *The Global
      Information Technology Report 2008-2009: Mobility in a Networked
      World* (Geneva: World Economic Forum/INSEAD, 2009), 75-80, 79.
9   S. Graham and S. Marvin, *Splintering Urbanism: Networked
      Infrastructures, Technological Mobilities and the Urban Condition*
      (London/New York: Routledge, 2001), 8.
10   Ibid., 115.
11   S. Graham, 'Software-Sorted Geographies', *Progress in Human
      Geography* 29 (2005), no. 5.
12   Baker, *The Numerati*.
13   S. Graham, 'Software-Sorted Geographies'.
14   N. Thrift and S. French, 'The Automatic Production of Space',
      Transactions of the Institute of British Geographers 27 (2002) no. 3,
      309-335, 331.

15 S. Graham and M. Crang, 'Sentient Cities: Ambient Intelligence and the Politics of Urban Space', *Information, Communication & Society* 10 (2007) no. 6, 814.

16 See http://senseable.mit.edu.wikicity/rome/ for a detailed project description, including technical details.

17 http://www.rotterdamopendata.org/

18 F. Calabrese, K. Kloeckl and C. Ratti, 'WikiCity: Real-Time Location-Sensitive Tools for the City', in M. Foth (ed.), *Handbook of Research on Urban Informatics: The Practice and Promise of the Real-Time City* (Hershey/New York/London: Information Science Reference, 2008).

19 Lynch, *The Image of the City*, 109-110.

20 Galloway, 'A Brief History of the Future of Urban Computing'.

21 http://www.intheair.es/

22 B. Latour, 'From Realpolitik to Dingpolitik: An Introduction', in: B. Latour and P. Weibel (eds), *Making Things Public: Atmospheres of Democracy* (Cambridge MA: MIT Press, 2005); N. Marres, 'Zonder kwesties geen publiek', *Krisis* 2 (2006).

23 Frei and Böhlen, *MicroPublicPlaces*; B. Bratton and N. Jeremijkenko, 'Suspicious Images, Latent Interfaces', in: *Situated Advocacy* (Situated Technologies Pamphlets 3), O. Khan, T. Scholz and M. Shepard (eds), (New York: The Architectural League of New York, 2008), 1-52.

24 Frei and Böhlen, *MicroPublicPlaces*.

25 Bratton and Jeremijenko, 'Suspicious Images, Latent Interfaces', 8.

26 Ibid., 16.

27 L. Bounegru, 'Interactive Media Artworks for Public Space: The Potential of Art to Influence Consciousness and Behaviour in Relation to Public Spaces', in: S. McQuire, M. Martin and S. Niederer (eds), *Urban Screens Reader* (Amsterdam: Institute of Network Cultures, 2009), 199-216.

28 http://www.pillowfightday.com/about (accessed 27 October 2010).

29 A. Mubi Brighenti and C. Mattiucci, 'Editing Urban Environments: Territories, Prolongations, Visibilities', in: F. Eckardt (ed.), *Media City: Situations, Practices and Encounters* (Berlin: Frank & Timme, 2008), 98; J. Nicholson, 'Flash! Mobs in the Age of Mobile Connectivity', *Fibreculture Journal* 6 (2005), http://six.fibreculturejournal.org/fcj-030-flash-mobs-in-the-age-of-mobile-connectivity/.

30 http://www.pillowfightday.com/about (accessed 27 October 2010).

31 http://www.pillowfightrotterdam.hyves.nl/ (accessed 27 October 2010).

32 H. Rheingold, *Smart Mobs: The Next Social Revolution* (Cambridge, MA: Perseus Publishing, 2002), xii.

33 Those charged with maintaining law and order are also concerned about this: see Nicholson, 'Flash! Mobs in the Age of Mobile Connectivity'.

34 Rheingold, *Smart Mobs: The Next Social Revolution*, 158-160.

35 M. Castells et al., *Mobile Communication and Society: A Global Perspective* (Cambridge, MA: MIT Press, 2007), 188.

36 Ibid., 189.

37 Ibid., 188.

38   Ibid., 191.
39   V. Rafael, 'The Cell Phone and the Crowd: Messianic Politics in the
      Contemporary Philippines', *Philippine Political Science Journal* 24
      (2003) no. 47, 3-36.
40   Ibid., 8.
41   Ibid., 15.
42   Ibid., 15-16.
43   Nicholson, 'Flash! Mobs in the Age of Mobile Connectivity'.
44   For critics who are less optimistic about the role of mobile media in
      self-organization, see: E. Kluitenberg, 'The Tactics of Camping',
      Tactical Media Files (2011); E. Morozov, *The Net Delusion: The Dark
      Side of Internet Freedom* (New York: Public Affairs, 2011).
45   For more on social dynamics and the mobilization of groups see: N.S.
      Glance and B. Huberman, 'The Dynamics of Social Dilemmas',
      Scientific American 270 (1994) no. 3, 76-81: Grannovetter, 'Threshold
      Models of Collective Behavior', *American Journal of Sociology* 83
      (1978) no, 6.
46   'Schaduwspel in Rotterdam', *Algemeen Dagblad* 3 September 2001.
47   M. McCullough, 'On Urban Markup: Frames of Reference in Location
      Models for Participatory Urbanism', *Leonardo Electronic Almanac* 14
      (2006) no. 3/4; S. McQuire, 'The Politics of Public Space in the Media
      City', *First Monday* 4 (2006), http://www.firstmonday.org/issues/
      special1 1_2/mcquire/index.html. For more on urban screens see: S.
      McQuire, M. Martin and S. Niederer (eds), *Urban Screens Reader*,
      vol. 5, INC Reader (Amsterdam: Institute of Network Cultures,
      2009).
48   M. Fernández, 'Illuminating Embodiment: Rafael Lozano-Hemmer's
      Relational Architectures', *Architectural Design* 77 (2007) no. 4, 78-87.
49   McQuire, 'The Politics of Public Space in the Media City'.
50   http://www.lozano-hemmer.com/body_movies.php
51   A. Adriaansens and J. Brouwer, 'Alien Relationships from Public
      Space', in: A. Mulder and J. Brouwer (eds), *Transurbanism*
      (Rotterdam: NAi Uitgevers, 2002), 138-159, 146.
52   Raymond Gastil and Zoë Ryan, *Open: New Designs for Public Space*
      (New York: Princeton Architectural Press, 2003), 97.
53   B. Massumi and R. Lozano-Hemmer, 'Urban Appointments: A
      Possible Rendezvous with the City', in: L. Manovich (ed.), *Making Art
      of Databases* (Rotterdam: V2_publishing, 2003), 29.
54   Ibid., 30.
55   McQuire, 'The Politics of Public Space in the Media City'.
56   N. Bourriaud, *Relational Aesthetics* (Paris: Les Presses du réel, 2002).
57   Adriaansens and Brouwer, 'Alien Relationships from Public Space',
      149.
58   Ibid.
59   Sennett, *The Fall of Public Man*, 213-215.
60   S. McQuire, 'Mobility, Cosmopolitanism and Public Space in the
      Media City', in: S. McQuire, M. Martin and S. Niederer (eds), *Urban
      Screens Reader* (Amsterdam: Institute of Network Cultures, 2009),
      59.
61   E. Paulos, 'Manifesto of Open Disruption and Participation', Paulos.
      net (2009) online.

Conclusion

1   Mayor of Rotterdam Pieter Oud in the foreword to *De stad der toekomst, de toekomst der stad: Een stedebouwkundige en sociaal-culturele studie over de groeiende stadsgemeenschap*, (Rotterdam: Voorhoeve, 1946), 5.

2   M. Chalmers and A. Galani, 'Seamful Interweaving: Heterogeneity in the Theory and Design of Interactive Systems', in *Proceedings of the 5th Conference on Designing Interactive Systems: Processes, Practices, Methods, and Techniques* (New York: ACM, 2004), 243-252.

3   P. Antonelli et al., *Design and the Elastic Mind* (New York: The Museum of Modern Art, 2008).

Bibliography

Aalst, I. van, and E. Ennen, *Openbare ruimten: Tussen activiteit en attractiviteit*, Utrecht: DGVH/NETHUR, 2002.

Adriaansens, A., and J. Brouwer, 'Alien Relationships from Public Space', in: A. Mulder en J. Brouwer (eds.), *Transurbanism*, Rotterdam: NAi Uitgevers, 2002, p. 138-159.

Aguiton, C., D. Cardon and Z. Smoreda, 'Living Maps: New Data, New Uses, New Problems', lezing voor conferentie 'Engaging Data', Cambridge, MA: SENSEable City Lab, 12-13 October 2009. http://senseable.mit.edu/engagingdata/papers/ED_SI_Living_Maps.pdf.

Alexander, C., 'A City is not a Tree', *Architectural Forum* 122 (1965) nr. 1, p. 58-62.

Anderiesen, G., and M. Martens, 'Continuïteit en verandering: Oude en nieuwe bewoners van de zuidelijke tuinsteden', in: A. Reijndorp and H. van der Ven (eds.), *Een reuze vooruitgang: Utopie en praktijk in de zuidelijke tuinsteden van Rotterdam*, Rotterdam: Uitgeverij 010, 1994.

Anderson, B., *Imagined Communities: Reflections on the Origin and Spread of Nationalism*, New York: Verso, 1991.

Antonelli, P. et al., *Design and the Elastic Mind*, New York: The Museum of Modern Art, New York, 2008.

Arendt, H., *The Human Condition*, Chicago: University of Chicago Press, 1958.

Auge, M., *Non-places: Introduction to an Anthropology of Supermodernity*, London: Verso, 1995.

Bahrdt, H.P., *Die moderne Grossstadt: Soziologische Überlegungen zum Stadtbau*, Reinbeck bei Hamburg: Rowohlt, 1967.

Baker, S., *The Numerati*, New York: Houghton Mifflin, 2008.

Beck, U., *Cosmopolitan Vision*, Cambridge, UK: Polity Press, 2006.

Bell, G., and P. Dourish, 'Yesterday's Tomorrows: Notes on Ubiquitous Computing's Dominant Vision', *Personal and Ubiquitous Computing* 11 (2007) nr. 2, p. 133-143.

Berman, M., *All That is Solid Melts into Air: The Experience of Modernity*, New York: Verso, 1987.

Bijhouwer, R., 'Ruimtewerking en ritmiek: Een analyse van het stedenbouw-kundige oeuvre van Lotte Stam-Beese', in: H. Damen and A. Devolder (eds.), *Lotte Stam-Beese 1903–1988: Dessau, Brno, Charkow, Moskou, Amsterdam, Rotterdam*, Rotterdam: De Hef, 1993, p. 94-95.

Blijstra, R., *Rotterdam, stad in beweging*, Amsterdam: Arbeiderspers, 1965.

Blokland, T., *Goeie buren houden zich op d'r eigen*, The Hague: Dr. Gradus Hendriks-stichting, 2005.

Blokland, T., *Het sociaal weefsel van de stad: Cohesie, netwerken en korte contacten*, The Hague: Dr. Gradus Hendriks Stichting, 2006.

Blokland, T., 'Van ogen op straat naar oog voor elkaar: Jacobs these en sociale veiligheid', in: S. Franke and G.-J. Hospers (eds.), *De levende stad: Over de hedendaagse betekenis van Jane Jacobs*, Amsterdam: SUN/Trancity, 2009, p. 95-106.

Blokland, T., and D. Ray, 'The End of Urbanism: How the Changing Spatial Structure of Cities Affected its Social Capital Potentials', in: T. Blokland and M. Savage (eds.), *Networked Urbanism Social Capital in the City*, Burlington: Ashgate, 2008, p. 23-40.

Blokland, T., and M. Savage, 'Social Capital and Networked Urbanism', in:

T. Blokland en M. Savage (eds.), *Networked Urbanism Social Capital in the City*, Burlington: Ashgate, 2008, p. 1-22.

Blum, A., 'Local Cities, Global Problems: Jane Jacobs in an Age of Global Change', in: C. Klemek (ed.), *Block by Block: Jane Jacobs and the Future of New York*, New York: Princeton Architectural Press, 2007, p. 51-53.

Boomen, M. van den, 'De stad als interface', *De Helling* spring 1996, nr. 1 (1996), http://boom.home.xs4all.nl/artikel/stad.html, accessed: 28-2-2013.

Boomkens, R., 'De continuïteit van de plek: Van de maakbare naar de mondiale stad', *Open* (Maakbaarheid) 15 (2008), 6-17.

Boomkens, R., *De nieuwe wanorde: Globalisering en het einde van de maakbare samenleving*, Amsterdam: Van Gennep, 2006.

Boomkens, R., *Een drempelwereld: Moderne ervaring en stedelijke openbaarheid*, Rotterdam: NAi Uitgevers, 1998.

Bos, A., *De stad der toekomst, de toekomst der stad: Een stedebouwkundige en sociaal-culturele studie over de groeiende stadsgemeenschap*, Rotterdam: Voorhoeve, 1946.

Botsman, R., and R. Rogers, *What's Mine Is Yours: The Rise of Collaborative Consumption*, London: Collins, 2011.

Bounegru, L., 'Interactive Media Artworks for Public Space: The Potential of Art to Influence Consciousness and Behaviour in Relation to Public Spaces', in: S. McQuire, M. Martin and S. Niederer (eds.), *Urban Screens Reader*, Amsterdam: Institute of Network Cultures, 2009, p. 199-216.

Bourriaud, N., *Relational aesthetics*, Paris: Les Presses du réel, 2002.

Boyd, D., 'Taken Out of Context', thesis Berkeley: UC Berkeley, 2008.

Bratton, B., and N. Jeremijenko, 'Suspicious Images, Latent Interfaces', in: *Situated Advocacy* (Situated Technologies Pamphlets 3), eds. O. Khan, T. Scholz and M. Shepard, New York: The Architectural League of New York, 2008, p. 1-52.

Brink, G. van den, *Prachtwijken?! De mogelijkheden en beperkingen van Nederlandse probleemwijken*, Amsterdam: Bert Bakker, 2007.

Burrows, R., and N. Gane, 'Geodemographics, Software and Class', *Sociology* 40 (2006) nr. 5, p. 793-812.

Buys, A., and J. van der Schaar, 'De woonplaats als gemeenplaats', in: J.W. Duyvendak and M. Hurenkamp (eds.), *Kiezen voor de kudde: Lichte gemeenschappen en de nieuwe meerderheid*, Amsterdam: Van Gennep, 2004, p. 116-131.

Calabrese, F., K. Kloeckl and C. Ratti, 'WikiCity: Real-Time Location-Sensitive Tools for the City', in: M. Foth (eds.), *Handbook of Research on Urban Informatics: The Practice and Promise of the Real-Time City*, Hershey, New York/London: Information Science Reference, 2008, p. 390-413.

Calhoun, C., 'Introduction: Habermas and the Public Sphere', in: C. Calhoun (ed.), *Habermas and the Public Sphere*, Cambridge, MA: MIT Press, 1992, p. 1-50.

Castells, M., 'The Culture of Cities in the Information Age', in: I. Susser (ed.), *The Castells Reader on Cities and Social Theory*, Malden, MA: Blackwell Publishers, 2002, p. 367-389.

Castells, M., *The Power of Identity*, Oxford: Blackwell, 1997.

Castells, M. et al., *Mobile Communication and Society*, Cambridge, MA: MIT Press, 2007.

Cauter, L. De, *De capsulaire beschaving: Over de stad in het tijdperk van de angst*, Rotterdam: NAi Uitgevers, 2004.

Cauter, L. De, and M. Dehaene (eds.), *Heterotopia and the City: Public Space in a Postcivil Society*, New York: Routledge, 2008.

Christiaanse, K., 'Een smeulend vuur dat oplicht in de duisternis', in: S. Franke and G.-J. Hospers (eds.), *De levende stad: Over de hedendaagse betekenis van Jane Jacobs*, Amsterdam: SUN/Trancity, 2009, p. 21-30.

College van Burgemeester en Wethouders, 'Het nieuwe elan van Rotterdam… en zo gaan we dat doen; Collegeprogramma 2002–2006', Rotterdam: Gemeente Rotterdam, 2002.

Conley, D., *Elsewhere, U.S.A.: How We Got from the Company Man, Family Dinners, and the Affluent Society to the Home Office, BlackBerry Moms, and Economic Anxiety*, New York: Pantheon, 2009.

Constant [Nieuwenhuys], 'New Babylon – Ten Years On', lecture Faculty of Architecture, Technische Hogeschool Delft, 1980.

Cook, P. (ed.), *Archigram*, New York: Princeton Architectural Press, 1999.

Cresswell, T., *Place: A Short Introduction*, Malden, MA: Blackwell, 2004.

d'Entreves, M.P., 'Hannah Arendt', http://plato.stanford.edu/archives/fall2008/entries/arendt/.

Davis, M., *Planet of Slums*, London: Verso, 2006.

Debord, G., 'Report on the Construction of Situations and on the International Situationist Tendency's Conditions of Organization and Action' (1957) http://www.cddc.vt.edu/sionline///si/report.html.

Deterding, S. et al., 'Gamification: Toward a Definition', in: *Proceedings of the 2011 Annual Conference Extended Abstracts on Human Factors in Computing Systems*, New York: ACM, 2011.

Dienst Volkshuisvesting, 'Onderzoek in tuinstad zuidwijk (Rotterdam) naar het oordeel van de bewoners over de nieuwe wijk', 1954.

Doorn-Jansen, M.J. van, 'Groei en gestalte van een nieuwe stadswijk: Verslag van een sociologische verkenning in Rotterdam-Zuidwijk', Utrecht: Rijksuniversiteit Utrecht, 1965.

Dourish, P., *Where the Action Is: The Foundations of Embedded Interaction*, Cambridge, MA, 2004.

Dowd, M. et al., *Applebee's America*, New York: Simon & Schuster, 2006.

DROS, 'Schouwburgplein: Van tochtgat tot uitgaanscentrum', Rotterdam: Dienstenstructuur Ruimtelijke Ordening en Stadsvernieuwing, 1984.

Duyvendak, J.W., and M. Hurenkamp (eds.), *Kiezen voor de kudde: Lichte gemeenschappen en de nieuwe meerderheid*, Amsterdam: Van Gennep, 2004.

Duyvendak, J.W., en J. Uitermark, *Sociale integratie: Straataanpak in de praktijk Ruimte maken voor straatburgerschap* (Essay Mensen Maken de Stad), Rotterdam: Gemeente Rotterdam, 2006.

Eade, J., *Living the Global City*, New York: Routledge, 1996.

Eisner, D., 'Neogeography', http://www.platial.com.

Ellin, N. (ed.), *Architecture of Fear*, New York: Princeton Architectural Press, 1997.

Engelsdorp Gastelaars, R.E. van, *Veertig jaar territoriale binding*, Amsterdam: Vossiuspers UvA, 2003.

Engelsdorp Gastelaars, R.E. van, and D. Hamers, *De nieuwe stad: Stedelijke centra als brandpunten van interactie*, Rotterdam: NAi Uitgevers, 2006.

Epstein, J., 'New York: The Prophet', *New York Review of Books* 56, nr. 13, 13 August 2009.

Es, E. van, 'Plannen Pendrecht 1948–1965', in: G. van den Brink, *Prachtwijken?! De mogelijkheden en beperkingen van Nederlandse probleemwijken*, Amsterdam: Bert Bakker, 2007, p. 225-265.

Fernandez, M., 'Illuminating Embodiment: Rafael Lozano-Hemmer's Relational Architectures', *Architectural Design* 77 (2007) nr. 4, p. 78-87.

Fierro, A., *The Glass State: The Technology of the Spectacle, Paris, 1981–1998*, Cambridge, MA: MIT Press, 2003.

Flichy, P., 'The Construction of New Digital Media', *New Media and Society* 1 (1999) nr. 1, p. 33-39.

Florida, R., *The Rise of the Creative Class: And How It's Transforming Work, Leisure, Community and Everyday Life*, New York: Basic Books, 2002.

Foucault, M., 'Of Other Spaces', *JSTOR* 16 (1986) nr. 1, p. 22-27.

Fraser, N., 'Rethinking the Public Sphere: A Contribution to the Critique of Actually Existing Democracy', in: C. Calhoun (eds.), *Habermas and the Public Sphere*, Cambridge, MA: MIT Press, 1992, p. 56-80.

Frei, H., and M. Böhlen, *MicroPublicPlaces* (Situated Technologies Pamphlets 6), eds. O. Khan, T. Scholz en M. Shepard, New York: The Architectural League of New York, 2010.

Fujimoto, K., 'The Third-Stage Paradigm: Territory Machines from the Grils' Pager Revolution to Mobile Aesthetics', in: M. Ito, D. Okabe en M. Matsuda, *Personal, Portable, Pedestrian: Mobile Phones in Japanese Life*, Cambridge, MA: MIT Press, 2006, p. 77-102.

Galloway, A., 'A Brief History of the Future of Urban Computing', thesis Ottawa: Carleton University, 2008.

Galloway, A., *Protocol: How Control Exists after Decentralization*, Cambridge, MA: MIT Press, 2006.

Gans, H., 'The Potential Environment and the Effective Environment' (1968), in: H. Gans (ed.), *People, Plans and Politics: Essays on Poverty, Racism and Other National Urban Problems*, New York: Columbia University Press, 1994, p. 24-32.

Garreau, J., *Edge City: Life on the New Frontier*, Garden City: Anchor, 1992.

Gastil, R., and Z. Ryan, *Open: New Designs for Public Space*, New York: Princeton Architectural Press, 2004.

Gaver, B., T. Dunne en E. Pacenti, 'Design: Cultural Probes', *ACM Interactions*, January-February 1999, p. 21-29.

Gemeente Rotterdam, 'Rotterdam Zuid: Zuidelijke Tuinsteden Wijkactieplan', 2003.

Geuze, A., 'Accelerating Darwin', in: T. Avermaete, K. Havik and H. Teerds (eds.), *Architectural Positions: Architecture, Modernity and the Public Sphere*, Amsterdam: SUN, 2009, p. 101-108.

Geyl, W. F., and S. Bakema-Van Borssum Waalkes, *Wij en de wijkgedachte*, Utrecht: V. en S., 1948.

Giedion, S., *Space, Time and Architecture: The Growth of a New Tradition*, Cambridge, MA: Harvard University Press, 2008.

Glance, N.S., and B. Huberman, 'The Dynamics of Social Dilemmas', *Scientific American* 270 (1994) 3, p. 76-81.

Goffman, E., *The Presentation of Self in Everyday Life*, New York: The Overlook Press, 1959.

Goldberger, P., 'Disconnected Urbanism', *Metropolismag.com* November 2003.

Goosens, J., A. Guinée and W. Oosterhoff (eds.), *Buitenruimte: Ontwerp, aanleg en beheer van de openbare ruimte in Rotterdam*, Rotterdam: NAi Uitgevers, 1995.

Gordon, E., 'Towards a Theory of Networked Locality', *First Monday* 13 (2008) nr. 10, http://firstmonday.org/htbin/cgiwrap/bin/ojs/index.php/

fm/article/viewArticle/2157/2035.

Gordon, E., and A. De Souza e Silva, *Net Locality: Why Location Matters in a Networked World*, Malden, MA: Wiley-Blackwell, 2011.

Graham, S., 'Software-Sorted Geographies', *Progress in Human Geography* 29 (2005) nr. 5, p. 562-580.

Graham, S., and M. Crang, 'Sentient Cities: Ambient Intelligence and the Politics of Urban Space', *Information, Communication & Society* 10 (2007) nr. 6, p. 789-817.

Graham, S., and S. Marvin, *Splintering Urbanism: Networked Infrastructures, Technological Mobilities and the Urban Condition*, London/New York: Routledge, 2001.

Granovetter, M., 'Threshold Models of Collective Behavior', *American Journal of Sociology* 83 (1978) nr. 6, p. 1420-1443.

Grünfeld, F., *Habitat and Habitation: A Pilot Study*, Alphen a/d Rijn: Samson, 1970.

Grünfeld, F., and L. Weima, 'Wonen in de nieuwe wijk Pendrecht (Rotterdam)', Rotterdam: Wetenschappelijk Bureau Dienst van Volkshuisvesting Rotterdam, 1958.

Haaren, V., *Constant*, Amsterdam: Meulenhof, 1966.

Habermas, J., 'The Public Sphere: An Encyclopedia Article' (1964), in: M.G. Durham en D.M. Kellner (eds.), *Media and Cultural Studies*, Malden, MA: Blackwell 2001, p. 102-108.

Habermas, J., *The Structural Transformation of the Public Sphere: An Inquiry into a Category of Bourgeois Society*, Cambridge, MA: MIT Press, 1991.

Hajer, M., and A. Reijndorp, *Op zoek naar nieuw publiek domein*, Rotterdam: NAi Uitgevers, 2001.

Hall, P., *Cities of Tomorrow*, Oxford: Blackwell, 2002.

Hampton, K., and B. Wellman, 'Neighboring in Netville: How the Internet Supports Community and Social Capital in a Wired Suburb', *City & Community* 2 (2003) nr. 3, p. 277-311.

Hebly, A., 'Op het ritme van de Horsten: Een stedenbouwkundig plan voor een buurt in Zuidwijk', in: A. Reijndorp and H. van der Ven (eds.), *Een reuze vooruitgang: Utopie en praktijk in de zuidelijke tuinsteden van Rotterdam*, Rotterdam: Uitgeverij 010, 1994.

Hendriks, F., and T. van de Wijdeven, 'Real-life Expressions of Vital Citizenship: Present-day Community Participation in Dutch City Neigh-bourhoods', paper presented at the Vital City conference, Glasgow, 2007.

Hill, D., 'The Street as Platform', in: *City of Sound*, 2008, http://www.cityofsound.com/blog/2008/02/the-street-as-p.html.

Hof, C. van 't, F. Daemen and R. van Est, *Check in / Check uit: De digitalisering van de openbare ruimte*, Rotterdam: NAi Uitgevers, 2010.

Horst, H.M. van der, J. Kullberg and L. Deben, *Wat wijken maakt: De wording van functionele, sociale en expressieve kwaliteiten van Vreewijk, Zuidwijk en Omoord*, Utrecht: Nethur, 2002.

Hortelanus, R.P., *Stadsbuurten: Een studie over bewoners en beheerders in buurten met uiteenlopende reputatie*, The Hague: Vuga, 1995.

Hudson-Smith, A et al., *Virtual Cities: Digital Mirrors into a Recursive World* (Working Papers Series), London: UCL Centre for Advanced Spatial Analysis, 2007.

Idsinga, T., 'Het Nieuwe Bouwen in Rotterdam 1940–1960: Wat is stedelijk wonen in een open stad?', in: W. Beeren et al. (ed.), *Het Nieuwe Bouwen in Rotterdam 1920–1960*, Delft: Delft University Press, 1982, p. 108-138.

Ito, M., D. Okabe and M. Matsuda, *Personal, Portable, Pedestrian: Mobile Phones in Japanese Life*, Cambridge, MA: MIT Press, 2006.

Jacobs, J., *The Death and Life of Great American Cities*, London: Pimlico, 2000 (1961).

Jansen, B., 'De ideale woongemeenschap in naoorlogs Rotterdam', in: K. Hage and K. Zweerink (eds.), *Van Pendrecht tot Ommoord geschiedenis en toekomst van de naoorlogse wijken in Rotterdam*, Bussum: Thoth, 2005, p. 20-25.

Jenkins, R., *Social Identity*, London: Routledge, 1996.

Johnson, S., *Interface Culture*, San Francisco: HarperEdge, 1997.

Kloos, M., 'Het Rotterdamse Schouwburgplein: voorbeeld van een uitdaging', ed. A. Hertzberger, 1977.

Kluitenberg, E., 'The Network of Waves', *Open* (Hybride ruimte) 11 (2007), p. 6-16.

Kluitenberg, E., 'The Tactics of Camping', *Tactical Media Files*, 2011, http://blog.tacticalmediafiles.net/?p=106.

Kracauer, S., *Orpheus in Paris: Offenbach and the Paris of His Time*, New York: Vienna House, 1972.

Kranenburg, R. van, *The Internet of Things: A Critique of Ambient Technology and the All-seeing Network of RFID*, vol. 2, Network Notebooks Amsterdam: Institute of Network Cultures, 2007.

Land, M. van der, *Vluchtige verbondenheid: Stedelijke bindingen van de Rotterdamse nieuwe middenklasse*, Amsterdam: Amsterdam University Press, 2004.

Landa, M. De, *A New Philosophy of Society*, New York: Continuum International Publishing Group, 2006.

Lange, M. de, 'Moving Circles: Mobile Media and Playful Identities', thesis Rotterdam: Erasmus Universiteit Rotterdam, 2010.

Latour, B., 'From Realpolitik to Dingpolitik: An Introduction', in: B. Latour and P. Weibel (eds.), *Making Things Public: Atmospheres of Democracy*, Cambridge MA: MIT Press, 2005, p. 14-43.

Latour, B., en P. Weibel (eds.), *Making Things Public: Atmospheres of Democracy*, Cambridge MA: MIT Press, 2005.

Lennard, S., and H. Lennard, *Public Life in Urban Places*, Southampton, NY: Gondolier, 1984.

Licoppe, C., '"Connected" Presence: The Emergence of a New Repertoire for Managing Social Relationships in a Changing Communication Techno-scape', *Environment and Planning D: Society and Space* 22 (2004), p. 135-136.

Lin, J., and C. Mele (eds.), *The Urban Sociology Reader*, London: Routledge, 2005.

Lindgren, T., 'Place Blogging: Local Economies of Attention in the Network', Boston: Boston College, 2009.

Ling, R., *New Tech New Ties*, Cambridge, MA: MIT Press, 2009.

Livingstone, S., *Audiences and Publics: When Cultural Engagement Matters for the Public Sphere*, Portland, OR: Intellect, 2005.

Lofland, L., *The Public Realm: Exploring the City's Quintessential Social Territory*, New York: Aldine de Gruyter, 1998.

Lofland, L., *A World of Strangers: Order and Action in Urban Public Space*, New York: Basic Books, 1973.

Lupi, T., *Buurtbinding*, Amsterdam: Aksant, 2005.

Lynch, K., *The Image of the City*, Cambridge, MA: MIT Press, 1960.

Marres, N., 'Zonder kwesties geen publiek', *Krisis* 2006, nr. 2, p. 36-43.

Martin, L., 'The Grid as a Generator', in: L. March and L. Martin (eds.),
Urban space and Structures, Cambridge, MA: Cambridge University
Press, 1972, p. 6-27.

Massumi, B., and R. Lozano-Hemmer, 'Urban Appointment: A Possible
Rendez-vous with the City', in: L. Manovich (ed.), *Making Art of
Databases*, Rotterdam: V2_ publishing, 2003, p. 28-55.

Matsuda, M., 'Mobile Communication and Selective Sociality', in: M. Ito,
D. Okabe and M. Matsuda (eds.), *Personal, Portable, Pedestrian: Mobile
Phones in Japanese Life*, Cambridge, MA: MIT Press, 2006, p. 123-142.

McCullough, M., 'On Urban Markup: Frames of Reference in Location Models
for Participatory Urbanism', *Leonardo Electronic Almanac* 14 (2006)
nr. 3/4, http://www.leoalmanac.org/wp-content/uploads/2012/07/
On-Urban-Markup-Frames-Of-Reference-In-Location-Models-For-
Participatory-Urbanism-Vol-14-No-3-July-2006-Leonardo-Electronic-
Almanac.pdf.

McKenzie, E., *Privatopia*, New Haven: Yale University Press, 1996.

McQuire, S., *The Media City: Media Architecture and Urban Space*,
Thousand Oaks: Sage, 2008.

McQuire, S., 'The Politics of Public Space in the Media City', *First Monday*,
2006, nr. 4, http://www.firstmonday.org/issues/special11_2/mcquire/
index.html.

McQuire, S., M. Martin en S. Niederer (eds.), *Urban Screens Reader* (INC
Reader, vol. 5), Amsterdam: Institute of Network Cultures, 2009.

Mesch, G. S., and Y. Levanon, 'Community Networking and Locally Based
Social Ties in Two Suburban Locations', *City & Community* 2 (2003)
nr. 5, p. 335-352.

Mitchell, D., 'The End of Public Space? People's Park, Definitions of the Public
and Democracy', *Annals of the Association of American Geographers*
85 (1995) nr. 1, p. 108-133.

Mitchell, W. J. *Me++: The Cyborg Self and the Networked City*, Cambridge,
MA: MIT Press, 2003.

Mommaas, H., 'Tussen verwording en wederopstanding: Het postmoderne
plein', in: R.V. Maarschalkerwaart and H. Mommaas (eds.), *Het Pleinenboek*, Utrecht: Hogeschool voor de Kunsten, 2003.

Morozov, E., *The Net Delusion: The Dark Side of Internet Freedom*, New York:
Public Affairs, 2011.

Moscoviter, H., *Een podium tussen de hoogbouw: Een halve eeuw hunkeren
naar een intiem schouwburgplein*, Rotterdam: City Informatiecentrum, 1997.

Moscoviter, H., A. Geuze and P. van Beek, 'Het genot van leegte', *Grafisch
Nederland,* kerstnummer 1992.

Mubi Brighenti, A., and C. Mattiucci, 'Editing Urban Environments: Territories,
Prolongations, Visibilities', in: F. Eckardt (ed.), *Media City: Situations,
Practices and Encounters*, Berlijn: Frank & Timme, 2008, p. 81-106.

Musterd, S., 'Ruimtelijk beleid bevordert maatschappelijke integratie niet',
Geografie 9 (2000) nr. 4, p. 12-13.

Musterd, S., and R. van Kampen, *De stadsbuurt: Ontwikkeling en betekenis*,
Assen: Van Gorcum, 2007.

Musterd, S., W. Ostendorf and S. de Vos, 'Neighborhood Effects and Social
Mobility: A Longitudinal Analysis', *Housing Studies* 18 (2003) nr. 6,
p. 877-892.

Nicholson, J., 'Flash! Mobs in the Age of Mobile Connectivity', *fibreculture*, 2005, nr. 6.

Oenen, G. van, 'Babylonische maakbaarheid', *Open* (Maakbaarheid) 15 (2008).

Okabe, D., and M. Ito, 'Technosocial Situations: Emergent Structuring of Mobile E-mail Use', in: M. Ito, D. Okabe and M. Matsuda (eds.), *Personal, Portable, Pedestrian: Mobile Phones in Japanese Life*, Cambridge, MA: MIT Press, 2006, p. 257-273.

Oosterhuis, K., *Architecture Goes Wild*, Rotterdam: NAi Uitgevers, 2002.

Ostendorf, W., S. Musterd and S. de Vos, 'Social Mix and the Neighbourhood Effect: Policy Ambitions and Empirical Evidence', *Housing Studies* 16 (2001) nr. 3, p. 371-180.

Ouwehand, A., 'Wonen in de wijken van de vooruitgang: Bewoners als dragers van de identiteit van de tuinsteden', in: K. Hage and K. Zweerink (eds.), *Van Pendrecht tot Ommoord: Geschiedenis en toekomst van de naoorlogse wijken in Rotterdam*, Bussum: Thoth, 2005, p. 26-33.

Ovink, H., E. Wierenga and M. Dings, *Ontwerp en Politiek*, Rotterdam: Uitgeverij 010, 2009.

Park, R., 'The City: Suggestions for Investigation of Human Behavior in the Urban Environment' (1915), in: R. Sennett (ed.), *Classic Essays on the Culture of Cities*, New York: Appleton-Century-Crofts, 1969.

Paulos, E., 'Designing for Doubt Citizen Science and the Challenge of Change', in: *Engaging Data: First International Forum on the Application and Management of Personal Electronic Information*, 2009, http://senseable.mit.edu/engagingdata/papers/ED_SI_Designing_for_Doubt.pdf.

Paulos, E., 'Manifesto of Open Disruption and Participation', *Paulos.net*, 2009.

Pentland, A., 'Reality Mining of Mobile Communications: Toward a New Deal on Data', in: S. Dutta and I. Mia (eds.), *The Global Information Technology Report 2008–2009: Mobility in a Networked World*, Genève: World Economic Forum/INSEAD, 2009, p. 75-80.

Perry, C.A., *Housing for the Mechanical Age*, New York: Russell Sage Foundation, 1939.

Perry, C.A., 'The Neighborhood Unit' (1929), in: R. LeGates and F. Stour (eds.), *Early Urban Planning*, London: Routledge, 1998.

Pinkster, F., 'Je bent wie je kent? Buurtgebonden sociale contacten, socialisering en sociale mobiliteit in een Haagse achterstandswijk', in: S. Musterd and R. van Kampen (eds.), *De stadsbuurt: Ontwikkeling en betekenis*, Assen: Van Gorcum, 2007, p. 109-120.

Rafael, V., 'The Cell Phone and the Crowd: Messianic Politics in the Contemporary Philippines', *Public Culture* 15 (2003) nr. 3, p. 399-425.

Ree, D. van der, 'Een deel van je leven', in: *Project Zuidelijke Tuinsteden*, Rotterdam: Dienst Stedenbouw + Volkshuisvesting, 1992.

Ree, D. van der, 'Van boerenzij naar stadswijk', in: A. Reijndorp and H. van der Ven (eds.), *Een reuze vooruitgang: Utopie en praktijk in de zuidelijke tuinsteden van Rotterdam*, Rotterdam: Uitgeverij 010, 1994, p. 105-118.

Reijndorp, A., 'De sociale ambities van het naoorlogse bouwen', in: A. Reijndorp and H. van der Ven (eds.), *Een reuze vooruitgang: Utopie en praktijk in de zuidelijke tuinsteden van Rotterdam*, Rotterdam: Uitgeverij 010, 1994, p. 35-59.

Reijndorp, A., *Stadswijk: Stedenbouw en dagelijks leven*, Rotterdam: NAi Uitgevers, 2004.

Reijndorp, A., and S. Lohof, *Privé-terrein: Privaat beheerde woondomeinen in Nederland*, Rotterdam: NAi Uitgevers, 2006.

Reijndorp, A., and E. Mik, *Stad in Conflict*, Groningen: Platform Gras, 2005.

Reijndorp, A., I. Nio and W. Veldhuis, *Atlas Westelijke Tuinsteden Amster-dam: De geplande en de geleefde stad*, Haarlem/The Hague: Trancity, 2008.

Reijndorp, A., amd H. van der Ven, *Een reuze vooruitgang: Utopie en praktijk in de zuidelijke tuinsteden van Rotterdam*, Rotterdam: Uitgeverij 010, 1994.

Reijndorp, A. et al., *Buitenwijk: Stedelijkheid op afstand*, Rotterdam: NAi Uitgevers, 1998.

Rheingold, H., *Smart Mobs: The Next Social Revolution*, Cambridge, MA: Perseus Publishing, 2002.

Rotterdamse Kunststichting, 'Rapport Schouwburgplein', 1977.

Ruitenbeek, J., B. Jansen and K. Zweerink, 'De wederopbouwwijken van Rotterdam', in: K. Hage en K. Zweerink (eds.), *Van Pendrecht tot Ommoord: Geschiedenis en toekomst van de naoorlogse wijken in Rotterdam*, Bussum: Thoth, 2005, p. 78-83.

Sadler, S., *Archigram: Architecture Without Architecture*, Cambridge, MA: MIT Press, 2005.

Schilt, J., '1947–1957: Tien jaar "Opbouw"', in: W. Beeren et al. (ed.), *Het Nieuwe Bouwen in Rotterdam 1920–1960*, Delft: Delft University Press, 1982, p. 139-170.

Schilt, J., and H. Selier, 'Van de oevers van de Oder tot Krimpen aan den IJssel', in: H. Damen en A. Devolder (eds.), *Lotte Stam-Beese 1903–1988: Dessau, Brno, Charkow, Moskou, Amsterdam, Rotterdam*, Rotterdam: De Hef, 1993, p. 10-37.

Schinkel, W., 'De nieuwe technologieën van de zelfcontrole: Van surveillance naar zelfveillance', in: M. van den Berg, M. Ham and C. Prins (eds.), *In de greep van de technologie*, Amsterdam: Van Gennep, 2008, p. 171-189.

'Schouwburgplein en Weena Oost', Rotterdam: Stadsontwikkeling Rotterdam, 1982.

Schuilenburg, M., and A. de Jong, *Mediapolis*, Rotterdam: Uitgeverij 010, 2006.

SCP, 'Zekere banden: Sociale cohesie, veiligheid en leefbaarheid', The Hague: SCP, 2002.

Seijdel, J., 'Redactioneel', *Open* (Hybride ruimte) 11 (2006), p. 4-5.

Sennett, R., *Classic Essays on the Culture of Cities*, New York: Appleton-Century-Crofts, 1969.

Sennett, R., *The Fall of Public Man*, New York: Knopff, 1977.

Sennett, R., *The Uses of Disorder: Personal Identity and City Life* New York: Norton, 1970.

Shepard, M., and A. Greenfield, *Urban Computing and its Discontents* (Situated Technologies Pamphlets 1), eds. M. Shepard, O. Khan and T. Scholz, New York: The Architectural League of New York, 2007.

Shirvanee, L., 'Locative Viscosity: Traces of Social Histories In Public Space', *Leonardo Electronic Almanac* 14 (2006) nr. 3, http://leoalmanac.org/journal/vol_14/lea_v14_n03-04/toc.asp.

Snels, B. (eds.), *Vrijheid als ideaal*, Amsterdam: SUN, 2005.

Soja, E. W., *Postmetropolis: Critical Studies of Cities and Regions*, Oxford/Malden, MA: Blackwell Publishers, 2000.

Solà-Morales, M. de, 'Openbare en collectieve ruimte: De verstedelijking van het privé-domein als nieuwe uitdaging', *Oase* 33 (1992), p. 3-8.

Sorkin, M. (ed.), *Variations on a Theme Park: The New American City and the End of Public Space*, New York: Hill and Wang, 1992.

Stam-Beese, L., 'Aantekeningen over Pendrecht', Rotterdam: archief NAi Rotterdam STAB, #17.

Stam-Beese, L., 'De stad als wooncentrum', in: *Studium Generale* maart 1959.

Susser, I., Castells, M. (eds.), *The Castells Reader on Cities and Social Theory*, Malden, MA: Blackwell Publishers, 2002.

Suttles, G.D., *The Social Construction of Communities*, Chicago: University of Chicago Press, 1972.

Thomas, P., 'The Chemist as Flâneur in Intelligent Architecture', paper gepresenteerd op het International Symposium of Electronic Arts, Singapore, 2008.

Thrift, N., and S. French., 'The Automatic Production of Space', *Transactions of the Institute of British Geographers* 27 (2002) nr. 3, p. 309-335.

Townsend, A., 'Life in the Real-time City: Mobile Telephones and Urban Metabolism', *Journal of Urban Technology* 7 (2000) nr. 2, p. 85-104.

Tuters, M., and K. Varnelis, 'Beyond Locative Media: Giving Shape to the Internet of Things', *Leonardo* 39 (2006) nr. 4, p. 357-363.

Uitermark, J., and J.W. Duyvendak, 'Over insluiting en vermijding: De weg naar sociale insluiting', in: *Over insluiting en vermijding: Twee essays over segregatie en integratie* (Werkdocument 6), The Hague: Raad voor Maatschappelijke Ontwikkeling, 2004.

Velzen, van E., 'Pendrecht opnieuw bezien: Ontwerpstudies voor de vernieuwing van Pendrecht', in: A. Reijndorp en H. van der Ven, *Een reuze vooruitgang: Utopie en praktijk in de zuidelijke tuinsteden van Rotterdam*, Rotterdam: Uitgeverij 010, 1994.

Vidler, A., 'The Scenes of the Street: Transformations in Ideal and Reality 1750–1871', in: S. Anderson (ed.), *On Streets*, Cambridge MA: MIT Press, 1978.

Vogelaar, E., *Actieplan krachtwijken: Van aandachtswijk naar krachtwijk*, Ministerie van Wonen, Wijken en Integratie, The Hague, 2007.

Waal, M. de, 'From BLVD Urbanism towards MSN Urbanism: Locative Media and Urban Culture', in: F. Eckardt (ed.), *Media City*, Weimar: Bauhaus University Press, 2008, p. 383-406.

Waal, M. de, 'The Ideas and Ideals in Urban Media', in: M. Foth et al. (ed.), *From Social Butterfly to Engaged Citizen*, Cambridge, MA: MIT Press, 2012, p. 5-20.

Waal, M. de, 'Nieuw gebruik van het mobiele telefoonnetwerk: Noodzaak om nuances van privacy te onderkennen', *Open* (Voorbij privacy) 19 (2010), p. 100-109.

Waal, M. de, 'The Urban Ideals of Location-based Media', in: *Cities of Desire: An Urban Culture Exchange between Vienna and Hong Kong* (2009), p. 24-31.

Weiser, M., 'The Computer of the 21st Century', *Scientific American* 265 (1991) nr. 3, p. 94-100.

Weiser, M., and J. Seely Brown, 'Designing Calm Technology', Palo Alto: Xerox Parc, 1995.

Wellman, B., 'The Community Question: The Intimate Networks of East Yorkers', *The American Journal of Sociology* 84 (1979) nr. 5, p. 1201-1231.

Wellman, B. et al., 'The Social Affordances of the Internet for Networked

Individualism', *Journal of Computer-Mediated Communication* 8 (2003) nr. 3, doi:10.1111/j.1083-6101.2003.tb00216.x.

Wentholt, R., *De binnenstadsbeleving van Rotterdam*, Rotterdam: Ad Donker, 1968.

Whyte, W.H., *The Social Life of Small Urban Spaces*, Washington, D.C.: Conservation Foundation, 1980.

Wiener, N., *Cybernetics or Control and Communication in the Animal and the Machine*, 2nd edition, Cambridge, MA: MIT Press, 1965.

Wiener, N. *The Human Use of Human Beings: Cybernetics and Society*, London: Sphere Books, 1968.

Wijs-Mulkens, E. de, *Wonen op stand: Lifestyles en landschappen van de culturele en economische elite*, Amsterdam: Het Spinhuis, 1999.

Wirth, L., 'Urbanism as a Way of Life', *American Journal of Sociology* 44 (1938) nr. 1, p. 1-24.

Wortmann, A., 'Tweesporenbeleid op het Rotterdamse Schouwburgplein', *Archis* 1993, nr. 4, p. 70-76.

WRR, *Vertrouwen in de buurt* (Rapporten aan de Regering nr. 72), Amsterdam: Amsterdam University Press, 2005

Zorbaugh, H., '"The Natural Areas of the City" from Ernest W. Burgess (ed.), *The Urban Community* (1926)', in: J. Lin en C. Mele (eds.), *The Urban Sociology Reader* (London: Routledge, 2005), p. 82-88.

Blogs

Adam Greenfield's Speedbird http://speedbird.wordpress.com/
Archined http://www.archined.nl/
BMW Guggenheim Lab http://blog.bmwguggenheimlab.org/
City of Sound (Dan Hill) http://www.cityofsound.com/blog/
Dpr-barcelona http://dprbcn.wordpress.com/
Engaging Cities http://engagingcities.com/
Monnik http://feeds.monnik.org/
Pasta & Vinegar (Nicolas Nova) http://nearfuturelaboratory.com/pasta-and-vinegar/
Planetizen http://www.planetizen.com/
Polis http://www.thepolisblog.org/
Pop Up City http://popupcity.net/
Postscapes http://postscapes.com/
Project for Public Spaces http://www.pps.org/
Putting People First http://www.experientia.com/blog/
Ruimtevolk http://ruimtevolk.nl/
Shareable http://www.shareable.net/
Tactical Media Files http://www.tacticalmediafiles.net/
The Mobile City http://www.themobilecity.nl
Theatrum Mundi http://theatrum-mundi.org/
Urbanophil http://www.urbanophil.net/
Varnelis.net (Kazys Varnelis) http://varnelis.net/index
Volume http://volumeproject.org/
We Make Money Not Art http://we-make-money-not-art.com/

Acknowledgements

This book is a revised version of my doctoral thesis *De stad als interface* ('The city as interface'), which I completed at the Faculty of Philosophy at the University of Groningen in 2012. It goes without saying that I am deeply indebted to both of my supervisors, René Boomkens and José van Dijck. I would also like to thank the members of the supervisory committee and opposition: Boudewijn de Bruin, Jos de Mul, Arnold Reijndorp, William Uricchio, Frank van Vree and Piet Pellenbarg. I am also extremely grateful to my colleagues Judith Vega and Martijn Oosterbaan with whom René Boomkens and I led the Netherlands Organisation for Scientific Research (NWO) funded programme New media, public sphere and urban culture research, and who were involved in my research from the outset.

As for the actual contents of this book, I am indebted to a number of writers whom I would like to mention here; after all, the themes in this book were not conjured up by me but elaborate on the work of researchers who preceded me. The central idea of refining the concept of the public domain by looking at the way publics are formed was derived from the work of Bruno Latour and Manuel De Landa. A number of essays in *Vrijheid als ideaal* (literally, 'Freedom as ideal') edited by Bart Snels provide more background to the republican political ideal. My ideas about the public domain were also strongly influenced by the work of René Boomkens, especially his books *Een drempelwereld* (literally, 'A threshold world') and *De nieuwe wanorde* (literally, 'The new disorder'), as well as the work of Arnold Reijndorp and Maarten Hajer. Richard Sennett's ideas also resonate in the background every now and then. I based the concept of the parochial domain on research by Lyn Lofland; the works of Jane Jacobs, Talja Blokland and, again, Arnold Reijndorp played an important role in my ideas about everyday urban life. It was Barry Wellman who introduced me to the idea of 'network individualism'. A number of influential thinkers preceded me when it came to new media and the city. The books, pamphlets and blogs by Howard Rheingold, Kazys Varnelis, Mark Shepard, Anthony Townsend, Nicolas Nova, Adam Greenfield, Dan Hill, Danah Boyd, Eric Gordon, Scott McQuire, Mimi Ito and Marcus Foth were particularly inspiring. My notions of interactivity build forth on the ideas of Rafael Lozano-Hemmer and Usman Haque. In the Netherlands, the works of Richard Rogers, Geert Lovink and Eric Kluitenberg in the field of new media theory are inexhaustible sources of new ideas.

It was – and is – a great pleasure to explore the themes in this book in the context of The Mobile City, the organization for researching urban media and urban design that Michiel de Lange and I founded in 2007. Our collaboration has always been inspiring. I also extend my thanks to the organizations that have worked with us over the years and for the faith in us expressed by Ole Bouman, Linda Vlassenrood, Saskia van Stein and Oene Dijk of NAi Publishers, Floor van Spaendonck of Virtueel Platform, Maaike Behm of Arcam and Alex Adriaanse of V2.

Many thanks, too, to all those who so generously gave of their time to answer my questions while I was carrying out my research. In Rotterdam, weblogger Mario Bosch gave me a guided tour of Pendrecht; Cees Bavius of the Pendrechttheater performed a series of wonderful plays with Pendrecht residents and engaged me in a number of conversations that provided me with a greater insight into the district; Bien Hofman and

Rieks Westrik also gave me a guided tour of Pendrecht; Anoek van den Broek, Kim Zweerink and Duco de Bruijn of the Rotterdam city council were exceptionally helpful; and Endry van Velzen of De Nijl Architecten received me at his office and gave me a greater understanding of the history of Pendrecht and his plans for its restructuring. In Songdo, Jonathan Thorpe and Scott Summers of Gale International gave me a warm welcome, and Cisco's Wim Elfrink and Munish Khetrapal answered my questions through TelePresence. Some of my research was also carried out at the Center for Future Civic Media at the Massachusetts Institute of Technology, and I would like to thank William Uricchio, Ellen Hume and Henry Jenkins for their hospitality during my stay.

I find it easiest to write in the anonymity of the city, and during the last few years many people provided me with accommodation so that I could work on my doctoral thesis and on this book. I would like to thank Luuk van Middelaar in Scheveningen, Joost Crouwel in Castricum, Henk and Els Elffers in Amsterdam, Kees and Margot de Waal in Dordrecht, Geke van Dijk and Bas Raijmakers in London and Amsterdam, Tracy Metz and Baptist Brayé in Barcelona, Attila Bujdoso and Melinda Sipos of Kitchen Budapest in Budapest, and Mandie Fox and Jason Fine in Watertown, MA.

The Netherlands Organisation for Scientific Research (NWO) funded my doctoral research. The Creative Industries Fund NL and the Rotterdam city council provided financial assistance for the translation and publication of this book. The Fonds Bijzondere Journalistieke Projecten and the Lira Auteursfonds Reprorecht made it possible for me to travel to New Songdo, a journey that also led to the publication of an article in the *de Volkskrant* newspaper. Without the generous assistance of these organizations, the publication of this book would not have been possible.

My last expression of gratitude has been reserved for my beloved Anna. Thank you for everything over these past few years – without you this book would never have been written.

Background information and discussion

For more background information and examples of the city as interface see: www.thecityasinterface.com

If you would like to join in discussions about this book on Twitter, the recommended hash tag is #cityasinterface

Credits

Texts: Martijn de Waal; *translation*: Vivien Reid/Bookmakers; *copy editing*: Bookmakers; *design*: Joseph Plateau; *lithography and printing*: die Keure, Bruges; *publisher*: Marcel Witvoet, nai010 publishers

Illustration credits
Cover: Keiichi Matsuda, video still from Augmented City 3D; Introduction: diagrams for the ideal Renaissance city, inspired by Vitruvius; Ch.1: Lotte Stam-Beese, design for Pendrecht Rotterdam; Ch.2: psynovec/ 123RF, New York black white city plan - street texture; Ch.3: Christian Nold, East Paris Emotion Map; Ch.4: Guy Debord and Asger Jorn, The Naked City; Ch.5: Three months on Foursquare, Rotterdam; Ch.6: MIT SENSEable City Lab Trash Track; Conclusion: Archigram, Computer City

This publication was made possible by financial support from Creative Industries Fund NL, Municipal Services for Arts and Culture, City of Rotterdam and Van Eesteren-Fluck & Van Lohuizen Foundation.

creative industries fund NL   Gemeente Rotterdam   EFL STICHTING

nai010 publishers is an internationally orientated publisher specialized in developing, producing and distributing books in the fields of architecture, urbanism, art and design.
www.nai010.com
    Available in North, South and Central America through Artbook | D.A.P., 155 Sixth Avenue 2nd Floor, New York, NY 10013-1507, tel +1 212 627 1999, fax +1 212 627 9484, dap@dapinc.com
    Available in the United Kingdom and Ireland through Art Data, 12 Bell Industrial Estate, 50 Cunnington Street, London W4 5HB, tel +44 208 747 1061, fax +44 208 742 2319, orders@artdata.co.uk

Printed and bound in Belgium
ISBN 978-94-6208-050-8

The City as Interface is also available as e-book and in a Dutch edition:
The City as Interface epub ISBN 978-94-6208-076-8
De stad als interface ISBN 978-94-6208-049-2
De stad als interface epub ISBN 978-94-6208-075-1